Please return or renew by

LOANS MAY BE RENEWED BY PHONE
657-7310

D1112491

THE AUTOBIOGRAPHY OF A WORKING MAN

From a Photograph taken at the Photographic Institution

A. Somerville

THE AUTOBIOGRAPHY
OF A
WORKING MAN

by

ALEXANDER SOMERVILLE

Edited and with an introduction by
JOHN CARSWELL

TURNSTILE PRESS

First published in 1848
This Edition 1951 by
Turnstile Press Ltd
10, Great Turnstile, W.C.1.
Printed in Great Britain at
The Bowering Press, Plymouth

CONTENTS

CHAP.   PAGE

INTRODUCTION   vii

NOTE ON SOMERVILLE'S WORKS   xxi

PREFACE TO THE FIRST EDITION   xxiii

I. FATHER—MOTHER—BROTHERS—SISTERS—SCOTTISH
RURAL LIFE   I

II. MY CHILDHOOD—'DEAR YEARS' OF 'SIXTEEN AND 'SEVEN-
TEEN—THE RADICALS   12

III. SCHOOL AND COW-HERDING—MY BLIND COMPANION   21

IV. I AM THE RUNAWAY BOY   31

V. I OBTAIN A GLIMPSE OF THE WORLD BY READING, AND
AM ELEVATED TO HOLD THE PLOUGH   42

VI. 1826 AND 1827—HARD WORK AND LITTLE WAGES   51

VII. INDUSTRIAL ADVENTURES IN 1828   57

VIII. 1829—MUCH HARD WORK—A LITTLE POACHING AND
SOME LOVE   67

IX. LOST IN A BOG   74

X. 1830—WORK IN A STONE QUARRY—EDINBURGH REFORM
RIOTS IN 1831   84

XI. I TAKE THE SHILLING   104

XII. FROM EDINBURGH TO BRIGHTON—FROM BRIGHTON TO
BIRMINGHAM   120

XIII. DAILY DUTIES OF THE DRAGOON WHILE YET A 'JOHNNY
RAW'   138

XIV. THE POLITICAL CRISIS OF 1832   147

XV. THE MILITARY CRIME   161

XVI. THE COURT MARTIAL—SENTENCE TWO HUNDRED LASHES   175

XVII. DISCHARGE FROM HOSPITAL—THE PUBLIC FIRST HEAR
OF MY PUNISHMENT—THE SENSATION   192

CHAP.		PAGE
XVIII.	AT THIS MOMENTOUS CRISIS, SINGULAR REAPPEARANCE OF A LONG-LOST BROTHER	205
XIX.	THE COURT OF INQUIRY—DISCHARGE PURCHASED	215
XX.	FROM LONDON HOME, AND FROM HOME TO LONDON—1832, 1833 AND 1834	230
XXI.	MARRIAGE	253
XXII.	POLITICAL DISCONTENT, PLOTS AND CONSPIRACIES IN 1834	256
XXIII.	THE PLOT FRUSTRATED	275

NOTES

The footnotes marked with an asterisk are Somerville's. The serially numbered references are to the Editor's notes grouped at the end of the chapters concerned.

INTRODUCTION

ALTHOUGH he survived long into Victoria's reign, neither Alexander Somerville nor his *Autobiography of a Working Man* should be classed as Victorian. They belong to the earlier age, which we call 'The Age of Reform'—a pleasing name, as if it were a time when old wrongs were at last righted in the light of truths for the first time clearly perceived. True, by the time the Corn Laws were repealed many of the staple ingredients of Victorianism were already there: the Queen herself, for instance; the Oxford Movement; middle-class radicalism; cheap books and steam trains. But the authentic stuffiness of the era had not yet descended. As Professor G. M. Young has observed, the thirty years from Waterloo to the repeal of the Corn Laws have their own inner dramatic unity. Their atmosphere is springlike, not stuffy, but it is a raw, blustering, spring.

They open with the scene into which Somerville was born—the long post-war repression, against a background of gathering industrial power; reach their emotional climax with the passing of the Reform Bill, when Somerville abruptly became a public figure; and their *dénouement* with the eclipse of the old Tories, the conversion of Peel, and the triumph of Cobdenism—the point at which Somerville's book was published. But though the plot is simple the characters seem bewildered, their voices call (amplified as never before), and each seems at the same moment reactionary and reformer. The industrial power which set their problems provided also unprecedented means of agitating them. Steam trains whirled anti-corn law lecturers in the first class, chartist agitators in the third, to the furthest corners of the kingdom; and the serial parts of *Nicholas Nickleby* and *Oliver Twist*, the Tracts of Newman and the Corn Law rhymes of Ebenezer Elliott, hot from steam presses, followed in the parcels van. Journalism moved from the metropolitan to the national scale, and the country-wide campaign became a political institution.

Somerville was born into the humblest stratum of the working class —a landless agricultural labourer. But he was a born journalist. He had a seeing eye, an imaginative mind, and an itching pen—which cost him a flogging and set him on the road to fame. The bewildering development of his views is typical of his age. Suddenly, just as he became a man, his spirits were released on reading in his *Caledonian Mercury* (half price, because it was a day old) that twenty-four years of Toryism had ended. Within two years he had been diverted to the trade of journalism from his original destination of Regimental Sergeant-Major of the Scots Greys, by becoming one of the few martyrs of the reform agitation; and in what he calls 'twenty years of political repentance' ran the gamut of politics from Chartism to Manchester Free Trade. Even so he might, but for the strange stubbornness of his character, have ended as a respected veteran—'Somerville the Scots Grey'—on the platform at Liberal and Trade Union meetings. Instead, after a long exile, he died penniless and discredited in a shack on the outskirts of Toronto.

Between the lines of his *Autobiography*, written, it must be remembered, twenty years after the events it describes, one can read why this was, and see the mixture of stubbornness and shame which enabled him to bear a savage punishment without flinching, and yet compelled him to carry the marks of it on his mind for the rest of his life. Other men would have cried out, and forgotten. But Somerville's narrative, at twenty years' distance, and after a radical change of views on the author's part, glows with a horrible distinctness. Yet in spite of his sufferings one dislikes him intensely, and he can infuriate to-day, just as he infuriated his officers in the spring of 1832. One cannot but turn from him (for instance) when he turns from the rum bought by his comrades and smuggled to him in the guard-room where he was awaiting flogging:

'Not one drop for me, Charley Hunter; I shall not sing out, I promise you, if they cut me to pieces. . . . Take away that rum; I shall not drink it; no, nor the half of it; nor a drop of it; I shall not touch it.'

No word of thanks. That is the key to Somerville's character as it was of his failure. He was a profoundly unsocial man. More than once he was to hear variations of the mortified reply of the drummer who brought the rum: 'Well there's no use losing it; if you won't drink it, I know who will.'

The blood of the seventeenth-century covenanters ran in Somerville's veins, and one must place beside his working-class origin, his

viii

upbringing in the narrow and obscure sect of the Anti-burghers, one of the many fragments into which refusal to compromise then divided Scottish protestantism. The eastern Lowlands, from which he came, were still, unlike the south-west, barely touched by economic revolution, and the traditions of the old Scotland still live in Somerville's evocative description of his youth. This part of the book is filled with accounts of working-class customs and scenes which there were few to chronicle. The young Somerville is accurate and impartial, a wandering labourer with a watchful eye, spectator and actor in a changing Scotland.

So deep was Lammermoor provincialism, that before Somerville could read Burns, he had to learn the Ayrshire dialect as if he had been an Englishman. But once known, Burns showed his liberating power on a young and intelligent Scot. And with Burns, Somerville catches the first straws in the wind of cheap periodicals, workmen's circulating libraries and incipient trade unionism. Then, in a lean year, and probably as a desperate step, though he does not say so, comes the comedy of the recruiting corporal with one shilling for two recruits, enlistment in the Scots Greys, and an account of life in a crack regiment during the longest period of peace Europe has known for centuries. The details he gives are worth ten times their weight in introspection; and though cork moustaches for those without natural hair are no longer insisted upon (so far as I know) by modern sergeant-majors, the carefully preserved clean straw used for no other purpose but to wrap round the dirty straw when stables were inspected, and the 'artistical' way of folding blankets will stir responses in readers whose military experience is separated from Somerville's by more than a century. His kit too included the button-stick and the canvas 'save-all', and he too wore hospital blue. All this tells the more because he entered whole-heartedly into the spirit of the army, even while noting its absurdities. His portraits of his N.C.O.'s are strictly fair, and though some are drawn as geniuses for the invention of misery, like Hospital-Sergeant William Sykes, the impartial memories of modern recruits will evoke a figure just like Somerville's Sergeant Keith, who commanded liking by his skill at arms, his patience and his sympathy.

The constant threads, which it is in nobody's interest to break, simply because they are so slight, connect the army of 1832 with the army to-day in such a way that it is almost possible to forget the great changes which have in fact taken place. In Somerville's day, in spite of stoppages far heavier than a modern soldier would stand, the man in the ranks was relatively much better paid, as well as more secure, than the average civilian working-man. Somerville tasted roast goose for the first time in his life when he joined the army. Naturally enough, men stayed as long as they could, once they had taken the initial social step; and the whole system was designed to encourage a life-time of service. Few men now serve with the colours so long as Michael Nelson, Somerville's Regimental Sergeant-Major, who had been at Waterloo, and soldiered for a full thirty-five years, to retire four years before the outbreak of the Crimean War. Just as the individual soldier was wedded to the army, and lacked roots in the community outside the barrack walls, so the army as a whole was largely ruled by a military hierarchy which had very ill-defined connexions with the civil government. Overshadowing this hierarchy stood the Duke, supported at the Horse Guards by his old subordinates of the Peninsula. The Tories might leave office, and a Whig Secretary at War succeed, but the veterans of the Horse Guards, now associated in the public mind not with Waterloo but with Peterloo, remained.

It was not at all clear to Somerville as a trooper of the Birmingham garrison in the early summer of 1832, which of his two masters he would have to serve. Although Lord Grey might well say in private 'Damn reform, I wish we'd never touched it', his Bill had become far more than a Whig proposal. It was the symbol of popular triumph. For a moment Thomas Attwood, the now forgotten Chairman of the Birmingham Political Union, could seriously be described as 'the most influential man in England'. It was true, as Somerville says, that for nine days, between the resignation and the return of the Reform Ministry, the Duke was trying to form an alternative government, which would have had to rely on military force. We know now that this plan broke on Peel's refusal to support it: whether the wavering in the ranks of the army, which Somerville describes, had any weight with the Duke, if he ever heard of it, is less easy to say.

Somerville only hints in his *Autobiography* at the conspiracy of which his fatal letter to the *Weekly Dispatch* formed a part. But he tells the story elsewhere*, and it was a serious matter. The conspirators intended, if the regiment was called out against Attwood's threatened reform demonstration, to go over to the demonstrators, carrying as many of the regiment with them as they could, and join the march on

* *Public and Personal Affairs*

London. Somerville's letter was not an improvised outburst, written during a sentry's turn off in the guardroom, but part of a calculated campaign of letters intended to discourage the authorities from going to extremes. Somerville later asserted that his letter was never intended for verbatim publication. If that is so, it was certainly naïve in him to send it to the editor of a leading radical weekly. The editor probably knew that in publishing the letter he was manufacturing a radical martyr, and saw both letter and what might follow as a story too good to be missed. This is the probable explanation of much of the otherwise puzzling bitterness and disingenuousness which from this point onwards stains and confuses Somerville's narrative.

The officers of the Greys were only too conscious of their position. From the point of view of internal security Birmingham was one of the most dangerous towns in the country. A month or two before, Bristol had been in flames because the officer in command of the troops had lacked initiative. But at Birmingham the decision, though made, was left to inexperienced men. The colonel, Lord Arthur Hill, was on leave, and the second in command, Major Wyndham, had seen no active service since he charged with the Greys at Waterloo as a subaltern. The adjutant, Lieutenant Ricketts, had taken over his job less than a month before.

So a delicate situation was crudely handled, by methods which bear signs of having been suggested first in the sergeants' mess. The farce of finding, indeed forcing, an offence, so as to punish a man for something that was not an offence, has all the low cunning of the most odious type of non-commissioned officer. Within a few days the maximum sentence a court martial could inflict for disobedience, two hundred lashes, was passed and partly executed.

Somerville's description of his flogging is the most notable passage in his book. Covenanting fortitude and a journalist's eye combine to give it what one contemporary reviewer of the *Autobiography* called 'painful and terrible minuteness'—a distinctness which is almost unnatural, achieved only by recollection of the powerful restraint under which the author must have placed himself in the teeth of torment. In Dostoievsky's *Idiot*, the executioner's frayed cuff, in Somerville's account *the green bag*, the sergeant-major's note-book and pencil for recording the lashes, provide the apparently harmless details which tell how suffering can heighten awareness.

Even in Somerville's day, military flogging had long been criticized by radicals and humanitarians. But it was long to endure, attacked, as it was defended, for motives which were not always disinterested. When Somerville's case came before the Commons on the petition brought forward by Joseph Hume, 'Orator' Hunt delivered an attack on corporal punishment which first bored, and then emptied the house. Fourteen years later, when a man died under the lash, the Duke, under strong pressure, and with the gravest misgivings, agreed to reduce the maximum sentence to fifty. Those fifty survived the Duke, the Crimean War, and the Indian Mutiny, to be banished from peace-time discipline (by the turn of a single vote) in 1868. But in the Navy (where the arguments for expeditious punishment were stronger, and tradition was even more deeply engrained), and in the Army when on a war footing, this economical but degrading punishment, though used less and less, was still possible in the closing years of the century; and vestiges of it remained in the Indian military code down to the war of 1939.

In taking up the cudgels on Somerville's behalf, the journalists of the *Weekly Dispatch* misjudged their man as much as Major Wyndham when he took a lash to Somerville's back. Officers and radicals alike found that they had to deal not with the simple peasant soldier, whom one could flog into submission and the other parade about the country as an obedient martyr to embarrass the government, but with a man of strong, if disconcerted opinions of his own. Somerville did not in the least want to help unseat Sir John Cam Hobhouse, the Secretary at War, or blacken the administration of the Army with words put in his mouth by copy-writers and fire-brands. He wanted his name cleared of the ignominy of a military flogging. One can understand his feelings when he saw his case before the Court of Inquiry ruined by the windy inaccuracies (which the Court was able to refute in detail) that his radical friends had written into the petition they got up on his behalf.

The proceedings of the Court of Inquiry have many of the elements of pure farce. The bench of peninsular veterans, carefully briefed not to stray without the advice of the politic Judge Advocate General; the embittered complainant, detailed by some N.C.O., as a soldier who seemed not to be 'on' anything, to polish his judges' boots; and finally his advocate, T. J. Wooler, one of the most grotesque radical journalists of the day, who had been gratuitously provided by the *Weekly Dispatch*. By then old in sedition, Wooler was famous as the former editor of the often prosecuted *Black Dwarf*. Somerville explains some of his differences with his representative; but refrains from mentioning the crowning damage that Wooler did to Somerville's cause, when, during a night of adjournment, the whole inn on which the Court was quartered was woken by the vapourings of counsel for the petitioner, stationed fighting-drunk in the courtyard:

'Where's Somerville? Where are his tyrant persecutors? Come forth to justice ye martinets in epaulettes—scarlet cloth—lashes—swords and daggers! Come forth and answer the demands of justice. . . . Bring out your judges from their snoozing dens, and let them face me! I'll do you justice. The *Weekly Dispatch* is here. I am the *Weekly Dispatch*. I am he who can crush tyranny! Annihilate tyrants! and—and—I'm the *Black Dwarf*, so help me God!'

Smith, the editor of the *Dispatch*, was smoother, but to a man of Somerville's temper, even more unbearable than Wooler, who had told him 'he knew best'. The editor's atttitude was that Somerville had become the *Dispatch*'s property, and we find him writing in pained surprise to 'the much injured man', complaining that a better account of the doings at Birmingham had been allowed to appear in *The Times*:

'Be so good, dear fellow, as send us a complete statement . . . as it must be at least satisfactory to you to see your detestable tyrants withering under our castigation. . . . We shall leave no stone un-turned to drag your infamous persecutors to justice. The proprietors of the *Dispatch* will move strongly in this cause, but need I remind you that in communicating with the press, it is to us that you ought to give your correspondence?'

Somerville escaped, as he explains, to Scotland, as soon as his discharge was purchased. But he was already famous. *The Times* considered that the results of the Court of Inquiry were important enough to allow the displacement of a whole column of front-page advertisements—a concession to sensationalism which even then *The Times* rarely permitted.

It is typical of the man that he brings his *Autobiography* virtually to an end with the episode which he spent the rest of his life trying to live down. But at least a sketch of what followed is necessary if the distortions and suppressions of *Autobiography* are to be corrected in the reader's mind. It is not a wholly honest book. Its author was far more deeply committed as a radical in 1832 than he cares to admit in 1848; and comparison of the actual text of his letter to the *Weekly Dispatch* with the version he gives in the *Autobiography* shows that he was not above making modest, but deliberate, alterations to important items of evidence. It has been suggested that he was a police spy.

The *Autobiography* ends with an account of Somerville's dealings with the Owenites and Chartists of 1834 in a tone of voice which gives a clear indication of the rightward course his politics was to take. From the bottom of his Lowland heart he despised 'political lunatics' with their half-baked plans of physical violence and their systematic incitement of the mob to emotions which he found it hard to believe they felt themselves. He did not easily forget the patronizing editors of the *Dispatch*. But his change of heart, and his frustration of the plot to murder Lord Melbourne (if indeed that danger was ever serious) are unimportant beside the fact that his notable descriptive powers have provided us with the best detailed account of the first major Trade Union demonstration ever held in London.

Then he was carried off on what is perhaps the most surprising adventure of all—to Spain with the so-called 'British Legion', which was forwarding Palmerstonian foreign policy by fighting for Queen Isabella against her uncle, Don Carlos. Somerville served through two years of one of the grimmest, and least publicized campaigns in which British troops have fought, rising to the rank of colour-sergeant in an army even worse found than the expedition to the Crimea. His officers, from General de Lacy Evans, the Commander-in-Chief, downwards, testified to his merit when he was discharged in 1837, with a bullet in his arm by which to remember war for the rest of his life.

He came back, still 'Somerville the Scots Grey' in the public mind, with the added experience of two years as a fighting soldier in a hard school, at a time when military amateurs were pushing Chartism to its first peak. Feargus O'Connor was trying to popularize the ginger-beer bottle filled with inflammable mixture (a version of the Molotov Cocktail to which Englishmen seem to turn when ammunition is short), and pikes, another favourite weapon of the hard-pressed Englishman; Count Chopski and Colonel Maceroni had appointed themselves advisers to the Chartists on street warfare. From rooms in Bridges Street, Strand, Somerville set about warning his countrymen of the risks civilians ran in fighting trained and disciplined troops. He spoke from experience, and from the heart. In a series of 'Dissuasive Warnings to the People on Street Warfare'—a penny each or eighteenpence a dozen 'for gratuitous distribution', he painted imaginative pictures of Birmingham and London in the grip of the kind of struggle which actually happened in Paris during July eleven years later. How right he was in his estimate of the Chartists to stand fire was demonstrated only a year afterwards in the fiasco of Frost's 'Welsh Rebellion' (on which Somerville says his military advice was sought and withheld), when a mob of several thousands was sent streaming back to the mining villages by two well-directed volleys from twenty-four muskets stationed in the shelter of the saloon bar and bedroom floors of the Westgate Hotel, Newport.

By 1838 he had publicly disowned Chartism in his pamphlet *Public and Personal Affairs*, and was on his way, with a capable pen already sharpened by controversy, into the fresh agitation of Cobdenism. This new cause, progressive but not radical, organized with greater skill, on a larger scale, and with a deeper purse, than any of its predecessors, was launched in 1839. By 1841 Cobden and his Leaguers had already spent £100,000 of Manchester money, and further expenditure of £50,000 was planned for 1842 alone. Their unprecedented propaganda was carried on not only by public meetings up and down the country, and by sheets which were openly the organs of the League, but also by the crookeder ways of journalism—inspired news items and comment floated in the columns of the supposedly independent press. The campaign had already conquered the industrial and middle classes of the towns, but the great voting power of the agricultural constituencies was still under the spell of Protectionism; and it was primarily on this decisive aspect of the struggle that there began the long association between Cobden and a mysterious agricultural adviser: 'R' of his correspondence, otherwise 'The Whistler at the Plough', otherwise again, Alexander Somerville.

The full story of 'The Whistler' would be in a history of the great Cobdenite propaganda machine itself during its most vigorous phase; and Somerville's own account of his connexion with Cobden, written after the inevitable quarrel between the two men, is an interesting item in it. Unquestionably these years carried Somerville to the zenith of his influence, both in public, as the author of the 'Whistler' articles, and in private, as Cobden's confidential adviser on agricultural subjects and his agent in Fleet Street. Cobden was a man who 'spoke to the top of his knowledge,' a brilliant advocate, but one who needed to be briefed. One can believe Somerville when he tells how he crammed Cobden for the meetings at market towns, when hostile audiences of farmers were converted in spite of themselves by the ready answers of the apostle of Free Trade.

Somerville goes further, and maintains that it was his unsolicited contribution to the *Morning Advertiser* (which became the first of the 'Whistler' series), that reorientated the League's propaganda policy from town to countryside. But it is easier to believe that he was recruited for the new campaign, than that he drew up its master plan, especially when it appears from Cobden's correspondence that 'R' was in touch with Cobden some six months before the first 'Whistler' article was published. Cobden clearly thought of Somerville's pen as wholly under his command, and meant at one time to use it to expose not only the fallacies of Protectionism but the wickedness of the Chartists. Manchester economics taught that hard work was among the greatest of virtues:

> 'We shall expect one or two good long articles from you this week as we have neither meetings nor advertisements; so get the steam up and let us have some spicy materials as early as you can.'

This from the editor of the Cobdenite *Morning Chronicle*. Work of another style was mentioned by Cobden himself in a letter to Wilson, later founding editor of *The Economist*:

> 'Could you not get a succession of notices in the papers similar to the *Globe* last evening? Might not "R" employ his pen in that way? Tell him not to be too rhapsodical, but to give from day to day a few facts and scraps of information which will induce the papers to insert the articles as news. There should be a description of the great trains filled with country Leaguers. In the next *League* let as long a list as possible of the people of rank who have attended be given. This is very important.'

The intimacy between Cobden and Somerville was beginning to languish when the *Autobiography* came out in the year of revolutions, two years after the League's battle had been won. On the whole, no doubt, Cobden approved of the *Autobiography*, especially its anti-chartism; but Somerville felt that his part in the repeal of the Corn Laws had received less than justice from his masters. Nor did his covenanting will bend to Cobden's interference with his ghost's opinions:

'You have touched on delicate ground in dealing with the question of the *productive* and the *non-productive* classes',

wrote Cobden of one of Somerville's leaders on the events in Paris during July 1848. The breach widened over an argument about an expense account, for which Somerville eventually managed to extort £50. Then, in 1852 came the prospect of war with Russia, and the peace campaign of Cobden and Bright, in which they tried to make use once more of the old anti-military legend of 'Somerville the Scots Grey'. This was too much. Within a short time of the publication in collected form of the 'Whistler' articles he had written for Cobden, and his official biography of the leading Leaguers, came the most offensive of Somerville's many splenetic pamphlets—*Cobdenic Policy the Internal Enemy of England*. He did more. He wrote to Palmerston repudiating the Peace Society's print of a million leaflets showing him triced to the flogging post, and the letter was read to a cheering House of Commons.

He denounced Cobden and Bright as humbugs and worse, printing every scrap of correspondence he possessed which could show them in a bad light or expose their methods of agitation. Absurdly, for his bitterness now runs deeper than is healthy, he allows the wheel to come full circle with a fulsome reference to his old commander, by then in dignified retirement as Lieutenant-Governor of the Tower of London, as 'one of the best and kindest gentlemen'. The worst he will say of the court martial is that it suffered from 'some informality'.

Though he said afterwards that he would 'carry to his dying hour a deep sorrow for having treated Richard Cobden with the bitterness of an enemy', his 'conscience is at ease as regards Mr. Bright'. He blamed them for his ruin, and no doubt their connexion with him, which they not unreasonably broke off, closed the market from which he had lived for so long. He had to move 'from comparative comfort at the foot of Haverstock Hill' to crowded lodgings in Islington. But his specific charges of persecution against the Manchester men lack precision and conviction. The truth was that his own mental powers were failing, and simultaneously, as often happens, he was engaging in vast projects—histories of Trade Unionism, studies in electro-magnetism, a critique of the trade cycle—for which he had neither the equipment nor a market.

For a few months he occupied the editorial chair of 'a great Scottish newspaper' at Edinburgh, and then, in 1857, by the intermediacy of a mysterious stranger (whom he afterwards maintained to be the emissary of a secret society), he prepared to emigrate to that dustbin of Victorianism, Australia. But suddenly convinced that he was again being drawn into a conspiracy, he refused to go at the last moment, and wrote wild warnings to the Colonial Office, where officials politely recorded that 'Mr. Somerville had supplied information which he believed to be of value'. Somerville himself, now under strong delusions, retired to St. Bartholomew's Hospital suffering, as he has the courage to say 'from a severe mental illness'. He emerged to renew his projects for leaving England, this time for Canada, and early in 1858 the ruined 'Whistler', now irredeemably eccentric and profoundly conservative, disembarked at Quebec. On 29 May, the anniversary of his flogging, and, as he noted 'making allowances for longitude . . . at the hour I was tied up', his wife died of phthisis.

The story of his long decline—he survived until 1885, his seventy-fourth year—is no more than a footnote to the history of Canadian journalism. Fame never visited him again, though he wrote as tirelessly and as miscellaneously as ever, founding, and for a time editing, *The Canadian Illustrated News*, corresponding with various English papers, and even taking the field once more (as a war correspondent) during the Canadian insurrection of 1866. But his style, now the vehicle for an embittered mixture of reminiscence and theorizing, had no longer the 'painful and terrible minuteness' which distinguishes his *Autobiography*. As he grew older and more incoherent he grew heavier—it was said that he weighed more than 20 stone—and stranger, the solitary inhabitant of hotel rooms where he slept, mountainous, on the floor among piles of newspaper cuttings. Porridge, on which he lived, he allowed to grow cold, and then ate seasoned with fragments of raw onion. And the obsession of his own importance grew with age. His solitary martyrdom had carried the Reform Bill and saved a bloodbath in 1832; his letter to Lord Melbourne had done as much again in 1834; so had his 'Dissuasive Warnings' in 1838. His pen had carried the repeal of the corn laws, and stilled the last waves of Chartism; and his obscure novels had inspired Dickens with the theme of a chancery suit for *Bleak House*, Thackeray with the characters of Lord Steyne and Becky Sharp.

It was a poetical justice (of the kind taught by Manchester economics) that drove Somerville, unfit to be a Victorian, out of England at the opening of the true Victorian age. In some ways, though he is far less likeable, he recalls Cobbett, with his agricultural background, military ambitions, and stern, simple morality, serving as foundations for a journalist's career. It is true that Somerville has not the lusty disinterestedness that attracts us to Cobbett: he is tinged with self-righteousness, and personal grudges disfigure his work. Sometimes, though less in the *Autobiography* than elsewhere, one can see that he wrote too easily and wrote to fill the column. But in the narrative gift, the eye for telling detail, the power to hold the attention, he is not far behind the author of *Rural Rides*, beside which much of his 'Whistler' is worthy to stand. And as with Cobbett, radicalism was superimposed on a saturnian conservatism—a conservatism to which Somerville eventually returned. It was a conservatism which was aristocratic almost, in some ways socialistic, rather than middle-class. In his later years he seems to be groping towards those very economic principles on which Marx and Engels were gaining a firm grip during those same years. 'My life has been spent', he wrote, 'in rescuing the Science of Political Economy from the soulless materialism which had made it, in the mouths of Whigs and Radicals, odious to the People. . . . I assert man to be the primary element in national wealth'; and again, 'Capital, though its achievements lie in the direction of civilization and a higher human destiny, is in its immediate influences cruel and cowardly'. His practicality, his unlikeable uprightness and attention to duty, his scorn of the 'physical force' Chartists for their inadequacy and idealism, all suggest a potential Communist born out of his time.

The present text follows the first of the two editions of the *Autobiography* which were published in the author's lifetime, apart from the chapter-headings (which are taken from the second edition, where they appear for the first time) and with certain reluctant omissions. A word should be said about these, though Somerville, as a journalist who rarely weighed his words very carefully, does not deserve minute textual apparatus. They are, firstly, the extracts from his Spanish memoirs which Somerville printed as appendices to his *Autobiography*. These are available, with the full text from which they are taken, in his published *Narrative of the British Legion*, for those who are interested in that grim but obscure campaign. Secondly, certain short passages which Somerville himself dropped from the second edition (presumably because they lacked interest, since it is so easy to agree with that verdict) are here left out, though it should be said that anything which adds substantially to Somerville's narrative has been allowed to stand, even though he himself decided to suppress it in his second edition. This he did, for instance, with his chapter on his marriage. Finally, for the omission of two chapters which Somerville included in both his editions, the present editor must take full responsibility. They digress into a description of the customs and superstitions of the Lammermoors, in a vein which Somerville found came very easily to him.

J.C.

October, 1950.

NOTE ON SOMERVILLE'S WORKS

The *Autobiography* is Somerville's best work, but he wrote a great deal else, and sometimes on subjects of more than transitory interest. His first work, the *Narrative of the British Legion in Spain* (1837), has its place in the not very plentiful class of war memoirs from the ranks; and his collected agricultural articles for the Cobdenite press, printed as *The Whistler at the Plough* in 1852, form a thorough and well-informed, if rather prolix survey of rural England and Ireland in the 'forties. His two best vituperative pamphlets, *Public and Personal Affairs* (1839) and *Cobdenic Policy the Internal Enemy of England* (1854), both written in white heat, one after parting with the radicals and the other after parting with the Manchester School, go far to supplementing the more cautious *Autobiography*; and although the work of an angry man, shed some light on the seamier side of the two movements. In Canada Somerville published what he described as *The First Complete Account of Somerville's Diligent Life* (1860). Much of this is a verbatim reprint of the *Autobiography*, with the addition of some details about his last years in England and his memoirs of 'coercion' in Ireland. But his main purpose in this book was to expound his peculiar brand of 'conservatism' as an economic and social theory. There is no published biography of Somerville; but a few personal notes about his later life are to be found in an article in the *Border Magazine* for 1913.

PREFACE

WITH the exception of a very few passages, this *Autobiography of a Working Man* was originally written to be read after the author's death, and not before. Personal circumstances which need not be further explained here, have changed this purpose. Public circumstances have also had an influence to decide the author on present publication.

The conspiracy of trades' unionists and political lunatics, in 1834, in which the author was solicited to take a part, which he did not take, but of which he had seen enough to know that calamities of direst peril impended over the lives of some of the highest personages in the kingdom, and that the vilest crimes which ever added atrocity to treason, were within the measure of a day, and a probable incident, of being ripe for action and development—that conspiracy is related in the latter chapters, which were written when the author had some apprehension that the time when they were to be read—the time after death—was precariously near at hand. He is now advised that the publication of these chapters may be of more use at the present, than at a future time. If they be of use to warn working men of the perils into which they are led by leaders whom they cannot control, he will gladly confess that good has been done.

If the earlier chapters, which relate the events of his boyhood, and of his farm-field life, be deemed satisfactory reading, and not obtrusive of puerilities, or of private affairs which have no public uses, he will feel sufficiently gratified.

If those chapters which contain a narrative of the author's military life in the Scots Greys fulfil the purpose he designs them to do, they will inform such readers as care to know what his motives were in doing what he and military associates did in Birmingham barracks, during the great national crisis of May, 1832, when Reform, in its troubled passage to the statute-book, was arrested, and thrust out of parliamentary doors.

All the chapters were, at first, written in letters of affectionate instruction for the use of the author's infant son, when he might grow to manhood; but, since it has been designed to publish them for public perusal, many of the reflections on men, on facts, on opinions, or on principles, have been omitted. The author doubts if he be qualified to make such reflections instructive to general readers. Wherefore he prefers, with a few exceptions, to give the incidents of the 'Auto-biography' in a continuous narrative.

LONDON
April, 1848.

CHAPTER I

Father—Mother—Brothers—Sisters—Scottish Rural Life

MY DEAR BOY, I cannot tell you of my own boyhood until I tell you something of your grandfather and grandmother, my parents.

There is a range of hills in the middle of Scotland called the Ochills, out of which a rapid running river called the Devon flows, tumbling headlong over linns and through chasms in its progress to the low country. Near to where this river is wildest, in the parish of Muckhart, your grandfather was born, in 1760. The place was an upland farm, called Nether-aichlin-Sky. Who were the last of the family in it I do not know; but all the sons and daughters were scattered to the world in early life, to work for the means of life elsewhere, the little farm being added to others to make a large farm. They have all died old men and women years ago. One of them, Lawrence, died at Perth within my recollection. I was to have been called Lawrence after him, but a change was made, and I was named after my mother's brother, a collier, living at Square, near Berwick-upon-Tweed—a worthy man, to whose name I may not have done all the honour I might have done. In my boyhood I used to regret that I had not been called Lawrence. I then thought my own name was a shabby one. Perhaps my dislike to it arose from it being so very common in Scotland.

My father settled in the town of Alloa, on the Firth of Forth, when a young man. He had a horse and a cart, and carted coals or lime, or such things, for hire. His horse had the common equine name of Dick, and was very much respected by his owner. But Dick took ill and died, and left that owner too poor to buy another. So Dick's hide, and the cart, and the harness, were sold, and your grandfather went to work as a labourer at the great lime works of the Earl of Elgin, near Dunfermline, whither his elder brother William had preceded him. This William was remarkable for strength, having been known to carry three bolls of barley, each boll filling a large sack, one boll by a rope round the sack in each hand, and another in his teeth.

The end of this strong man was melancholy, and decided the period of your grandfather's stay at those works. An extensive shipping trade of lime was carried on from that place. The trimming of the lime in the holds of the vessels was so disagreeable and dangerous, that none of the workmen would do it unless compelled. The custom was to order certain picked men to do that work, or submit to be dismissed from employment. William, the strong man, was ordered to this duty, and one day was taken out of the hold either dead, or so much affected by the dust and fumes of the lime that he died soon after. Upon which his brother, my father, left the works, and crossing the Firth of Forth journeyed southwards to Berwickshire. There he obtained work as a farm labourer, in which capacity he continued until within a few months of his death.

He found my mother a young blooming woman at or in the vicinity of Ayton—a pretty village as you will say if you ever see it. She was a servant in a farmhouse previous to marriage, and the daughter of John Orkney, a working man. She had a female ancestor, reputed as a witch, who is still remembered for her sayings and doings. People in Ayton to this day, to justify something unusual said or done by themselves, add to it, 'As old Eppy Orkney said,' or, 'As old Eppy Orkney did.' Perhaps my progenitors who lived nearer to her time than I, did not feel much honour in Eppy's reputation for witchcraft. But for myself I confess to have always had a veneration for this, the only one of my progenitors who was in any way distinguished above the common level of men and women. I have no doubt that she was a woman of superior energy and intellect, whom narrower minds around her could not comprehend. Had she been remarkable only for her weakness of mind, her sayings and doings would have perished with her or soon after her.

My parents being a careful pair, began housekeeping with a good stock of furniture. But I have heard them tell of the wretched hovel of a house they lived in. The houses of the labourers in the south of Scotland are generally only sheds to this day, even most of those newly built; but they were much worse then. My father and mother had a window (the house had none) consisting of one small pane of glass, and when they moved from one house to another in different parts of Berwickshire in different years, they carried this window with them, and had it fixed in each hovel into which they went as tenants.

I do not know all the places they lived at in that shire. But if you should ever visit Berwickshire, and for crops of corn it is well worth visiting, you will find a place called Edencraw. I know they lived there. Between that place and Chirnside, the next village, you will see some fine farm land which was, up to a late period, a wet moss, or bog. This was a celebrated place for witches, in days of yore; and if I mistake not, my friend and correspondent, Mr. James Bruce, of Ayton, once made a poem about those witches and this bog. This place, known as Billy Mire, is however, more remarkable for having once nearly swallowed up David Hume, the historian, who was a native of Ninewells, in the neighbourhood. Hume missed his footing in the mire, stuck fast, called for assistance, and was at last heard by some people, who ran to give help; but when they saw it was Hume, 'the unbeliever', though he was in other respects an amiable man, they turned back, saying, 'Na, na, the deil has him, let the deil keep him.' David Hume got out, by some means, and wrote his famous history after that time.

My father and mother were in principle and practice strictly religious. They were of the party of dissenters then known as Anti-burghers, afterwards associated with the Burghers from whom they had split, and now known together as the United Associate Synod of the Secession Church of Scotland.* The secession originated more than a hundred years ago, on a charge of laxity of moral discipline brought against the church in a sermon preached before the general assembly of ministers by the Reverend Ebenezer Erskine. The assembly censured him for his sermon, but he again justified it and would not submit to the censure. He dissented from the church. Others adhered to him at the time, and in the following year his more celebrated brother, Ralph Erskine, followed him. Those two great preachers were natives of Chirnside, in Berwickshire, near to Billy Mire, of which I have been speaking. Their father was parish minister. Their mother gave birth to one or both of them after she had been buried, as dead, in Chirnside churchyard; so the common story goes. But I have heard of so many places which have had a lady buried in a trance, and a sexton who opened the grave at night to take the ring from her finger, and so allowed her to escape from the grave (which was said to have been the case with her), that my belief of this legend belonging in reality to Chirnside and to the Erskine family is somewhat shaken.

* Since this was written, a union has been effected between the Relief Synod, a numerous body of Scottish dissenters, and the United Associate Synod, and they are now in one body designated the United Presbyterian Church.

3

In process of time that party of dissenters disputed upon the burgess oath which freemen of corporations were required to take. Part of it provided that they would uphold the church as by law established. Some thought this law was harmless to a dissenter's conscience, and some thought not. The first were called Burghers, and the latter Anti-burghers. The last were in all things the strictest sect: to them my parents adhered.

Removing from Edencraw, which is on the south side of the Lammermoors, my father went to the farm of the Cove near the sea side, north of the Lammermoors. He was barn-man or thrasher there, as he had been at other places, threshing-mills not being then common as they now are. Six children had been born then, and three buried— the latter in Ayton churchyard. My brother James was born in the Cove; Peter was born a year or two after, in Thorntonloch; Janet was born next, in Wood Hall; Mary next, in Thornton Mains, a place now pulled down and its site a corn field; and, lastly, I was born at Springfield, in the parish of Oldhamstocks: this event occurred on the 15th of March, 1811. Your uncle William, my eldest brother, rode for the midwife. I was the eleventh and last, and came into the family at a time when I could have been very well spared. By a table of prices hanging beside me where I now write, I perceive that the price of wheat was that year £5. 5s. per quarter; and, in the following year, it was at the enormous price of £6. 5s. per quarter, the barley, and beans, and oats, upon which such families as ours lived, or shifted to live, being dear in proportion.

But I need not refer to historical tables: my father has told me, that in the year after I was born, he paid no less a sum than £20 to John Bathgate, the miller, of Oldhamstocks, for hummelled corn, that was barley and beans, to make bread. This, besides what he must have paid for oats or oatmeal, and for the schooling of the children—for the latter was never neglected, must have kept the backs and feet bare. He could not, he has told me, spare a shilling to the parish clerk of Oldhamstocks to have me registered, as all the other children had been in the respective parishes where they were born, and so my name does not exist in any register. I was baptized by the Rev. Andrew Bayne, of Eastbarns, the Anti-burgher minister.

When I was born, and for a year or two after, my father was working at Dunglass House as a barrow-man, or mason's labourer, at 15s. per week, the highest wages which he ever earned. Sir James Hall, of Dunglass, father of the late eminent and amiable Capt. Basil Hall[1], of

4

the Royal Navy, whose voyages and travels you will, I hope, live to read, as I hope they will live to be read by you—Sir James Hall rebuilt that splendid mansion overlooking the romantic scenery in Dunglass Dean, about that time, and my father assisted to carry many a stone of it up the gangways. His reputation as a mason's labourer was that of one who never lost any time, if time could be made. An old stone-mason once told me, that when rain came on, and every one went home, or went to the public house, my father always found something to do at the works. He needed it all for the hungry mouths at home. Mr. Yorston, of London, the eminent potato salesman, was a youth working alongside of my father then, and remembers him not only for his industry and sobriety, but for his cheerful anecdotes and jokes; which accords with my own knowledge of him. He had not 'spent forty shillings on drink for forty years'; such was his truthful boast. His economy and foresight was such, that though always on the verge of want, want never came; not even in tobacco, of which I never knew him without an ounce to begin to, as the last ounce was done, though the kind of tobacco he used in chewing (he only smoked once a week, and that was on Sabbath evenings, listening to some one of the family reading a sermon), could not be obtained nearer than Dunbar, six or seven miles distant. He used tobacco, however, very sparingly, and only because, as he said, 'it cheers my old heart, and helps me to get through the hard labour.' Though so practically religious that the hardest day's work never prevented him from having family worship at night, which consisted of a preliminary prayer, singing a psalm, reading a chapter, and giving an extempore prayer of considerable length, nor the usual early rising, from having both the family prayers and his 'private duty' in the morning; though the wettest, windiest, and coldest storm that ever blew in those regions did not keep him from the meeting-house on the Sabbath, no matter what the distance might be, and the distance from most places where he lived was from five to ten miles; though deeply imbued with religious sentiments at all times, and though struggling with poverty on one side, and his affectionate love for his family on the other, continually, yet was he one of the most lively companions to work with, or walk with, always ready with an anecdote that had a point in it. At the annual 'winter suppers', or the 'kirnes'—harvest homes—which our master gave to his workpeople, my father was always the life of the company; ready with droll stories, witty jokes, and songs with a meaning in them; the only drawback on his pleasure was that these festivities being usually held on Saturday night (that the master might not lose the work of any of his men through intemperate headaches the next day), he felt the more serious responsibility of encroaching on the Lord's Day. No persuasion nor entreaty, nor enjoyment of fun, nor the trick of putting the clock back, would keep him after ten o'clock. Nor would he allow any of us to remain later. We were always on those occasions taken home to have family worship over, and be in bed by twelve.

My mother was not less remarkable, as a woman, for the labour she encountered and overcame, in domestic toil to keep our clothes mended —no easy task in such a family, where all the earnings might have gone for food without our having too much—and to add by out-field labour to the income. At the time I was born all the family were at home, consisting then of eight children. The eldest, Margaret, now no more, mother of those five excellent young men, the Doughtys (all rising in the world, and some of them risen as regards social station), she was then as she was to her dying day (and I helped to lay her in her grave, when her sons, mere children, all wept around us and their bereaved father); she was always a helpful creature to everybody who needed help. She sacrificed her life by going from her own house in a delicate condition, to help an afflicted family to bake and wash, and to watch and nurse the dying father of that family. This she did from pure charity, and died herself in the effort. When I was born, Margaret was the only daughter able to work. She worked daily in the fields and the barns, and, morning and night, in the house. She was my first tailor, and the first clothes which she made for me were made from the old corduroys of my brother William. When we lived in Springfield, the house rent was paid by finding one shearer for the harvest, no matter how long the harvest might be; also an out-field worker winter and summer for the farmer; and, in addition to the latter, a 'stack carrier', whenever the threshing mill was going. This last might happen thirty or forty days in the year, and usually in the winter months. For the shearer in harvest, and for the carrying of the stacks into the barn, no wages were paid; but the shearer was allowed breakfast and dinner in harvest time, and a bushel of grain called 'supper barley'. The other worker, called the 'bondager', was paid ten-pence per day, the hours being usually ten, but later whenever the farmer chose.

The carrying of the sheaves from the stackyard into the barn, which was a part of the house rent, was heavy work. My mother did that all the winter before I was born and the winter after, besides shearing in harvest time—the hours being in harvest between sun and sun. The stack carrying was done thus: Two women had a barrow made of two poles, with canvass stretched between the poles; upon which canvass were laid ten or twelve sheaves. The two women then carried that load through the yard and up a gangway to the upper floor of the barn, meeting another couple going down empty. They laid down their barrow, and rolled the sheaves out of it on the floor, where another woman was 'loosing out' and laying the loosened sheaves upon a table, where the man who 'fed in' to the mill stood. One woman stood on the stack outside and forked down the sheaves to the ground; while another on the ground assisted to load the women who carried the barrows. At this work and in the harvest field did my mother bear the burden of heavy labour and of me. After I was born I was carried to her on such occasions to be suckled. My brother James has told me that the duty of carrying me devolved chiefly on him.

Should you ever be in Scotland and see Springfield, you will find a row of shabby looking tiled sheds, such they continued to be when I was there last, the centre one of which is about twelve feet by fourteen, and not so high in the walls as will allow a man to get in without stooping. That place without ceiling, or anything beneath the bare tiles of the roof; without a floor save the common clay; without a cupboard or recess of any kind; with no grate but the iron bars which the tenants carried to it, built up and took away when they left it; with no partition of any kind save what the beds made; with no window save four small panes on one side—it was this house, still a hind's house at Springfield, for which, to obtain leave to live in, my mother sheared the harvest and carried the stacks.

How eight children and father and mother were huddled in that place is not easily told. The worst of it was, that food was so very dear, clothes were so very dear, as to us not to be obtainable, and national glory was so very dear—that glory which Europe was mad about at that time, and for which we, like others, had to pay, that even those bare walls, for which so much of my mother's labour had to be paid in rent, were less comfortable than they might have been.

Next to Margaret was your uncle William, who from boyhood to this present year of his age always contributed to, and never detracted from, the assistance and comfort of our parents, and such others of the family as needed his brotherly aid, and who, as if it were an ordinance of Providence that the dutiful son shall be rewarded even in his own life, has prospered in every thing to which he has put his hand. He was a stripling when I was born, and worked for such wages as a youth could obtain in that part of the country. When he came home at night, my father has told me, he stripped off his coat, took off his hat, put on his night cap, got down the 'elshen box', with awls, hemp, rosin, scraps of leather, lasts, tackets, and hammer; and taking all the children, one by one, as if he had been the father of the family, examined their feet to see which of them had shoes most in need of mending—for all needed repairs, new shoes being in those dear years out of the question. He would then sit down and cobble the shoes by the light of the fire until near midnight, while our mother would mend the other clothes of those in bed, or spin lint to make yarn for the weaver to weave shirting, or card and spin wool for stockings, or darn stockings that were daily decaying. William would then end the day with his private prayer, and go to bed. He would rise at four o'clock in the mornings, and do the heaviest part of James's work amongst the farmer's cows and other cattle, before going to his own day's work two or three miles distant. James was too young for the heavy task of cleaning the cow-houses every morning, which had to be done; but as he could make shift, with the assistance of one or two of the other children nearest him in age, to carry straw and turnips to the cattle, and give them water; and as the payment of the few pence per day was an object of importance to the family (I do not now remember what James got per day; it was, however, less than I subsequently got when a boy for the same kind of work, and my wages were sixpence per day), William got up every morning to do part of the work to keep James in the employment.

This uncle James of yours I have always looked upon as the most intelligent member of our family. He was such an excellent reader when a mere child, so fond of reading, and possessed of such a memory for saying catechisms, psalms, and chapters without the book, that our poor fond father used to lay his hand on his head and say, 'Ah! if I had siller I would make my Jamie a minister.' James, when a young man, went to work as a journeyman cooper at Leith, and almost instinctively, being for the first time within reach of intellectual associates, joined a debating club, where, if he was not distinguished for his style of speaking, he was at least deemed superior for his sound sense.

Neither he nor I have the gift of making speeches. I am too timid and forget in my timidity what I was going to say. This fortunate defect has kept me from being a political orator, so that I have been restricted to the less dangerous sphere of a political writer. The same defect may have kept my brother from political speech-making. Nor has he been a writer. He is possessed of a delicate literary taste, which, even if he had been reduced at any time to write for bare bread as I have been, would have most probably prevented him from rushing into print as I have done.

Whether the world is the better in having a tradesman who puts hoops upon its barrels, saws its timber, makes its bedsteads, and nails its coffins, and does all those things honestly and to the best of his mechanical ability, instead of contributing to its literature and philosophy with a graceful pen and a strong mind, I shall not determine. But if it be a loss to the world not to have more literature and philosophy than it possesses, it has sustained a loss in the mis-employment of your uncle James.

Those three of our family, Margaret, William, and James, were the only ones who could earn anything in addition to my father and mother when I was born, and for several years after.

At Whitsunday term, 1813, we moved from Springfield to Thriepland Hill, where by father lived until that bright summer morning, when in the happiest belief of a glorious resurrection, he died in the month of May, 1834; and where my mother lived until my sister Mary, the last who remained with her, was married in 1840. This Thriepland Hill is the farm and farmery belonging to the small landed estate of Branxton, then a single property, but purchased and added, some years ago, to the more extensive territory of Hunter of Thurston. The stackyard, threshing mill, and cattle sheds, with three houses (now only two), were at Thriepland Hill, while the 'big house', the stables, and some other offices, with three houses for work people, were at Branxton, three quarters of a mile distant. The woods, shrubberies, gardens, and pleasant places about Branxton showed that it had once been the residence of a rich and tasteful proprietor. These had grown wild when I was a boy; and it was amid their wildness and decay that I grew up. Long summers of my boyish life were spent amid these woods, and in the rocky ravine of the Ogle Burn, with the cows which I herded, in almost unbroken solitude, with only the birds singing in the trees, and my dreamy thoughts, and the incessant invention of my organ of constructiveness to amuse me. In the farm fields, sheltered by those woods, I drove the harrows, and held the plough, when I grew out of the office of herding cows.

The earliest recollection that I have of my existence or individuality, was at Thriepland Hill. My mother had spun yarn, and had got the yarn woven into a web for shirting; had cut the web into three pieces, and was bleaching the pieces at the Lady's Well. This was a beautiful spring of soft water, issuing from a green hillside, with a 'bobbing well', or quick moss at the bottom of the hill. No plough had ever broken a furrow there at that time; the boulder stones showed that, and the stone coffins of the chieftains slain in battles long ago, confirmed it. I used to play on the green grass, and gather gowans with my curly haired sister Mary, while our mother watered her webs, or put them through the processes of bleaching. But at that early age I had a propensity to seek to know something more than I knew. The strong spring that gushed into the Lady's Well, puzzled me greatly, as to where it came from, and when it would leave off running. I would lie beside it, and watch it bubbling; and one day in getting nearer and nearer it, to look up into the dark passage from whence it came, I tumbled into the well head foremost. How I was pulled out, or when, I never knew of my own knowledge.

An old man, Thomas Brown, and an older woman, Mary Edgley, his wife, lived next door to us, and they lived alone. They were in their dotage, and were fond of telling the recollections of their youth to the only listeners they could obtain, who were seldom more than my sister Mary and myself. It was some years after that time before I could speak plainly. In my effort to call the old woman Mary Edgley, I called her Essel, which name everybody else took up; she lived ten or twelve years after that time, and was always called Essel. Her most prominent recollections of early life were the love passages. She would sit on one side of the old-fashioned fire-place, telling of the young men who had made love to her, and the young women who had been maids at service with her. While old Thomas, sitting on the other side of the fireplace, poured out—the two speaking together—all his recollections of early life, which chiefly told of how he had been dealt with by the fairies; how the fairies had taken the horses out of the stable and turned them loose to the hills; how one spring-time, the fairies came and took a loan of the harrows to harrow in their corn-seed in fairy land; how he waited and waited for the harrows to be brought back, to get his own corn seed sown; how it was not sown until it was too late to grow and ripen; how, when the harvest failed, and they had no bread, they used to cry 'Fairy, fairy, come bake me a scone; and I'll give thee a spurtle[2] to turn it off and on.' He would continue for hours at such tales, while Essel as uninterruptedly continued to tell how she had been a beauty in her young days, how she had been courted, and how she wondered that 'Old Tam there ever got her.' She was however, ten years older than he was, and he was nearer eighty than seventy at that time. They would have been a study, and their recollections of peasant life in the middle part of last century, a treasure to those who could have appreciated them. But I, being only a child, saw nothing in what they revealed of that world which I did not know, but mystery. We had no intercourse with the social world. Save my sisters Mary and Janet, I knew and saw no children.

When old Thomas Brown died, and Essel was taken elsewhere to live out her great age and die, our next neighbour was old Lizzy, who had an elderly daughter with her. Both professed to have the art of fortune telling, and the oldest of the two travelled through the country after that time and subsisted by telling fortunes. The world, as opened to me by that couple, during two—perhaps three—years that they were our next door and only neighbours, was not the world which I have since found existing beyond Thriepland Hill. The old woman had some grandchildren who occasionally came to see her. One of them told me of the towns he had been in, and of a place called Stobby Castle, where he had lived, and of the things he had seen between that place and Edinburgh, and at Edinburgh; but I had quite as clear a comprehension of the land of the fairies, and of the fairies themselves, as told of by Thomas Brown; and, as Thomas Brown had known the fairies personally, I had as complete a belief in their existence as I had of the people who lived at Stobby Castle, or at Edinburgh, or anywhere else beyond Thriepland Hill and Branxton.

[1] 1788–1844. The travels were in North America.
[2] A stick (not a spoon) for stirring porridge.

CHAPTER II

My Childhood—'Dear Years' of 'Sixteen and 'Seventeen —The Radicals

THE dear years of 1816 and 1817 were now upon us, and they were hard times for the poor, ill times for everybody. The potatoes were bad and few. Our dinner consisted of these potatoes, and one or two salt herrings, divided among five or six of us—all who were at home. My father worked two miles off at the Skateraw lime kilns; went away every morning before light and came home after dark, having taken a piece of bread made of oatmeal and a bottle of milk with him, the usual bread of barley and beans being too hard for his decaying teeth. This was for his day's subsistence. Yet upon such fare as that he had the reputation, as I have since learned from those who worked with him, of being one of the best borers in the limestone quarry; and he was certainly by far the best skilled in books of divinity and general reading, which was of some importance even as regarded the working of the quarry. The *Marrow of Modern Divinity*, a favourite book with him, might not be in all respects a substitute for a marrow bone, but he was strong in conversation or controversy, and kept his spirits up for hard work on that strength. Another reader in the quarry was Robert Wallace, whose wife taught him to read after marriage, and who at the time when my father was in the quarry had read eighteen different authors on astronomy, besides many others on other subjects. Robert Wallace had never seen the stars through a telescope, but he knew all that books could tell him of the celestial system. He would travel twenty miles on a Sunday, and back again, to borrow a book on astronomy. He was rather deaf and seldom went to church. He would get a wheaten flour loaf (having no partiality for the hard bean and barley scones), and would scoop out part of the inside of the loaf, fill the vacancy with treacle or with sugar, go out on the Sunday mornings and find a retired spot inside some cornfield, and lie there all day reading about astronomy and eating his favourite feast of bread and treacle. The last time I was in that vicinity I saw this lost genius, aged and frail, raking the mud off the turnpike road, for a very small sum of wages, near Dunbar. I believe he still lives, and is very poor.

To return to the dear years of 1816 and 1817. I remember that on one occasion our potatoes had dwindled to very nearly none. Those left lay in a corner in the pantry behind the door, and my mother never went into the pantry without drawing a heavy sigh and saying that she 'wondered what in the world would come of us when they would be all done'. Our door opened into the straw close where a number of large, hungry, horned cattle were eating straw. They should have been eating turnips, but the turnip crop had been a failure that year as well as the potato crop. One of these animals had, unseen, made his way into the pantry, and was fast engaged in making a finish of our little stock of potatoes. I and my sisters Mary and Janet—all children, and the only creatures near, except our mother, heard a noise in the pantry and ran to see what it was, and there was our poor mother battling with this horned ox to get him out, and to save the potatoes, he almost too large to turn, even if he had been willing to turn; but he was not willing. His hide and hair were so thick that he cared nothing for all the blows which our mother could give him. He kicked out with his hind feet, and kept eating. In desperation to save the potatoes, my mother got up to his head between his large horns and the wall, and backed him out with blows of the tongs, while he butted and tossed his head. It was a dreadful sight to us; when the brute was dislodged, our poor mother sat down and cried over the loss of the potatoes. We all cried too, and bitter tears they were which we shed, one and all of us.

The next epoch in my life was going to school. This did not occur until I was in my eighth year, partly because I was taught to read at home, partly because the school was two miles away, and there were no other children to accompany me, and *take care of me;* for a notion prevailed, not altogether unfounded, that I could not take care of myself. I had all the appearance of a soft, helpless lad, that could not meet a stone without stumbling, or a pool without going into it to the knees. But the chief reason for not being sent sooner to school, I believe, was the want of clothes, such as the affectionate feelings of my father and mother wished me to go in—simply something else than rags; and these were not to be had until 1818, when markets fell, and food being cheaper, it became possible to get clothes.

My sister Mary was also to go to school for one quarter. We went off one Monday morning, and our mother with us. I see her now before

13

me with her red 'stamped' gown on, and her shawl, and her velvet bonnet. I see the gown as if it had never been absent from my eyes. The place of the school was Birnyknows, a hamlet of about twenty houses, forming a kind of square fifty yards wide, the square filled with pigstyes, dunghills, stagnant pools, and stacks of firewood. The houses in the square were all miserable thatched sheds, save one, the house of George Dickison, a weaver. Outside the square were two or three better houses and weavers' shops. The thatched hovels were chiefly inhabited by the hinds and other labourers of the great farmer of the neighbourhood, who at that time occupied three farms, each of them large. One of the oldest and most infirm of the thatched houses was the school-room. The schoolmaster was a lame man, and was a teacher only because he was lame. It was not a parish school; but he had a local fame as a good teacher, and though, as will be seen, I have no reason to remember him with much respect, I must say that, excepting the inordinate and cruel use of the *taws* for punishment, his system of teaching was better than that of any of the parish schools near us at that time.

My mother saw the schoolmaster in the house of George Dickison, the weaver, and some of the pupils, pleased to see 'new scholars' come, took us into the school, and so my education, having got a twopenny spelling book, began. The first six weeks were consumed in learning to forget to name the letters as my father and mother had named them; that once accomplished, I got on pretty well; for though the spelling books were made up of lessons with no meaning in them, or a meaning of sheer nonsense, I had a desire to know what that nonsense was. In short, I read as well as I could, and tried to read better, and ran before the lesson I was at, to see what the next one said. In this way I was getting on, and had not got much punishment, not so much as several other children reading with me, when one day I came in rather late in the morning. I was instantly called up and questioned as to why I was too late. The schoolmaster was a very polite man in his own way, but he had never taught us the polite designation of vulgar things. After some hesitation, I, in my innocence, gave him an answer which offended him; upon which he took his great leathern belt, thirty inches long, two and a half inches broad, which was split half way up into six thongs, the end of each having been burned in the fire to make it hard; the other end of the belt having a slit in it, into which he put his hand and wound it round his wrist. With this instrument, called the *taws*,

14

he thrashed me on the hands, head, face, neck, shoulders, back, legs, everywhere, until I was blistered. He wanted me to cry, but I would not, and never did for pain or punishment then nor since, though my flesh is nervous and extremely sensitive. I have cried when excessive kindness has been used to me, not when cruelty was used. I sat sullen and in torture all the day, my poor sister Mary glancing at me from her book, she not crying, but her heart beating as if it would burst for me. When we got out of the school to go home, and were away from all the other scholars on our own lonely road to Thriepland Hill, she soothed me with kind words, and we cried then, both of us. We could not tell at home what had happened; our mother would have deeply grieved, and our father, we supposed, would think it all right what the schoolmaster had done, for he believed in his infallibility as a teacher.

My sister went no more to the school than that quarter, having to go to the fields to help to work for the family bread. When the summer of 1819 came, I left school also, to herd the farmer's cows. In the winter of 1819 I again went to school, and got into severe trouble with the teacher on one occasion. It happened thus: some sons of farmers, and sons of other people who read newspapers, told one another of a terrible set of men in some part of the kingdom, called radicals, who were threatening to take the lives and destroy the property of all good people; that only for the soldiers, who stopped them, the radicals would have come to Birnyknows before that time, and would have burned it, and killed everybody. And then one boy would say he was not afraid of the radicals, for he had an uncle who was a soldier, and another had a brother a soldier, and a farmer's son would say that his father was in the yeomanry and had a sword, and saddle with holster pipes, and pistols in the holster pipes, and neither he nor his father were afraid, he would get his father to kill all the radicals who offered to touch him, for they were only ragged weavers, half starved and not able to fight; and the other boys whose brothers and uncles were soldiers, would say that they would go to such brother or such uncle, and get him to kill the radicals that offered to touch them; though, for aught the foolish boys knew, their military relations might be in the East or the West Indies, while those people called radicals, were, so far as Scotland was concerned, located about Glasgow, seventy miles from us.

Perhaps, before I go further, I should tell you who and what the radicals were. They were people who complained that the country was not governed as it should be, that the laws were not made by those who should have made the laws. They were grieved to be excluded from voting for members of parliament, and they felt at the same time that food was dear, wages low, and taxation very high. They said that those circumstances must be altered, and in changing them they must go to the root of the evil, and effect a radical change; the word radical meaning 'original' or 'primitive', and they meaning by using it that they must reform the laws of the country by beginning at the beginning, by pulling down the constitution to the foundation and building up a new one. Many persons used the term 'radical reform', who did not mean to destroy the constitution, or existing form of government, but only to lop off such portions of it as they deemed corrupt. The great body of the radicals was composed of honest working people; but there were attached to them a few persons of wealth and high social station, while all below the working classes, that is to say, the idle, and dissolute, and the rambling makers of speeches, who went from town to town exciting the industrious people to rise against the law and effect a radical reformation, or revolution, by force of guns, pistols, and pikes, were as a matter of course called, and were proud to be called radicals. Those last succeeded in getting many of the more honest men and youths to join them with pikes, pistols, guns, old swords, old scythes, cudgels, and other weapons of offence, in the neighbourhood of Glasgow; from which place they marched into the country to do, what, they hardly knew, and were abandoned by those leaders and instigators who had given information to the authorities where and when the radicals were to be met with, and who then slunk away to live on the rewards paid to them, leaving the radicals with their guns, pistols, pikes, swords, scythes, and cudgels, to be dispersed, slain, or taken prisoners, some of them to be afterwards tried, condemned, and hanged, and beheaded after they were hanged, for high treason.

In other parts of the kingdom, particularly in London and Manchester, there were radicals rising against the law, and the law was rising against them. It is probable that there was undue violence on both sides, and that more forbearance on the side of the law might have been safely practised. Yet when we look to the position which men, charged with maintaining the peace of the country were placed in, we need not be surprised that they adopted every measure which they at the time deemed the best to deter the rebellious and avert revolution. It is easy for us to say, when the danger no longer exists, that *this* other step, and *that* other milder course, would have been better, but it was not so easy for the rulers in those times to know what to do. If, however, there is one thing clearer than another now which they should have done and did not do, it is that they should have opened the doors of the constitution, and admitted some of those who were assembled in multitudes at its doors demanding to be let in. This was done in 1832; the doors were opened by the Reform Act, and a goodly number were let in. I have no doubt that the doors will be opened again and again, allowing all to come in gradually and safely.

But to return to the time of the radicals of 1819, and the rumours that came to Birnyknows school, that 'they were coming'. The term 'ragged radicals' was a common one in newspapers of that time, and the boys who heard their fathers read the newspapers or talk of the news, brought this name of reproach to the school. It was suggested one day by some of them, that an excellent play might be got up in the Eel Yards, a meadow with some large trees in it, if the scholars divided themselves into soldiers and radicals. As the soldiers were the most respectable in the eyes of the better dressed sons of farmers and tradesmen, and as they took the lead in everything, they made themselves soldiers; and, in addition to that, took upon themselves to pick out those who were to be radicals. This was done according to the quality of the clothes worn, and I, consequently, found myself declared to be a radical. The first day's play passed with no greater disasters to me than the brim torn from an infirm hat which I wore, my trousers split up, all the buttons torn from my waistcoat, and my neck stretched considerably on the way to strangulation. For being a radical who seemed inclined to look upon the treatment I received as too serious for play, I was condemned to be hanged. It happened that the clothes I wore were not of the usual corduroy worn by the sons of farm labourers and always worn by me, save in that year. Mine had been remade the year before from some cast-off clothes given a year or two before that to the brother next to me in age by his master. There was a brown coat which had been reduced in size, but it was still too large for me; trousers which had once been of a very light blue or grey; and the infirm hat already named, which came to our family I do not remember precisely how; but it had so broad a brim at first, that my mother cut part of it away to let me see from below it, and still it was so broad that some of the boys nicknamed me after some people whom I had never seen nor heard of, but who were said to wear broad-brimmed hats. These clothes having been old when I got them, and having been worn by me all the summer in the woods herding the cows, and all the autumn, they were not in sound condition. But my poor mother always kept them patched up; and I never once went out then or any time, with an open rent or a worn hole in my clothes. As she spun wool for stockings, and lint for shirts, herself, and my father knitted stockings at night, and my sisters made shirts, I was equal in those articles to any one in the school; and I was only so badly clothed otherwise because the second year was running on between my father and a master for whom he then worked without a settlement of accounts; the said master allowing my father to get oats for meal, and barley and beans for bread, but being sadly embrraassed as a land-owner, with his land mortgaged—not able at that time to pay up the arrears of wages.

When I went home on that first evening of my ragged radicalship, my poor mother stood aghast, lifted her hands, and said, in a tone of despair, 'What shall I do with those rags?' They were stripped off, I got an early supper and was sent to bed, while she began to mend them—putting in a piece there and a piece here, sewing up a rent, darning the worn holes, and ending some hours after midnight, not far from the usual hour of rising from bed, by sewing the luckless brim upon my infirm hat. Her motherly affection for me, and natural pride in the good appearance of her family, had led her to suggest to my father that I should not be sent again to school until we had got the 'siller' we were waiting for to get new clothes. But my father, though not less affectionate, and not less anxious about the appearance of his family, was stern upon that point. 'If the laddie lives to be a man,' said he, 'he will need his education, and more than we can give him. If I had got schooling myself, as I am trying to give to all my sons, it would have helped me through the world more easily than I have got through. The laddie must go to the school.'

So I went to the school, my mother begging of me, with tears in her eyes, not to get my clothes torn again, else it would kill her to see me in such rags, and to have to sit up every night to mend them. But 'soldiers and radicals' was again the play, and again I was the radical upon whom the greatest number of soldiers concentrated their warfare. They had seen me thrashed by the schoolmaster until I was blistered,

18

without crying or shedding a tear, which made them think I could stand any amount of punishment or torment, without feeling it; in short, I was believed to be a great stubborn lad, who had no feeling in him. Had they seen me after leaving my mother that morning, and carrying her injunction with me, in a heart that was bursting with her words, they would have seen whether I had tears in me or not, and whether they would not come out.

As soon as I made my appearance, the cry of the 'ragged radical' was raised; the soldiers charged on me, and knocked my infirm hat over my eyes with my head through the crown of it. Some laid hold of me by the feet to carry me off to be hanged and beheaded, *as the real law upon the real radicals had taught them to imitate in play*. I made a violent effort to free myself, and the rents of yesterday, which my mother had so carefully sewed, broke open afresh. The hat I raised from where it had sunk over my face, and saw part of the brim in the hands of a lad who was a kind of king of the school, or cock of the walk, with some of my poor mother's threads hanging from it. He was older than I, and was a fighter. I had never fought, nor had heard of two human creatures going together to fight, until I came to that school. Yet neither had I heard of the divine principle of forbearance and forgiveness, as regards blows upon the body, and the laceration of feelings worse than blows upon the body—my father, who gave me many good precepts, never having contemplated the possibility of my being a fighting boy. (My child, you will be brought up where there are policemen and law, lawyers and magistrates to take your part if you are injured; never raise your own hand against any one.) But I was a strong boy for my age, and I had received very bad treatment. My honour and the remembrance of my affectionate mother's toils made me feel like a giant. I amazed the king of the school by giving him a blow in the face that laid him flat on his back, and amazed the onlookers by giving several of them as much with the same results. Not that I escaped without blows myself. I got many, but they were returned with principle and interest. Some one ran to the schoolmaster and told that I was thrashing 'Master' Somebody, for he being a gentleman's son was called 'Master', while I had to submit to a nickname, derived from the state of my clothes. The school was summoned in at once, it being near the schoolhour in the morning. Some of those whose noses were bleeding ran to school with them in that state to let their disasters be seen. Another one and myself tried to get water to wash our faces, for mine was in as bad a condition as the worst of theirs; but the frost was so hard, that we could not break the ice to get water, and at last were compelled to obey the repeated summons to school in the dreadful guise we were then in; my clothes being torn half off me in addition to the hideousness of the blood streaming from my face.

The schoolmaster stood with the *taws* ready to flagellate the moment I entered the school. He inquired who began the fight, and every one named me. He at once ordered me to hold up my right hand, which I did, and received a violent cut on the edge of it, given with his whole strength. He ordered my left hand up, and up it went and received a cut of the same kind; then my right, which got what it got before; next my left, which also got what it got before; and so on he went until I had got six cuts (skults we called them) on each hand. He had a way of raising himself upon his toes when he swung the heavy *taws* round his head, and came down upon his feet with a spring, giving the cuts slantingly on the hand. He saw me resolved to take all he could give without a tear, whereupon he began to cut at the back of my hands. I drew them behind me to save them, which seeing, he cut at the open places of my torn clothes, where my skin was visible; and always as I wriggled to one side to save those bare places, I exposed other bare places on the other side, which he aimed at with terrible certainty. After a time he pushed me before him, still thrashing me on the bare places, and on the head, until he got me to the farther end of the school, where the coals lay in a corner. He thrashed me until I got on the top of the coals. Here he ordered me to sit down and remain until he gave me liberty to leave that place, which he did not do until evening. The day was piercing cold. The house was an old place, with no furniture nor partition in it. I sat at the end farthest from the fire-place, and near to the door, which was an old door that did not fit its place, and which allowed the wind to blow freely through. It blew through and about me as if it had been another schoolmaster, and was as partial to the farmers' sons, and as cruel to the ragged boys of farm labourers, as he was.

CHAPTER III

School and Cow-herding—My Blind Companion

THE misfortune which befel me, as related in the last chapter, happened on a Friday. It was the custom at our school on that day to re-read all the lessons of the week, and say over again all the spelling lessons. The teacher kept slates with every pupil's name written on them, and against each name, he, during the week, put a mark for being too late for school, for being deficient in any lesson, or hymn, or question; and on the Friday he put a mark for each mistake in reading or spelling, on the afternoon of which day he read out the names, beginning with one which had no marks, if such there was, or with a name which had fewest, if there was no name with none. He gave a half-penny to each of those in junior classes whose names were read by him with the word 'none', and to those of the superior classes he gave a penny, or more commonly a penny-worth of paper or quills.

I had often got the half-penny, for I must do him the justice to say that he was impartial in allowing the best reader to get to the head of the class. I made little progress in arithmetic or writing, either at his school or elsewhere; but in reading and spelling, and in learning cate-chisms, psalms and hymns, I may be said to have rushed up, 'ragged radical' as I was, like a weed that over-topped the most tenderly-nourished plants. Some of those who were in the shilling spelling-books when I went first to school with my two-penny book, had been over-taken by me and left behind; and I was now in a collection called the Tyro's Guide, which I had already mastered, every word of it, whether to read or spell, and should have probably been put forward to the next class reading in the Bible and Barrie's collection, if my parents could have afforded to buy Barrie's book, which they could not do at that time.

On this eventful Friday I was made to read my share of the lesson from the top of the coals; which I did with the usual correctness, though I was very cold, and a far way out of good humour. I spelt all my own share of the words; and the words which others stuck at, on their being put to me, I spelt for them. I was in hopes that this good work on my part would lead to my free pardon, and redemption from the coal-hole, and I watched with tremulous expectation the reading of the names of my class. The teacher called silence, and when silence was obtained, he began slowly and emphatically, 'the bad boy who sits on the coals, *none*; at the *bottom* of the class, and to sit on the coals until he behaves better.' And the next, who had several marks to his name, was read off thus—'at the top of the class in the bad boy's place.' I can hardly say if I would not have had another thrashing with the taws rather than have suffered this renewed disgrace.

I need not tell what was said or done when I got home with my poor clothes once more torn. I could not conceal that I had been fighting, for my face showed it; nor that I had been severely flogged by the schoolmaster, for my body, blistered and cut in every direction, showed it. My mother and sister, from fear that my father would also punish me if he knew that I had been fighting and had come home with my clothes torn again, kept the disaster secret, got me to bed out of the way, and patched my dilapidated rags together when my father had gone to sleep.

One good resulted from it—the hat which had brought so much ridicule and so many enemies on me, was too far gone to be repaired, and some old highland bonnet, which once belonged to James or Peter, was rummaged out and mended for me. This, though it did not come over my ears as the ample hat had done, saved me from that biting ridicule which was worse than biting frost.

On going to school next day, I found matters quite as hopeless as the day before, as regarded the teacher, not as regarded the soldier and radical business; there was no more of that. But some of the young gentry had gone home with bruised faces and other wounds, and had told terrible tales of a bully who fought them all out of the school, and who was so ragged and foul in the school that they could not sit near him. Orders were at once sent to the teacher that I was to be separated from those boys and girls, else they would be taken from the school. The charge of uncleanness was an audacious libel, for a child more tenderly cared for, and kept in more healthful cleanliness than I was by my mother, never entered that or any other school; but the outward appearance of my clothing gave rise to the libel and continued it.

I was put on a form by myself, in the middle of the floor, and there I sat day after day, for about six weeks. My father had such a good opinion of the teacher, that I could not tell him, and my mother would have grieved so much, that I could not muster courage to complain to her. It came to a termination thus: The form had four pins in it for its feet; these pins were loose, and it was the custom of one of the sons— the eldest, of the the great farmer of the neighbourhood—to kick it down whenever I stood up to read my lesson, so that I had to put the feet in it again, and doctor it up, before I could sit down. In the mornings, when I entered the school, one foot would be in the coal hole, another up the chimney, another beneath the schoolmaster's chair, and so forth. I had to gather them together and make my seat amid tittering and laughter, in which the teacher often joined. He would rebuke the whole school for the mischief, as if he did not know which one, or which of two or three did it, and tell them what he would do if the mischief was repeated. One day, the young gentleman who amused himself most frequently at my expense, came with his brothers, in new clothes, all very smart and fine, and in his gaiety of spirits, at being so finely dressed in new clothes, he was more than usually frolicsome and mischievous. Having the run of the school, his father being its chief patron, and landlord of the house, he went about doing anything his fancy led him to do. Twice that day he came behind me, unseen, and knocking a foot from the form, with a violent jerk, let me fall down on the floor, and twice all the scholars and the schoolmaster laughed at me. He did it a third time, when I started up, and seizing hold of one of the loose feet of the form, would have probably struck him with it, had not the teacher come behind me and held me. He made me lay it down, and spoke very angrily to my tormentor, and that soothed me considerably. But on going out at the midday play hour, the young gentleman, still bent on mischief, snatched my bonnet off my head, and ran away with it. I pursued with the bounds of a lion, and soon came up with him, though he was a fast runner (I had never run so fast before, and probably have never done so since). As I was reaching him, he threw my bonnet into a filthy pool of stagnant water, thinking I would follow it. I followed him and caught him in my arms, and though he was taller, older, and generally stronger than I, and though he kicked and bit me, I bundled him along and soused him into the filthy pool, new clothes and all, where he wallowed in a most wretched plight, and bellowed like a young bull. He gathered himself up at last and ran home to tell of his disaster, while I made up my mind for a terrible thrashing from the schoolmaster. Sometimes I thought of running home, but the fear of my father deterred me; then I thought of running away somewhere—anywhere, and never going home again, but the thought of my mother, and how she would grieve, overcame that. I slunk away alone into the eel yards among the trees, and rubbed my hands with clay to harden them, that I might not feel the taws to be so terribly severe. I was thus employed, when one of the weavers came and called me to come to him. I felt sure that he was going to take me to the school to be flogged, for I had no doubt that everybody would look upon the deed I had done as a great crime. I viewed it so myself by that time. Nothing on earth seemed to me, in those times, so precious and so much to be desired as new clothes, and I had destroyed a youth's new suit of the finest clothes I had ever seen. I did not go to the weaver, so he came towards me. I began to walk away; he began to run, whereupon I ran too. He called to me to stop, that he was not going to hurt me, he only wanted to speak to me: but I continued to run. Ultimately he came up with me, and assuring me that it was not to have me flogged, but to prevent it, that he wanted me back with him, I returned.

The end of this was, that the weavers, hearing how I had been treated for a long time, and particularly of the provocation I had got that day, and sympathising with me as one distressed (and probably because I was the son of an Anti-burgher, who went to the same meeting-house as they went to), interfered in my behalf, and I was not flogged, nor made to sit any more on the solitary form.

That dismal period of my life soon passed over. I got new clothes; the early summer months soon came; I was sent again to the leafy woods to herd the cows, where I made water-mills and wind-mills, built houses large enough to creep into, and some of them small enough, with carved stones shaped in imitation of masons' stones, to be curiosities. I did not go to Birnyknows school again; I went to the parish school of Oldhamstocks, where, if I did not learn much, I had leave to live and learn without punishment. My brother James had been resident for a year or two in Leith and Edinburgh, had returned to the country, and set up in business as a cooper at Innerwick, where, besides being accounted one of the most intelligent men of the district, and one of the best business men in the parish in such things as benefit societies, and in organizing a parish watch for the church-yard, to prevent resurrectionists from disturbing the repose of the dead, which watch exists, as he organized it, to this day—besides doing such things as these, he opened evening singing classes in the parish school of Oldhamstocks, introduced new songs, and taught more people church music than had ever been taught before, which led (in addition to the reputation I now enjoyed as a lad who could play at foot-ball with any one, and take my own part in anything) to my being looked upon by other lads as not a common boy, because I was the singing-master's brother! When playing at fox and hounds I could go through as deep pools in the burn, get over as steep rocks, take refuge in places as unapproachable, and head, if I was a hound, lead, if I was the fox, as long a chase right up into the Lammermoor hills, as any one.

Two years before that I had been permitted to go to Oldhamstocks fair, for the first time, under care of my sisters, Janet and Mary. My money given to spend was a penny, Mary's money two pennies, and Janet's three pennies, our ages being so related. I had never before seen a town, nor village, nor shop, nor a stall, nor a coin of any kind spent, nor an article of any description purchased. The fair consisted of about one hundred head of cattle, and perhaps two hundred people, and as I had never seen such an assemblage before, I was amazed, and we stood the greater part of the day gazing at the riches of a stall of gingerbread, upon which we had expended all our fortunes, and it was still not sold up.

But now I had no less than fourpence given me to go to the fair with, by my mother; and in that fair stood the cooper, my brother, with a cart-load of cooper's ware of all descriptions, selling them to the lady wives of farmers; and to the farmers in top-boots and spurs, and passing jokes with them, and I could stand so near to them without being awe struck at the fine clothes they wore that I could actually touch a farmer's top-boots if I chose. And again, when my fourpence was spent, and I conveyed that information to the cooper, by the roundabout method of telling him that I knew some other boy who had spent all his money; he never hesitated for a moment to understand me, but gave me a sixpence, and afterwards bought a knife himself and gave it to me for my 'fairing'. To be the cooper's brother in Oldhamstocks fair was to make me be looked upon with respect even by some of those youths who once used me ill, and who happened to be there. But the strangest change of all was, that on going with my brother in the evening to get a biscuit at the village inn, while he and others had bottled ale to drink, the terrible schoolmaster who had thrashed me so, and the very sight of whom used to make me quake with dread, was sitting there drinking ale, and did not look terrible; on the contrary, he was actually singing, and with the parish schoolmaster and my brother took part in glees and other songs.

He is dead, and I would rather have buried his ill treatment of me in a grave within myself; but his kind of schoolmasters still live in Scotland, and so I write of him. Besides which, I could not tell the story of my life correctly if I omitted this portion of it.

Of those boys who were hardest upon me, one has spent a fortune, and is or lately was poor. Two or three are dead. Two or three are hinds to farmers. Two are in America, and 'going a-head' wonderfully, as I have heard, both in wealth and station. Of those who were punished with a severity most nearly approaching my punishments, one was a sailor, and fell from the topmast of a ship on the deck and was killed. One enlisted into the Scots Greys, and I believe is a soldier in that regiment still. This was rather a dull boy in learning, and whatever intellectual life he had in his boyhood was thoroughly thrashed out of him. His name is J. G. and if any one can bear me witness as to the awful punishments at Birnynows school, he can. Another of the sufferers is captain of a trading ship. A few more were the sons of fishermen, who have all gone to sea as their fathers did, and have shared the same destiny—have been drowned in the pursuit of their perilous profession, or are still following it, sometimes poor, sometimes not poor, all of them fathers of large families.

It seems that, as by a law of nature, those fishes which are most exposed to enemies and impending extinction, breed the fastest and most numerously, so does that law of nature apply to fishermen. Many a gallant boat's crew I have known on that stormy coast go out to sea and never return; but each of the lost men usually left a young boat's crew growing up. Before I went to school it was dreaded that, being unprotected by companions who knew me and would take my part against the rough fisher lads, I should be in danger of ill usage from them. But they were the only lads who took my part, and who never ill-used me. I have in after years, when we were men, been employed with them, and they were then the same daring, generous, gallant fellows that they were when boys; not much the better for having been at school to be thrashed, perhaps, and knowing little of books; but knowing more of the volume of nature opened on the sea shore and on the sea, and in the firmament above them and the sea, than most other men. Ignorant of the very name of German literature and German philosophy, but more familiar with the deep mysteries of the German ocean, upon which they go many hundreds of miles for cod-fish, than any metaphysician is with the mysteries of the deep ocean upon which he embarks.

My first acquaintance with the subjects of books, not with the books themselves, but with the history and geography of the world as known through books, was while herding the cows in the wooded solitudes of the Ogle Burn. The only persons whom I saw during the long summer days were the women who came to milk the cows at midday, the gipseys who were occasionally encamped in those woods, and an aged blind man, James Dawson. James did not rise from bed until midday, as his aged wife worked in the fields for daily bread, and did not get home to help him to put on his clothes until the dinner hour— his limbs being too stiff with old age for him to dress himself. If the afternoon was fine, he made his appearance at the foot of the Ogle about two o'clock. He either whistled to himself, or sung, or talked, as he came slowly along in quest of me and the cows; most commonly he talked. He had been a shepherd when he had his eyesight, and had read history and geography extensively. In his best days he had been a man of strong imagination, and now that he was blind, his memory and imagination peopled his path with beings from history with whom he held conversation. I had read no history then, and no books of any kind but the first school books. My father's library consisted entirely of divinity, and it was nearly all controversial, which I did not understand; the exceptions to controversy were sermons. On a stone at the foot of the Ogle Burn, and on a green sod which overgrew a low wall at a place on the verge of Branxton estate, in the upper woods, James Dawson used to sit down and call to Sir Walter Raleigh, Essex, Burleigh, and other courtiers of Elizabeth to come to him, and when they came he sent them to fetch her majesty. He would then go into political arguments with them about Philip of Spain and the other personages and subjects of Elizabeth's reign. He would listen as if some one spoke into his ear, for their observations, and would interrupt them at times impatiently, if they did not seem to be holding a sound argument. Intermingled with such converse he would speak aside to some shepherd or farmer whom he had known in his younger days, and ask him what he thought of Burleigh's opinions. The next minute he would address me by name, and ask a question as to what I thought of Queen Elizabeth's dress.

Since I have grown to manhood, and read history and geography, I have been often surprised to find the persons and places which James Dawson used to make me familiar with. One of his most frequent associates in those imaginary conversations was Washington. The Empress Catherine of Russia was another. One time, when he came to me, and I, in the usual way, asked, 'Well, James, how are ye thi' day?' he said, 'Man, Sandy, I'm glad I've met ye. You're a clever callant, and you must go this minute to the Empress, and tell her that Frank Horne must not be made a slave. If you go down to Linkheads, you'll meet Paul Jones, and he will take ye in a Russian man-of-war to the Empress. Tell her, if she does not liberate Frank Horne, and all her slaves, I will be obliged to take her through hands myself.' This Frank Horne had been a lad in Branxton, and James had the idea that he was about to be made a slave in Russia. I had never until that time heard the term, slave, spoken, and did not know its meaning. I inquired what a slave meant, and to this day I have a distinct recollection of the stories he proceeded to tell me of slaves, slavery, the slave countries, and the slave trade. His descriptions I have since found were realities.

Thus, in the solitude of the Ogle Burn, and the Cocklaw planting, in the company of this singular old man, he believing himself and me surrounded with the personages of history and romance, did I first learn anything of the world which is laid before us in books—anything of countries beyond our own—anything of other ages, and other classes of society.

James Dawson was then near his eightieth year. He was a tall man, two or three inches above six feet; wore a broad blue bonnet, with his white hair hanging from beneath it behind; a long broad skirted coat of light blue cloth, with a leathern belt girded around his waist; a grey checked plaid thrown around his shoulders, and a staff five feet long, with a pike in the lower end of it. He stepped slowly, with his staff in his right hand, at a wide angle from his body, his left hand being in the folds of his plaid. In his venerable head there was a great store of book knowledge; but what with a lively imagination, and many years of blindness, the knowledge had become disordered—the facts of everyday life mingling with the images of beings and of actions that were unreal. I heard the neighbours speak of him as 'superannuate', and not knowing that the historical personages with whom he believed himself to associate in the woods had once been real, I believed less in them than I did in some of the more spiritual of those to whom he addressed himself—the '*Enemy*', for instance. One day, my father, on meeting him, inquired about his health, and how he had been for some time, during bad weather, when he could not get out of doors. He said the weather had been no hindrance to him; he had been on a visit to paradise, where there was no bad weather. 'Aye, have ye been there?' said my father, inquiringly. 'Yes,' replied the other; 'but I did not see any of your folk there'; meaning that he did not see any of the dissenters—known as Anti-burghers, there; and he immediately added, 'but I heard that W—— B—— was there; but he had gone out to get a dram, and I did not see him: he still sits late at his dram.' There was a cutting irony in this, which was quite sharp enough even for him to whom it was addressed, with all his philosophy and general good humour. For James Dawson was a churchman, and had no high opinion of dissenters; while the Anti-burgher dissenters were very rigid, and, taken as a body, were not indisposed to believe themselves better than other people. An elder, who belonged to the congregation of which my father was a member, was the party alluded to as having reached paradise, from which he had thought fit to steal away to get a dram, and had not returned.

Jean Crombie (it is the custom for married women, in Scotland, to retain their maiden names, a custom which sounds strangely in English ears), was one of the happiest and kindest of human beings whom I have at any time known. Though sixty years of age, she worked in the fields or barns during the year almost daily, and supported herself and her infirm husband on the wages of her daily toil, with the exception of the allowance of twelve shillings per quarter, which was received from Innerwick parish. The parish allowance was at first only six shillings per quarter. My father went several times, on behalf of the poor blind man, to the Rev. Mr. Logan, the parish minister, and ultimately succeeded in getting the aliment augmented to twelve shillings. And this, to the discredit of the Scottish Poor-law of that day, was considered a good allowance. The indefatigable industry and happy contentedness of Jean Crombie, however, kept her almonry always supplied with food, and her house always clean, the floor being scoured and sanded, and the door steps whitened; every article of furniture in the house being an example to any housewife to look at; while the blind man never wanted his tobacco, of which he made a most liberal use in chewing. In the latter years of the life of this amiable woman, one, and sometimes two, of her grand-daughters lived with her, eased her toil, and aided her in house-keeping.

I remember reading a book of travels which gave an account of the hideous idols worshipped in India. I wondered why, if people fell down on their knees, and worshipped something else than the one God, they did not make choice of idols that were pleasing and lovely. I thought that if I lived among idolators, and fell upon my knees to worship anything that was of earth, I would pay divine honours to one of those grand-daughters. She, however, never knew this, nor did any other human being. I was only a boy, and as yet had no idea of the feeling called love; my thoughts took this idolatrous turn from a love of the beautiful. She was married before I was half grown to manhood, and has a family now grown to men and women.

CHAPTER IV

I am the Runaway Boy

I WAS in my fourteenth year when an occurrence fell in my way, or I fell in the way of the occurrence, which may be related at length. It was harvest time, nearly the end of harvest. The men of the farm, and two hired strangers were carting the corn sheaves from the fields, and I was on the stackhead in the barnyard, lifting each sheaf on a fork as it was thrown from the loaded cart by the carter, to the stack in process of being built, and laying the sheaf at the hand of the stackbuilder, that he might get hold of it readily to put it in its place with his knees above it, without having to rise from his knees. The shearers were at the last field of corn on that day. In the afternoon it was seen that there was more to shear than they could do at the usual rate of working. Wherefore the master sent some bottles of whisky to the field, to be mixed with water, and given to the shearers, partly in honour of it being the last day of shearing, but chiefly to make them drive on at great speed with their work to get it done.

The whisky had its desired effect. All the people, male and female, home hands and hired hands, Scotch and Irish, slashed down the corn, and strove with one another at the work more like mad people than workpeople. The men carting the corn from some other field to the barnyard where I was at work, passed this scene of laborious strife going out and coming in with their carts, but got none of the whisky, at which they grumbled a good deal. They said to me that if they could run as well as I could, and were *as clever as I was*, they would run down the side of a certain hedge, and get one of the bottles, which were still in the basket, in no time. On another man coming in with his loaded cart, and hearing what had been suggested to me, he also urged the adventure; and off I ran down the hedge side, across the field, and, amongst the sheaves at a certain place which had been named, found the basket, and brought off one of the bottles of whisky. Being fleet of foot in those days, I was soon in the barnyard with the purloined mischief, and it was soon dealt out and drunk by the men; for my own part I abhorred the very flavour of whisky at that time, and tasted none of it. But I was in a full flow of animal spirits, through the exertion I had used in performing the feat, and from the praise awarded me by those who had enjoyed and were made talkative by the hot spirit of the bottle; so I thought nothing was wrong about it, and worked on with vigour and gaiety.

We had nine or ten men, who came annually to the harvest-work from the county of Antrim, in Ireland, six of whom were named Michael—old Michael, young Michael, big Michael, wee Michael, singing Michael, and Michael the laird. They were all good shearers save the last; old Michael, the head of the lot, being a favourite with most of us. The laird was so called from having owned a piece of land in Ireland. He had dissipated it, however, and was perhaps poorer than any of the others, because not so good a worker. He was fond of drink, and a cunning man. On this occasion he had dropped behind the shearers, who, striving with one another, did not observe him; and he, having seen me approaching, hid himself in a stook of corn sheaves near to where the whisky bottles and basket stood. He saw me take a bottle. His own design being to drink or hide a bottle until a convenient time to remove it, he did so with more confidence, and probably to a greater extent than at first intended, because he saw the blame could be laid on me.

In due time three bottles, the greater part of the store in the basket, were missed. A general outcry was raised, and all the Michaels and their party exclaimed at once, Michael the laird having informed them, that 'Sandy from the stack-yard done it'—that 'he came down from the stack-yard and done it.' Added to this, one of the carters going past was questioned by the master if any of the whisky had been taken to the barnyard; and he, seeing the affair beginning to look serious, and fearing for himself, said that he saw me bring some to the barnyard; that he drank some of it thinking it had been sent to them. The master said he did not like a trick of that kind, because he was always ready to give the men a glass of whisky (which he certainly was).

Upon which my father, who was binding the sheaves to six shearers, as is the custom, and no doubt vexed at the slashing nature of the shearing, and the bad bands made to tie the corn, which again was thrown into the bands, heads and tails, in the wild work of that day, giving him much trouble and fourfold work; he having also, on principle, a dislike to work of that kind being so executed—people cutting their own hands, and cutting the hands of their neighbours, and quarrelling by the power of whisky; he having those causes to put him out of a happy humour, felt himself and the whole family to be terribly disgraced by my having carried away the whisky. Those who did not know otherwise, and he was one of them, supposed that I had taken all that was missing. He came up to the stack-yard, and commanded me to come down from the stack-head, where I was at work. I saw there was something of fearful importance to me in his face, and I would rather not have faced him; but I went down the ladder, and asked what he wanted with me, though truth to tell, it was no mystery, for he had in his hand a formidable cudgel, a fork shaft. He struck me a grievous number of blows with it. He at last left off, telling me I had disgraced myself and the family for ever: the only words he spoke. He burst into tears, and went away. I was much nearer to the shedding of tears when I saw him in that condition than when he was giving me blows, but I kept myself silent and gloomy, weeping not, speaking not. Some of the men asked why I did not run from him, when he was striking me; another said if his father had ever struck him that way, he would have struck his father, and would have knocked him down if he had been able, and he was sure that I was strong enough to have done so to my father. Only one of them, the builder of the stacks (David Lyall, long since settled as a farmer and flockmaster in the region of Buenos Aires, in South America), seemed to condole with me; none of them had the sense of fairplay in them to make a statement of the whole truth; and I was by this time too much troubled in spirit to do so myself. They did not understand the nature of my mind, who either thought that I might have run away or have battled with my father. It might have been an unworthy obstinacy that made me firm, but I took that as I have taken all other punishments, in silence. This feeling I can account for; but not quite so easily can I account for my standing as if willing to receive punishment. There was a kind of fascination, or if that is not the name, an influence without a name, that rooted me to the one spot of space whenever my father commanded me to stand there, or which made me involuntarily move towards him if he commanded me so to move. It was not easy to believe, when one's bones and skin were sore with punishment, that it was done in parental love; but my poor father was at all other times affectionate to me and to all his family, and showed it in so many ways of hard endurance on his part for our sakes, while I, on calm reflection, could always see within

33

myself that I had done something reprehensible before he punished me. Still I do think that a milder course might have been more effective.

We were at this time working at Thriepland Hill, near to which was our house. I was victualled that year in the master's house at Branxton, but came home to sleep at night. On this evening I did not come home. I did not come home to sleep. I did not sleep at all. I lay down amongst the straw in the stable at Branxton, where the master's riding-horse stood, and planned during the night what I should do with myself. I was deeply affronted at having been so punished in the presence of so many people, and some of them strangers; and I resolved to go away and leave home for a long time, and not return until I had lived to be a man, and had done something that would entitle me to respect. To go to my brother James was to be too near home; to go to my brother William, who lived in Yorkshire as forester to the Duke of Devonshire, seemed as undesirable as staying where I was. He had always been a kind of second father in our family, when at home, and to the family when away. He was now in a situation above that of a working man, and would expect any relation to come to him *dressed* (so I fancied), which I could not be, for my Sunday's clothes were at home where I could not get them, and I had on my ilkaday breeks, my highland bonnet, and tacketed shoon (nailed shoes). Besides which disadvantages, I would have to tell, so I reasoned, why I had left home, and why I had given offence to my father, which offence would appear to William to be a punishable one, I had no doubt. Accordingly I decided against going to Yorkshire.

The next bent of my thoughts was to my brother Peter, who was a soldier in the Royal Artillery; had been serving in the West Indies, but was now supposed to be returned to Woolwich, and serving there. What I could do if I reached Peter was by no means clear to me, nor did I know how I was to reach Woolwich, nearly four hundred miles distant. I had one penny, and one penny only in the world. I had but a poor notion of what the life of a soldier is, but I had read of wonderful adventures and successes, and I thought, foolish boy that I was, that if I could reach Peter, he and I might yet become captains, colonels, or great generals. Yet, again, I doubted if one so young as I was would be admitted into the army; and I doubted if I would find Peter at Woolwich if I got there; and then I doubted if I should ever find Woolwich.

But I resolved to go, and travel somewhere. It was Sunday morning,

34

and the day was breaking. I knew nobody would be astir for several hours, as people did not rise early on the morning of the day of rest in harvest time, and that I might remain later and still go unseen. But I resolved to go soon, and go far away that day. The master's riding horse neighed when it heard me moving about the stable; and as I was its groom, in addition to many other offices which I filled on the farm, I opened the corn chest, of which I carried the key, and gave it a feed of corn. It knew me well, and I hung my arms around its neck as it ate the corn, and told it I would never see it more.

I then took a pice of chalk, and wrote on the top of the corn chest, 'Fare ye well, Branxton, I am away, never to come back.' My heart had been beating all night quick and strong, and my mouth was feverish and thirsty. I went to the pump to have a draught of cold water, and with all seriousness and sorrow, I bade the pump farewell. Coming away from it, my eyes caught sight of my old wheelbarrow on the dunghill, with which I wheeled the clearings from the stables; I turned it upon its feet, lifted it, and put it down again, and said, 'Poor old barrow, I shall never wheel you again.' Coming out of that close, I had to pass the cart in which I had taken the breakfasts and dinners, the porridge and bread and beer, so often to the fields to the shearers during that and other harvests. Taking my chalk, I wrote on the bottom of it, 'Parritch cart, I am done with you.' Then going up the coach-house road, between the high holly hedges, which overshadowed the road, and under the large trees which met and overshadowed the hedges, I stood a few minutes considering which way I should go, and bitterly regretting that I could not take farewell of something belonging to my mother. All at once the thought struck me, that I would go up into the Fir Knowe, and see the cows, and my mother's cow in particular, and bid it farewell. I did not find them in the Fir Knowe, so I went down the steep hill side, amid the holly bushes, rabbit holes and high trees, to the meadow—a lovely green, framed, as it were, in rows of dark spruce trees, the timber of other varieties rising on the high ground behind the rows of spruce. Here, as I expected, I found the cows. Some of them would have nothing to do with me, but others knew me well, and were kind and gentle, and allowed me to lay my hands on them. My mother's was one of these. I put my hands on her head and neck, and said to her I was going away and would never see her again. The poor animal knew not what I said, but in her usual kindness she licked my hand with her tongue, and I felt as if it was a friend that sympathised with me. I tried to come away from her. I had left the master's riding horse, the pump, the wheelbarrow, and the cart which I used to work with, all of them with heaviness of spirit, yet without a tear. I could not repress tears as I quitted poor Kidley; she was my mother's favourite, and licked my hand, and I thought of my mother. I turned back to the kindly animal again, and put my arms around her neck, and gave her my hand, which she again licked so gently with her tongue, that I cried outright, and blubbered like a great foolish boy as I was.

I left her, and going up the wooded acclivity, with my face towards the Rabbit Hill, where the rabbits, starting before me and running to their holes, seemed to turn round and look as if they knew I was not their enemy now, and was going away from them, and was never coming to shoot them again. The birds that twitter and sing in the early morning were all in voice and upon the fluttering wing, as if they had got up to see me away. Every creature seemed to be up and astir but human creatures, and I felt a melancholy pleasure in seeing at my parting so many living things and no human thing. I was gloomy, and anxious to shun human beings.

Coming down the road called the avenue, my face eastward, I remembered a large beech tree in the Pond Planting, by the side of the road not far from the dismal deep pond, on which tree all of our family who had herded cows in those woods had carved the initials of their names, with the dates and other memoranda. I paid a visit to that tree, and once more put my name on it, and then turned away. The sun was rising; the top of the little thatched house where slept my father, mother, and sisters, was just visible through the trees, with the first beams of the glowing sun glorifying the old thatch. Were they sleeping soundly under that roof, or were they awake and mourning for me who had not been home all night—the first night I had been a fugitive from their roof? I thought the glowing sun upon the house, seen so soon after the dark night of trouble which I had wasted in wakefulness, might indicate that there was now forgiveness, and welcomes, and warm affections for me under the thatch; and that, like the night, all displeasure had disappeared. And this thought enlarged itself. Perhaps, said I, that sunshine on my father's roof at this very early hour (it hardly seemed the natural time for sunrise), is the face of God looking upon me, and signifying that that is the place I should go to. With which thought in me I remembered that I had not once, in the momen-

36

tous resolves I had been making, prayed, or thought of praying. I tried to pray now, but could not. The unformed words refused to be formed into prayer. I felt myself to be a rebel against my father and against God, and the very prayers which I had once used now rebelled against me, and would not be uttered. They fled even from my thoughts in their very spirit when I tried only to think them, without saying them word by word. I could not pray. It was awful; yet I could not. Neither could I undo my resolves and remain at home. I made a sudden start and away I went.

My face and feet went towards England. Berwick-upon-Tweed was about twenty-five miles distant. I was over the half of that distance while it was yet early. I reached Ayton, eight miles from Berwick, before the church-going hour of eleven o'clock. I had once been at Ayton with my mother. I saw little of it then, and knew it better from my mother's description. I had heard her tell at home of the time when she was a young woman in that pretty village; of the washing and bleaching of clothes by the banks of the little river Eye, and sitting up with the clothes all the night, she and other young maidens, beneath Ayton bridge, to lay them out again in the summer mornings, when the first glimpse of sun appeared; the night being spent in story telling, and sometimes in the society of lovers, who came and kept the maidens company.

I now stood upon this bridge, and looked over its parapet upon that bold rivulet, its ledges of rock, and grassy banks, and pools of shining water, and fancied my mother there. Then I remembered that there was family dust of ours in Ayton churchyard, and that my mother's affections often dwelt there, though she herself dwelt beyond the broad hills of Lammermoor. My two brothers and a sister, who parted with the world in their childhood, but whom I never knew, were buried in that place. I found the green spot of their early graves by finding the tombstone of John Orkney, my mother's father. I sat down on the old man's grave, wondering what kind of man he had been, and what kind of men my two brothers, and what like a woman their infant sister lying beside them would have been, had they lived until then. Would those brothers have been like William in Yorkshire—grave, upright, and like a father; or would they have been like James—less stern, keen readers of books, excellent singers of songs, and tellers of good stories; or like Peter—clever as mechanics, but adventurous and unsettled? Would they, had they lived, have been apprenticed to trades like

James and Peter; or would they have been mere hedgers and ditchers, as William had been, rising above ditching and spade labour to offices of trust, by self-instruction, unswerving integrity, and sheer perseverance? Would they have been a solace to our parents, and a help in time of need, as William had been; or would they have caused grief to them by running away, like Peter and me? These were bitter thoughts as I sat on the grave of my grandfather, with my own wayward feet over the dust of those children. I rose from the place and returned to the bridge to see the pools of clear water once again, which my mother, when young and blooming, had looked into instead of a looking-glass, to do up her luxuriant hair in the early summer mornings, when she bleached her linen there. I leaned over the bridge and felt more sick at heart about my journey than I had yet done.

But I said at last, this is not the way to get on. So I started to the road and reached Berwick, where I spent my penny in the purchase of a loaf, which I ate at about two o'clock, a mile or two from the town on the English side. I had an uncle Peter Orkney in Berwick, and an uncle Alexander Orkney at the Square, two or three miles from that town, both brothers of my mother, and the latter my name-father. I might have just conceived the thought of calling on them, but a glance at my working clothes and nailed shoes forbade a repetition of the thought. Besides, they would ask why I had come away from home, and I could not tell that it was because my father gave me a 'licking'; it was the shame I felt at that which had made me leave home.

After eating my pennyworth of bread—swallowing my all, at once—I proceeded on my journey. I was several miles on the road to Belford, when being thirsty, I went into one of several poor-looking houses standing in a row by the roadside, and asked a drink of water. A motherly woman took a bason to get me some water, but stopped short of the good errand and asked if I would prefer milk. I said yes, if she pleased. Whereupon she gave me a bason of milk, and bade me sit down and rest if I were tired. I sat down and was drinking the milk, when her husband said, 'Perhaps the lad would like a bit of bread to his milk; do thee, lad?' I was blockhead enough to say, 'No, I thank ye; I am not hungry'—which is considered good manners among young people of my condition in Scotland, no matter how hungry one may be who says so. But the good man of the house said, 'The lad is blate, and wunnot tell; I see he's hungry; give him a piece of bread to the milk.' So I got bread and ate it, and answered many questions as to where I came from, and why I was travelling into England. On my telling what kind of work I had been used to, the man said that his master, a farmer, would give work to such a lad as I, and he directed me to his house. Thither I went, and after getting through a yard, terrible with dogs, I reached the kitchen door, and asked to see the master. He was not at home, but the mistress came and asked what I wanted. I told her I wanted to work, if they needed any harvest hands. To which she said angrily, 'Go away, go away; we have too many idle tramps of your sort already.'

So I got through the yard full of dogs, and proceeded on the road to the south.

Nearly opposite a large house, the greatest house I had ever seen—greater than Sir James Hall's of Dunglass, greater than Lord Lauderdale's at Dunbar, and they are both large ones—I came up to a man going in the same direction with myself, and inquired what house that was. He wondered where I could have come from not to know Haggerston. 'That,' said he, 'is Sir Carnaby's house.' Finding that I had come a long way from the Scotch side, he said he could wager his life I was going to Newcastle to get a ship. 'Lad,' he continued, 'ye'll rue that; they'll rope you until thou won't be able to stir thysel. I once went to sea at Newcastle, but I soon ran away again. Go thou home again, lad.' I told him I could not go home; but he said as I was tired, and had nowhere to go for a lodging, he would put me in a stable where he lived, let me sleep there, and think of what he had told me in the morning.

We went on a mile or two farther, and arrived at his house. He was a hind to a farmer, and lived with his mother. His mother gave me broth and bread, and I went to the stable, got straw where he directed me to get it, and lay down in it, sleeping soundly until he called me at sunrise in the morning. He and his mother were going to the fields to the harvest work; they had their own breakfasts of oatmeal crowdy made, and said they would give me part of it if I would promise to go home. I would not take the crowdy on that condition, and went out to the road, my face again southward. They called me back, and said they could not let me go away without some crowdy; so I had crowdy with them, and then set out on my journey towards Belford.

I passed through that town and got to the fourth milestone on its south side. Near to this was a small bridge, and I sat down on the ledge of this bridge, and pondered over and over again on what I was doing.

The want of a change of clothes, not having even changed the shirt I had been working in, and the want of money, but above all the thoughts of my poor mother, how she would be distressed on my account; how I was grieving her who was no party to what I had suffered, who on the contrary would have willingly saved me from the suffering; all those things came into my thoughts, rushing one on the other; and for the first time since I had left home I prayed to God to direct me what to do, and where to go. I had not so employed my thoughts many minutes, when I felt fully assured that it was best to go home. I started at once, my feet going faster than they had gone before, and my thoughts absolutely happy.

I reached Berwick Bridge without halting, and stood a few minutes looking over upon the Tweed, and then passed through the town. As soon as I got out of Berwick, I took off my shoes and stockings, and ran bare-footed. Soon after this the Union four-horsed coach came up. It was a fast coach; but so light-footed and light-hearted was I now, that I ran as fast as it. I kept up with it six miles, running about twenty yards behind. The guard once looked back to me, and asked if I had any money. I said 'No', whereupon he sat down on his seat and did not look at me again. It got away from me at Ayton. I was not able to run up hill with it; but I walked on as fast as I could, and got over the remaining eighteen miles between ten and eleven o'clock at night.

I did not feel enough of confidence to go to my father's door, but being outrageously hungry, having ate nothing since the crowdy at sunrise, and having walked and run over fifty-two miles of road since then, I was obliged to go to a neighbour's house to get something to eat. Here were two young women, Jean and Alice Dawson, who lived with their blind grandfather, old James Dawson. They rejoiced as much over my return as if they had been my sisters; got out of bed and made tea for me, and laid me down to sleep; told me how glad my mother and father, and every one, would be to know I had returned, and were inquisitive as to where I had been. The distance I had travelled over that day surprised them, as it may do many, considering the want of food; but the number of fifty-two miles is correct, including what I walked in the morning, before I turned.

I got up early, and went round a back way to Branxton, not to be seen by the men whom I expected coming with their horses to resume the leading of the corn to the stackyard. They happened to come by the very road which I took. I got behind the holly bushes at the bottom of the Horse Hill Planting to avoid them. They were talking of me, and saying they wondered where I could have gone. They thought I must have gone with the Irish shearers, for I had been often in the barn where they slept, and seemed fond of their company.

The only man I wanted to see at that time was David Lyall, as he was the only one who had not made a jest of the punishment I received. Fortunately he was behind the others. I called 'Davy' as he passed. He looked into the bushes, and said 'Is that you; where in the world have you been?' And without saying another word, bade me go along with him. He turned back to Branxton, and going up to the master's bed-room, told him I had returned, and that he hoped he would not refuse to allow me back again to his service. The master soon came to me and bade me get to work, but I had begun work in the stable before he came. He said that although I did not choose to go home to my father, that was no reason why I should run away from my service.

I did not feel confidence to go home that night; but was anxiously expected home when my day's work was done. My mother had come and entreated me to go home; but I had not seen my father, and could not go. I again slept in the stable among the straw. While I was yet in the straw, in the early morning, my father came to me. He said he had been lying awake all the night, and nearly the whole of every night I had been away, and so had my poor mother. With his eyes wet, and the tears running down his venerable face, he asked me to forgive him for the wrong he had done; for he had since found that the men sent me to take the whisky for their use, and that they drank it. For me to be begged of for forgiveness by my father! It was worse—aye, far more painful—than the hasty punishment was which he inflicted on me. I never again saw him raise his hand in punishment or rebuke; and, so far as I can remember, he never again spoke a severe word to me.

CHAPTER V

*I Obtain a Glimpse of the World by Reading, and am
Elevated to Hold the Plough*

W HEN I was a boy, the periodicals which are now so common,
cheap, and useful in supplying young minds with information,
did not exist. Such books of popular instruction as then existed, and
might have been useful for me to read, were out of my reach. Not
knowing them, I did not seek them, nor feel their absence, and my own
loss. My earliest acquaintance with a book subject, one which took a
lodgement in me, and remained from its first entrance to this day to
receive new comers, and admit them to a place beside it, but never to
be dislodged itself, was the story of Joseph and his Brethren. It was
told by my mother. My father had been sent to Edinburgh market, a
distance of thirty-four miles, with sheep or cattle. On such journeys
he was absent a day and night going; a day and night there, and a day
to come home. It was one night when he was thus absent that my
mother, when we were preparing to go to bed, answered some questions which I put to her, by telling the whole narrative from the selling
of Joseph to the Ishmaelites, to the Egyptian bondage of the children
of Israel, and their escape to the desert. To this day I remember the
very manner of myself and sisters, sitting around her on our creepie
stools³ on the hearth stone. To this day I can see the fire of logs and
coals as it burned behind the bars of the grate; and I see the bars also
as they were then, and the fancied figures of Egyptians and Israelites
which I then saw in the fire. It was the first time that I felt an intellectual
ecstasy. It came from my mother as did many other pleasing, good, and
holy feelings. Who can tell all a mother's goodness, or all her power
to do good?

This occurred in my eighth or ninth year. About three years after,
at the end of harvest, on a moonlight evening, when the corn was
nearly all in the stackyard, and the carters were still at work in the
moonlight, to get the corn carried from the fields while good weather
lasted, I was with James Wilson, who was then the stacker, laying the

sheaves to his hand as the carter forked them to the stack from his cart. We had some spare time between the departure of the emptied cart, and the arrival of the loaded one; and James Wilson, who was a reader of books, asked me as we sat on the stack together, if I knew Burns's poem of 'Halloween'. I said, no: that I did not know what people meant when they spoke of Burns's poems. What was a poem, and what was Burns? Halloween I knew about; for we had pulled cabbage *runts*[4] that night blindfold, and burned beans on the bars of the grate, and put three basins on the table, one with clear water in it, one with muddy water, and one with none, and the young women and men had gone blindfold to choose a basin—the maiden who got the basin with none being destined to live without a husband, she who got the muddy water being destined to marry a widower, and she who got the clear water having in store for her a lover who had loved no other. I had seen such ceremonies gone through at Halloween (though never in my father's house, or in his presence), so I told the stacker that I knew what was meant by Halloween, but not what he meant when he spoke of Burns's poems. What was Burns's poems, was it a book, or a song, or a story?

He said he would tell me; and saying so, he recited all the poem of 'Halloween'. Seeing that I was delighted with it, he gave me that of 'Death and Doctor Hornbook', which pleased me still more. And then he told me some part of Burns's life, which excited an interest in me far stronger than the recital of the two poems had done. He then reminded me that I had heard the songs of 'Auld Lang Syne', 'Of a' the Airts the Wind can Blaw', 'My Nannie O', and some others which he named; and that they were songs made by Burns, and were included in the book called *Burns's Poems*, which he would bring with him to-morrow, and lend me to read.

Tired as I was with late work, which had lasted from daylight in the morning until ten at night, I was now so eager to see that famous book, from which he had kindled in me intellectual sensations so new, so delightful, and irrepressibly strong, that I could not go home to supper and to bed, until I had accompanied him to his home, three quarters of a mile distant to get the book; I could not wait until he brought it in the morning. It was a volume that had been often read, well read, and well worn. It had been in tatters, and was sewed again together, and I had special charges to take care of it, as it was not every one that it would be lent to. I got it, and if each leaf had been a

43

bank note, I could not have hugged it in my breast pocket more closely and carefully. At first I felt a difficulty with the Scottish dialect of the poems, as I had never seen the dialect in print before; and my education, such as it was, had been exercised only on English reading. Moreover, the dialect of Burns was that of the west of Scotland, while in our every day speech we used that of the Lothians and of Lammermoor in the south-east of Scotland, a dialect differing in many respects from that of the west. Yet I was soon able to read the poems with facility; and though I now know that I did not then feel the force of the poetry, I then read them under sensations of pleasure entirely new. Unfortunately, as regarded my father's approbation of such reading, the most witty of the poems of Burns are directed satirically against the ministers of religion of that rigid body to which my father adhered. Still, rigid as he was in moral discipline, and believer as he was in the orthodoxy of those whom the poet had satirised, the genius of Burns subdued him. He took that old volume from me, and read it again and again, his grave countenance relaxing, and the muscles of his face curling into a smile, and the smile widening to a broad laugh at certain passages, which having read to himself, he would read aloud, that we might all laugh. And I remember his saying, 'It's a pity Burns was so coarse on some good men, for he was a droll fellow, and after all there is so much more good than ill in the book.' Still he was not willing for me to become familiar with Burns. He said when I grew older I might read him to advantage, when I could know what to admire and what to reject; it was hardly fit for me to read poetry while so young. But I had felt new sensations so exquisitely delightful, that even this admonition, good though I knew it to be, was not strong enough to separate me from Burns.

Seeing that I continued to read everything of verse kind which fell in my way, my father resolved to get me a book of poems to read, which he thought would do me good—the *Gospel Sonnets*. It was no small thing for a poor man like him to pay half a week's wages, and send all the way to Edinburgh for a book of verses for his boy, because he saw that boy eagerly laying hold of every printed poem, song, ballad, or verse, that could be reached, and in the exuberance of his enthusiasm making rhymes for others to listen to. The *Gospel Sonnets* were received and read, but there was something wanting either in me or in them. We stood, the book and I, in positions of respectable friendship, but I rushed not into it to live in it, with it in me, to hold

44

companionship with it in the lonely woods, in the green loaning, or lie with it on the grass and the gowans beside the well, drinking from the well of water when I was thirsty and tired—drinking from the book of poetry always, as in Burns. Also in respect of the gospel sonnets of Ralph Erskine, I had an imperfect opinion then, which has grown into a confirmed opinion now, that the gospel of the God of Grace is too sacred a subject for trifling rhymes; for, great as Ralph Erskine was in preaching (his published sermons, and the history of Scotland in the days of his life, attest his pulpit greatness), he was but a small poet. Perhaps the best of his verses were those on the tobacco pipe. I remember one of the stanzas was somewhat to this effect:

> And when the pipe grows foul within,
> 'Tis like thy soul defiled in sin,
>   For then the fire
>   It doth require;
> This think and smoke tobacco.

The next book which came in my way, and made an impression so strong as to be still unworn and unwearable, was *Anson's Voyage Round the World. Gospel Sonnets, Burns's Poems*, old ballads, and self-made doggerel, everything gave way to admit the new knowledge of the earth's geography, and the charms of human adventure which I found in those voyages. I had read nothing of the kind before, and knew nothing of foreign countries beyond the glimpses of them opened to me by old James Dawson when he held converse with the personages of history, and the imaginary beings whom he associated with in the solitudes of the Ogle Burn. I got Anson to read in this way:

James Wilson was at Innerwick smithy one day, getting his horses shod, and his plough irons laid. He saw a thick, aged-looking volume lying on the wall head under the tiles; and taking it down, read parts of it between the heats of the iron, it being his business, as of other men like him at the smithy, to wield the fore-hammer, when the iron was red-hot on the anvil. John Watt, the smith, had borrowed that book, and was reading it at resting hours. In working hours the book lay where James Wilson saw it. The account of it given to me was such as to make me try to get it and surmount all difficulties in the trial. Those difficulties were all the greater that my *blateness* (bashfulness) was at this time oppressive, and almost ridiculous. I was now nearly fourteen years old, but had mingled in no company, and did not know above twenty people, and not even the half of twenty familiarly. If I were going an errand, and saw men at work on the road, laying stones on it, perhaps I would go half a mile round by some other road, or through fields and over hedges and ditches, rather than pass them. If I had to pass people on the road, I could not look them in the face, nor, if they had asked me a question, could I answer them without my face reddening as if with shame. If my errand was to a private house, I would go past and return again, and pass it once more, and still be unable to muster courage to go in to tell what I wanted. This want of self-confidence, I am sorry to confess, has not been supplanted as it should be unto this day. True, I have done things which should make ordinary observers think that I was largely supplied with confidence, or self-esteem. In those circumstances I have, however, been impelled by other impulses, or opinions, or necessities, which by their strength made me forgetful of my inherent weakness. I cannot now tell how much I have suffered in the toil of spirit, far less the silly things which I have done and allowed others to do for me, in the absence of that self-confidence which looks the world in the face boldly, when boldness is a virtue, which shrinks only from the world when it is modest to do so.

Perhaps the writing of this autobiography (and above all its publication, now that I have allowed it to be published) may suggest that if my self-confidence was once weak it abounds in strength now. To this I cannot well reply. I feel that there are other moving causes to this act of publication; but this is not the page on which to write the confession of them.

At all events, whatever I may be now, I was bashful to the extent of being ridiculous when I was younger; and the struggle I had with the desire to go to the owner of *Anson's Voyages* to borrow the book to read, and the shame of the thought that a boy like me, who only wore corduroy clothes, nailed shoes with thick soles, and a highland bonnet, should presume to go to the house of those who had a back door and a front door, was a war of thoughts that allowed me no peace for several weeks.

But the effort was made. It was successful; and I got the book to read. It was in summer, in the month of July, and I was then one of about ten persons employed in turnip hoeing. The turnips were that year in the large field called the Under Floors. The other workers went home to their dinners, but I carried a bottle of milk with me and a piece of hard bannock of bean and barley meal and would not go home, not though there was the great temptation of new potatoes just come in, or curds and cream, or some of the other summer delicacies which our mother was so pleased to provide for us at that season of the year. I remained in the fields, and lay on the grass under the shadow of the trees and read about the *Centurion*, and all that befel her. When the afternoon work began, I related to the other workers what I had read; and even the grieve[5] began to take an interest in the story. And this interest increased in him and in every one else until they all brought their dinners afield, so that they might remain under the shadow of the trees and hear me read. In the evenings at home I continued the reading, and next day at work put them in possession of the events which I knew in advance of them.

About this time a parish library was established at Innerwick, and we got books from it. But the larger part of them were silly stories, of that silliest kind of literature—religious novels. Intermingled with these, however, were a few useful works of divinity, history, and biography. Since that time the library has been much improved.

There was a remarkable library established in my native shire of East Lothian, by Mr. Samuel Brown, of Haddington, which I cannot omit to notice, though I obtained no advantage from it. Mr. Brown is a philanthropist of the first order of merit. He formed, at his own expense, a collection of books, and put them in divisions; retaining the newest at Haddington; and sending a division to each of the principal villages of the county. When a division had remained in one place a certain time (about twelve months), it was removed to a distant village, and the division of that village was sent to take its place. Thus the books were kept in circulation, the readers each year having a set of books which they had not read before. The charge for reading was exceedingly small, not more than sufficient to keep the books in repair. The librarians to whose custody they were committed acted gratuitously. In my early reading days, none of those divisions came within our district.

Another eminent servant of mankind was Mr. George Miller, of Dunbar, who certainly lived before the age was ripe for him, and died, I fear, before he was fully appreciated. George Miller was the father of cheap literature. Nearly forty years ago he brought out several serial works at prices so low as to secure the hostility of all booksellers, and to make the learned and the literary look upon them as worthless. One was the *Cheap Magazine*, published monthly at Dunbar, price fourpence. It had ceased to exist long before I became a reader. Its object was solely to do that which such men as Charles Knight and William and Robert Chambers began to do with success twenty years after. But George Miller had the misfortune to live in a small provincial town, and to be bound to that town by his other business of a shopkeeper. It was impossible, and still is, to force the sale of a publication against the current of trade. The current of bookselling goes outward from metropolitan reservoirs, not inward. Moreover, the religious readers of the *Cheap Magazine* took alarm at it, because it aimed at popularizing philosophical and purely literary subjects, and did not give a predominancy to religion. This defection and opposition sealed its fate; and after several years of heavy struggles, mental and pecuniary, George Miller left off publishing, a poorer man in purse and reputation than he began. Yet again he published. He was a geologist and naturalist, and to give liberty and currency to thoughts which would not lie dormant in an active mind like his, he compiled and published a work called *The Book of Nature Laid Open*. It came out about the time that I was beginning to seek after books, and I bought a copy of it, price 10s. 6d. I believe there were not six other copies of it sold in the three parishes of Cockburnspath[6], Oldhamstocks, and Innerwick, the geology of which it was chiefly devoted to. Like all Mr. Miller's adventures in literature, it entailed loss upon him. He subsequently published an autobiography, entitled, if I mistake not, *The Life of a Sexagenarian*, in which he reviewed the sixty years of his life, and the thankless struggles he had made for popular instruction; but even that book, I believe, was not bought to an extent sufficient to pay the printer; and unrequited and unappreciated, George Miller died and was buried.

The postage of letters was dear in those days, but my brother William, then living in Yorkshire, sent us frequent letters; they were all post-paid. It was a welcome thing to see the letter in the hands of somebody who had been in Dunbar and had brought it from the post office. The exclamation of 'A letter rhae Wull!' was like an electric shock in the family, only it was a pleasant one. Sometimes a letter would contain a five pound note. That was also welcome. But it being an English note, and new and clean, as Bank of England notes usually are, it was a task incredibly difficult to get it changed. Had it been dirty and well worn, like the Scotch notes, it would have been less suspiciously looked at; yet, even then the fact that it was 'English' was against it.

One of the letters 'rhae Wull' contained a suggestion that I might possibly, if I had some more education, join him and become a forester. Here was new delight. I was recommended to get *Hutton's Mensuration*, and learn it, and to practise measuring and account keeping. But where to get Hutton, and how, was the question. I had no money of my own, and my mother at that time had none; the cow had not calved, and there was no butter selling to bring in money. Yet I could not rest: if I could not then buy Hutton I must see it. One day in March I was driving the harrows, it being the time of sowing the spring corn; and I thought so much about becoming a good scholar, and built such castles in the air, that tired as I was (and going at the harrows from five in the morning to six at night on soft loose land, is one of the most tiring days of work upon a farm), I took off my shoes, scraped the earth from them and out of them, washed hands and face, and walked to Dunbar, a distance of six miles, to inquire if *Hutton's Mensuration* was sold there, and, if possible, to look at it—to see with my eyes the actual shape and size of the book which was to be the key to my future fortunes. George Miller was in the shop himself; and told me the book was four shillings. That sum of four shillings seemed to me to be the most precious amount of money which ever came out of the mint; I had it not; nor had I one shilling; but I had seen the book; and had told George Miller not to sell it to any one else; and so I walked over the six miles home, large with the thought that it would be mine at farthest when the cow calved, perhaps sooner.

It was mine sooner. I occasionally got a sixpence as stable boy, when I took out the horse of a visitor. And whenever Mr. Rennie, of East Craig, came, I got a shilling. He was the only visitor at my master's house who invariably gave me a shilling for each night he staid. The master had a beautiful sister, Isa; and George Rennie was her lover. He began about this time to come often; and the oftener he came the longer he staid. He took her away at last; and a loving and lovely pair they were. It was a great day in Branxton that wedding day; though many eyes were wet when they saw Isa going away—happy bride though she was. Alas! that she was so soon to be a widow! The love visits of George Rennie, so frequent and so long-continued, soon produced me four shillings, and more. I groomed his horse well; he knew it; and was kind to me. As soon as I had four shillings, I proceeded once more to Dunbar; and bought Hutton.

I need hardly say that my studies in mensuration did not result in my being a forester with my brother. But in subsequent years of my life, when I became a wood sawyer, I found that it was useful to have learned how to measure our work, and to cast up the accounts.

The chief reason why I did not go to be a forester was that my father was now old: all the family but one sister were away; and both parents were anxious that I should stay with them. In the year following, also, it happened that one of the ploughmen left his service with our master midway between the terms of Martinmas and Whitsunday; and as no other man could be conveniently obtained at that period, I was promoted to the office of a ploughman. I was only fifteen, but I had gone many yokings at the plough during the two previous years. This unexpected advancement in fortune, to have a pair of horse given me, and these to be no less than Nannie and Kate, the most lively and sprightly pair on the farm, at once decided that I should neither go to be apprenticed to any trade, as had occasionally been talked of, nor to Yorkshire to be a forester.

[3] A redundancy. *Creepie* by itself means a low stool.
[4] Cabbage-stalks no longer sprouting: by extension, an old woman, not, as in English, a small man.
[5] Foreman.
[6] Pronounced *Coppersmith.*

CHAPTER VI

1826 and 1827—Hard Work and Little Wages

THE next few years of my life have little variety in them beyond the variations of hard work. So far as ploughing was concerned I might have continued to work a pair of horses; but in the carting department—going to the corn merchants' stores, for instance, and carrying sacks of wheat up the stairs of four or five stories, I was not strong enough, in my fifteenth year. A full grown man was hired at Whitsunday, and got the horses which I had ploughed with in the spring. During the summer months of that year, 1825, I was chiefly employed in horse-hoeing the turnips—that is, holding the one-horsed shovel plough in the turnip drills. At harvest I was a binder and shearer, and when the leading in of the corn began, I got the pair of horses belonging to the stacker, and his cart, and loaded the cart and drove the horses.

When harvest was over, I got a quantity of draining to do, and now worked by the piece. Sometimes I could earn 9s. a week at the drains, but in the deep ones there were rocks to be encountered and overcome; and in some parts the clay was so wet and greasy, that it slid in before the drains were filled with stones. Those drawbacks brought my wages down to an average of 7s. a week.

In the winter, and during two months in the following spring, I engaged to break the stones on a division of the public road in the vicinity of Thriepland Hill. I took them at 1s. 4d. a cart-load. My father warned me that I had taken them at a price too low. But work was exceedingly scarce that winter, and seeing no chance of getting employment elsewhere, I contracted to break the stones at the price offered to me. I took advantage of every minute of daylight, save about half an hour for dinner; and when it was moonlight, I occasionally took a few hours at night. But all I could do did not produce me on an average more than one shilling a day. Out of that I had to provide myself with hammers, and get them steeled and repaired at the smithy from time to time. The stones were hard water-worn fragments, gathered from the farm land; stones which lasted well on a road when once broken, but very difficult to break. I was a happy lad when I got them all done, and my contract was finished. This was at the end of February, 1826.

During March and April of that year, I was chiefly employed by the master in his garden, digging, planting, sowing, pruning, and so forth. I also hired a piece of vacant garden ground from him, for which I paid him 6s., and planted it with potatoes. I intended to buy a pig in the autumn, feed it on these potatoes, and sell it in the spring. But that summer was so dry that nearly all kinds of vegetation, save wheat, were withered away. I did not get as many potatoes out of my piece of ground as were equal to the price I paid for it. So that my father's having also failed, I was but too glad to do for mine what I had intended a pig to do—eat them.

In May of this year, I was one of nearly a hundred persons employed by Mr. John Liddell, of Cockburnspath, the joiner, at a *hag*. This was at Bowshiel, in a glen stretching into the interior of the Lammermoor hills. A *hag* is to cut down the oak trees, peel the bark from them, dry the bark, stack it up, and cross cut and sort the timber. The nearest way I could go to the place of the *hag* from our house, at Thriepland Hill, was between six and seven miles. I had to be out of bed, and have breakfast, and be on my way over the moors by four o'clock, to be ready for work at six. I did not get home till eight, or half-past it. This, for 1s. 4d. (towards the latter end of it for 1s. 6d. per day) was heavy work. The weather was intensely hot, and the hill-side on which the oaken wood grew, rose direct against the midday sun. During the last two weeks of the *hag*, being completely worn out with the long journeys night and morning, I took a lodging; but the nearest I could get was at Harelawside, two and a half miles distant from the work. I took oatmeal with me from home, and as much of bean and barley bannocks as served me three days; at the end of three days I went home for one night, to get a fresh supply. I also took a piece of butter from home, and bought each morning a bottle of new milk at Harelawside. I paid ninepence a week for my lodgings, for which I also got boiling water night and morning, to make my brose. The weather being so dry and hot, and oatmeal brose night and morning, with bannocks for dinner, being very dry food, I suffered greatly from thirst. Water running out of the peat bogs, could be obtained at no great distance, but it was of bad quality, and to get at it, we were in danger of being bit by adders. They abounded like a plague in that district. Frightened from the wood where we were working by the din of saws, hatchets, crashing of trees, and shouting of human voices, they took refuge in the heath, by the bog sides, and seemed determined to defend themselves against intruders there. They would hiss, and coil themselves up, ready to leap upon us when we approached. But as they had always a dread of the human eye and voice, they usually retreated, and allowed us to get at the water to drink.

The women employed in peeling at this *hag* got 1s. a day. Those who *snedded* the branches from the trunks, such as I, got 1s. 4d. and 1s. 6d. a day. The superior hands who sawed down the trees got 2s. a day. Some of these were joiners who had been working at their trade in Edinburgh during two or three previous years, for high wages. The building speculations in Edinburgh during the few years of commercial excitement which ended with the panic of 1825, were excessive. From the country everybody seemed going to Edinburgh to get work. And now in 1826, everybody was coming back again, and were obliged to take work at any wages which were offered. Labourers returned to the country as well as the skilled artisans; and while fifteen months before I had been made a ploughman, men being so scarce, I could with difficulty get work of any kind now.

When the *hag* was over about the middle of June, I got employment as a great favour, and solely on my father's account, at the Skaterow limekilns, where he had been a workman some years before. I was put on the kilnhead, enveloped in smoke, to throw in stones and coals. This work began at three or four o'clock in the morning, sooner or later, according as the burning mass had slackened down. We were seldom later in beginning work than four o'clock; and as I had to walk two miles, and take breakfast before I went out, it was necessary to be out of bed soon after two o'clock. I got home at five or six in the afternoon. For this work the wages paid were 8s. and 9s. a week. I was on the lowest scale—that of 8s. The best hands who worked in the quarries from which the limestone was raised, got 10s. a week. In some years they have had 11s., I believe. A great summer trade used to be done in lime at these kilns. The farmers of the Merse[7] of Berwickshire sent their carts from distances varying from ten to twenty-five miles, for lime to be used as manure. Many of them came and lay at the kilns all night, there being a stated hour to begin to draw the kiln and load the carts in the morning. The carters competed for the privilege of getting first loaded. I have known as many as three hundred carts waiting to be loaded at once. To see the racing; the carters whipping their horses to the gallop, those on the post road, to get before others who were galloping down the cross roads to get before them; an axle-tree breaking, or a wheel going off; sometimes a cart *couping* at the sharp turns, and all the others thundering past, leaving the unlucky racer to his fate—was a sight which I have not since seen the match of; and which could only be matched by men of the same combative energy as the men of the Scottish borders, by horses of the same strength and lightness of form as the horses of the Merse.

Both men and horses in Berwickshire differ in their habits from the men and horses of East Lothian—the county in which the limekilns now under notice are situated. The Lothian horses are large and heavy; the Lothian men do excellent work, but go more slowly and steadily about it. The men of Berwickshire still partake of the habits and character of their free-booting forefathers, so far as vivacity and energy of action are concerned; to which may be added their propensity to change of place and change of service. The Lothian hinds often live with a farmer throughout his lease of nineteen years, and if he takes a new lease they still remain on the farm. If a new farmer takes the farm, he will often retain the hinds who were hired to his predecessor. In any case, taking an average view of the periods of service in Lothian, they are long compared with the periods served by hinds in Berwickshire. A period of one, two, or three years is seldom exceeded there— the hind changing or *flitting* most commonly at the end of one or two years. They go through more work in the same space of time than the Lothian men; they are obliged to do more by their masters. But at the same time, they have themselves to blame for much of the overwork they do. At harvest especially, they get so excited by a spirit of combative competition, as to who shall work fastest, and be before his or her neighbour, that the masters have to threaten to 'pay them off', to get them to take time to do the work as it should be done.

The harvest of 1826 was early. As soon as it began I left the limekilns at Skaterow, and went to the shearing at Branxton. It was pulling rather than shearing. The wheat was long enough in the straw to be shorn, but oats, barley, and beans were so short that we had to pull them. No rain had fallen during the space of three or four months. The harvest was soon over. When it was done, I, as in the previous autumn, took a quantity of draining. When I had drains which went well, I could earn from 8s. to 9s. a week. But I had some very bad ones, boggy in parts, so as to close in upon me and give double or triple work; rocky and hard in other parts, so as to make blasting with gunpowder necessary. Taking the bad with the good I did not make over 6s. a week.

During all that winter of 1826, and during the spring and summer of 1827, I worked as a labourer for our master. Sometimes in the garden, occasionally going at the plough, sometimes pruning a hedge, and now and again scouring a ditch. My wages were one shilling a day. In harvest I got the usual allowance of victuals with the other shearers, and the men who 'led in' the corn to the stackyard; and I did the work of a man at 'leading in', part of the time as a carter, and the remainder of the time as forker to the carts in the fields. There was, however, some misunderstanding about my working for a shilling a day. My father had made the agreement for me, and was not clear in his recollection whether that agreement included harvest work. I held that it did not; the master held that it did. As soon as harvest was over, he told me the agreement might be at an end if I chose: that he had no particular use for me, and that he had only engaged me at a shilling a day, at the beginning of the year, because I was out of work and could not get employment elsewhere.

There being still harvest work to do in the hilly districts, I left him, and went into the Lammermoors, among the hill farms on Whitadder side, and got three weeks of shearing, and an additional week as forker to the carts, at ten shillings a week, and the usual victuals. This was at the farm of Mr. Darling, of Millknowe.

It was near to the hiring days of Martinmas term when this last work was done. Returning home and giving my mother the two pounds I had received at Millknowe, I went to the hiring market at Dunse, with a piece of whip cord in the ribbon of my hat, and a piece of straw in my mouth, as signals that I wanted to be hired. But with the exception of one person, nobody even asked how much wages I expected. Men were more plentiful than masters. Men of full years, and experience as carters and ploughmen, were only offered from three pounds to four pounds ten shillings, with their victuals, for the half-year. And the person who offered to hire me, the miller's wife of Strawfountain Mill, would not go beyond two pounds ten shillings. I would not hire for that amount of half-yearly wages, particularly to be loadman at a mill. So I took the straw out of my mouth, and the cord out of the ribbon of my hat, and walked home to Thriepland Hill, distant from Dunse sixteen miles.

I went also to Dunbar fair, which is on the first Tuesday after the 22nd of November, and tried to get hired there, but had not a single offer. So also to Haddington market on the Friday following, with no better success. Every farmer could get more men than he wanted—men of full growth and good practice, while I was only aged seventeen. I had, however, done the work of a man for two or three years; and being as tall and as strong as most men, I was not disposed to return to the pay of a boy, which was my only alternative at Branxton.

My brother James, hearing the difficulty I was in, suggested that I might get employment with him as a wood-sawyer, at Edinburgh. The payment for wood-sawing was very low at that time, as all trade was in a state of stagnation. The price for sawing pine was only 1s. 8d., in some few cases 1s. 10d. per 100 feet; and for hard wood, not more than from 2s. 9d. to 3s. per 100 feet. Still, as there was work to go to at those prices, and as double as much could be earned by a full day's work at the saw than could be earned on a farm by a day's work, I resolved to go to Edinburgh; and had the full consent of father and mother to do so.

[7] The third of the natural divisions of the Counties of Berwick and Haddington, the others being Lammermoor and Lauderdale. The Merse is the extreme south-eastern tip of Scotland, and is said to be the largest piece of level ground in the country.

CHAPTER VII

Industrial Adventures in 1828

I WAS prepared for my journey to Edinburgh before old Handsel Monday of 1828; but I did not think of leaving home before that day, nor would those whom I was to leave at home have permitted me to be absent from the family feast of old Handsel Monday. This family feast occurred annually on the first Monday of the new year, reckoned by the old style. The feast was simple; but in regard to the number of persons assembled, and their usual tastes and habits, it was bountiful. Our visitors were chiefly brothers and sisters living from home. The children of my eldest sister, Margaret, and their father, came; and for several years, while I was yet a boy, they made me feel to be more than a boy by calling me 'uncle'. And there was our uncle, John Temple, the weaver, of Chirnside. He was identified with our family by marriage with our mother's sister; but in my mind more identified with our family by always visiting us at happy Handsel Monday. It seemed to me then, and by memory it still seems, that Handsel Monday would have been joyless, and would have declined and become an ordinary day, but for the coming of John Temple. The moment that the sound of his cheerful voice was heard in the house, until the next day, or next again that he went away, except, perhaps, a few hours in the night, the time was one continuous stream of story-telling, anecdote, and laughter. The moment John took his departure, and was out of sight, and his merry voice out of hearing, Handsel Monday was over, and the old, sober, working days reigned in its stead.

But he was yet at Thriepland Hill on the Handsel Tuesday of 1828, and was only talking about taking his departure, when, according to previous arrangements, I took mine. I walked to Loanhead, near Stenton, in the afternoon, and spent the night with my nephews, David, James, Thomas, William, and Robert Doughty. They were by this time motherless boys, but their father kept house with them, without any female assistant. This he continued to do for years; the eldest boys, besides going to school in winter, and to work in summer, assisting the younger ones to cook and to do the household work. For their early industry and perseverance they already have their reward.

Next morning their father, who was a stonemason, and chiefly employed on Biel estate, went with me several miles on the road towards the town of Haddington. It was a hard frost, the ground covered with snow, from one to three feet deep. He wished me to remain a day or two with them, until the snow melted, or was tracked down on the roads to make walking more easy; but I was too strongly bent upon reaching Edinburgh as soon as possible, to relax in my determination by a storm of snow. As he could not go out to do mason's work in such weather, he went the farther with me, and the farther he went the more good advice he gave; warning me of the dangers of Edinburgh, and cautioning me against continuing my journey, if the snow-storm increased.

We parted, and after a journey which was almost an overmatch for me, of twenty-five miles in the soft snow, I reached Edinburgh. It was dark when I got within sight of the streets; and the lamps newly lighted, stretching out in long chains of fiery links, amazed me more that I can now tell. I was not long there until I heard complaints of bad trade; that 'everything was flat'; 'nothing was stirring', and so forth; to which I could not help saying, that I wondered what like the town must be when everything was 'brisk' and 'stirring'; for it seemed to me that the stir, the din, and bustle were excessive and never-ceasing.

But it was a dull time for trade. Edinburgh was then, had been for two years, and continued to be for years after, depressed beyond almost every other place, especially in the building branches of its trade, from the excessive extent of building speculations previous to the commercial crash of 1825.

I was kindly received by friends, some of whom I knew previously, some of whom I did not know. Most of them wondered why I should have left, what they, being town bred, believed to be a happy country life, to come and work in a saw-pit in a town. The sawyers objected greatly that my brother should at such a time of depression introduce a new hand; and they were disposed to prevent me from working. They said little to him; but on several occasions they told me I might probably get my head broken, and would possibly be found by somebody dead in the Cowgate Burn. Had it been at a busy time, they would have struck and refused to work for my brother; but as it was otherwise,

58

so many being out of employment and suffering dreadful privations, they were powerless. In the country where I had come from, men were without work; it was the difficulty of getting employment at anything which would yield me higher wages than I had received as a boy, and the certainty that there was not constant work at such wages, that had caused me to go to Edinburgh, to add one more to those who competed for a livelihood at sawing timber.

In the course of five or six weeks the sawyers became reconciled to me. One who had been readiest in secretly telling what I had to fear from some unknown enemy, intimated that this unknown person or persons and himself would protect me on certain conditions which were hinted at, though not explicitly named. A neighbouring publican came and explained the matter more fully; and I found that the chief article in the conditions of friendship and brotherhood which the sawyers wished to establish with me was whisky. A certain quantity of whisky was to initiate me into the mysteries of brotherhood, and to secure the good will of the whole body. This condition being complied with, I was allowed to work without hindrance or molestation.

Soon after my arrival in Edinburgh I went with some relatives to the theatre. The Christmas pantomime was still played, and that season it was *Mother Goose*. I thought it funny, clever, wonderful. But the pantomime had less charm for me than the house, especially the chandelier. I had seen nothing of lamp kind brighter than my mother's oil lamp at Thriepland Hill, until I saw the rows of gas lights in the Edinburgh streets; and now it seemed as if all their brightness had been concentrated within the theatre. But on the next occasion (the only other occasion, I believe, of my going to the theatre during that residence in Edinburgh) I saw *Rob Roy*. The *Rob Roy* of Pritchard, the matchless *Bailie Nicol Jarvie* of Mackay, the *Diana Vernon* of Miss Noel, the *Major Galbraith* of Murray (the manager, who for many years has been celebrated for having the best dramatic company out of London); all these might have afforded a theatrical treat to old play-goers; what, therefore, must this have been to me? I loved music, but had never heard a female voice so good as bare mediocrity. When Miss Noel, with her powerful and rich voice, opened out with the song, 'A Highland lad my love was born', the electric effect was as great upon me as if heaven had opened, and a singing angel had descended. Horn-castle was the musical *Osbaldeston*, and began, if I mistake not, with 'Oh, my love is like a red, red rose!' I had heard some good male singers, as precentors in the churches; but none had a voice like him. The memory of that delightful entertainment served me to think upon, and refresh my spirit with, as I toiled in the saw-pit at the long saw, for weeks after.

One of the chief intellectual treats which I enjoyed was that of going, on Sundays, to hear the most celebrated of the Edinburgh ministers preach. I was disappointed in every effort to hear Dr. Chalmers. But the late Dr. Andrew Thomson I heard; and wondered how a *kirk* (established) minister should be such a famous preacher as he was reputed to be, and as I believed him to be! The dissenters were not inclined to be liberal, perhaps not even just, to the ministers of the establishment in those days; and I had partaken of their teaching and tone of thought.

But the greatest entertainment of an intellectual nature was enjoyed in attending the sittings and listening to the debates of the Synod of the United Secession Church, which met in May. On more than one occasion their debates lasted until daylight in the morning. I remained all the time in the gallery listening, and proceeded from the gallery where I had listened direct to work in the saw-pit. It was not so much from the interest attached to any single topic under discussion that I remained there; as from the fact that many of the debaters were ministers of whom I had heard; whose reputations for piety and ministerial ability stood high, and whose very names were always uttered by my father and others like him with accompanying expressions of veneration; and whom I could now look upon face to face, at least I could look down from the gallery upon their heads, grey heads, bald heads, and wigs: and as they debated I wondered at the grey heads, the bald heads, and the wigs.

During the previous two years, I had now and again, but with no regularity, seen a newspaper. It was the *Edinburgh Courant*, and came three times a week to our master at Branxton; but, as other farmers got it from him, it did not often fall into my hands. But now, in Edinburgh, I could see the successive numbers of a newspaper, and see the continuation of the news, and the political disputes between two different newspapers. The first event which I had learned from the papers, and which made much impression on me, was the battle of Navarino. James Wilson borrowed a newspaper from some friend at that time (latter part of 1827), when the right and the wrong of that battle was under discussion. We wondered why any body should doubt the right or propriety of Sir Edward Codrington destroying the Turkish fleet. The claims of the Greeks, or the principles of international law, we knew nothing of. It was enough to us, that the enemy which the English had fought and vanquished was the Turks, and that the Turks were Mahommedans, and not believers in the same religion as ours. The more ignorant that any people are, the more ready are they to reason in this way, or in passion to overcome all reason. James had, however, read more history than I. He was old enough to remember the French war, and had been a militia man and a volunteer, and had been drilled to help to defend the sea coast of Lothian from the threatening French —a needful and a patriotic purpose: but at the distance of fourteen years after the French were no longer able nor willing to invade East Lothian, he and many more still talked about the French. When, therefore, we read that at the battle of Navarino the French and Russians were allied with the English in defeating the Turks, it was thought to have detracted greatly from the honour of England to have had anything to do with the French, unless to give them a thrashing.

One evening, when I was still at Thriepland Hill, James Wilson came to our house with a letter which had come from London to one of his friends. It was written in a running hand, and was crossed over, and was so difficult to read that it had been sent to him, and he came to me, to see if I could assist in deciphering it. We found after two or three hours of orthographic labour, that it was written to inform his friends in Scotland, that all London was in consternation and mourning at the sudden death of the Right Honourable George Canning; and that some terrible trouble for the nation might be expected, as strong suspicions existed that he had not come by his death fairly. This was the first time that I knew anything of Mr. Canning, even by name. I was not satisfied until I learned more, which I did soon after I went to Edinburgh, from a gentleman with whom I became acquainted through an accidental circumstance. He had been editor of a daily newspaper in London during some part of Canning's career as a statesman. It was more common then for statesmen to have a newspaper engaged as a special organ than it is now. He had waited on Canning, at the Foreign Office, to receive his instructions, when the minister had any to give; this paper being favoured, for a considerable length of time, when there was anything special to go forth to the public. In the ante-room, where the persons seeking audience waited, there were new faces every day, but some old ones. One of the old ones began to eye the editor anxiously, not knowing who he was nor his business. This was an eminent foreigner, a capitalist. He seemed resolved to know who the gentleman could be who was always favoured first with an audience, no matter who was waiting. 'You must be a great man—pardon me, sir; the minister always sees you, and always sees you first. I am M ——, whom people say is de richest man in Europe; but you are de greater man—pardon me, sir; this great minister sees you first. If I might be permitted to beg the honour of your acquaintance?' The editor presented the capitalist with his card, to which the latter replied, 'Mine Got! but you are de great man!' But he meant quite the contrary. When he found that the gentleman to whom the minister gave such ready audience was only the editor of a newspaper, he never looked at him again.

From this gentleman I learned much that has been of use to me; at all events, much in a very short space of time.

The trade in timber and the cutting of it got worse and worse as the summer of 1828 came on. The prices of work were not only low, but there was no demand for men at any price. Where I was working, it became as profitable to leave the timber in the log in hopes of better times, as to cut it up. When the month of June arrived, it was proposed to me by Adam Skeldon, a working man who had once been overseer of the parish roads in my native district, and who was now on a limited scale a cowkeeper in Edinburgh, and occasionally a sawyer, to go to the hay harvest which begins early in the vicinity of Edinburgh. I had not mowed much at home, but had tried. So Adam and I got new scythes rigged, and went off to look for mowing. We had only got to Duddingston, when Mr. Pendrigh, who keeps a tavern there, told us that Mr. Scott, a farmer, with a large farm on the east side of Arthur's Seat, had been inquiring for mowers. We went to him and engaged to cut his hay, a mixture of clover and rye-grass, at 3s. 6d. the statute acre. We were about ten days at it. During this time Adam went home to Edinburgh to sleep at night, a distance of two miles and a half. But I could not. I obtained leave from Mr. Scott to sleep among the straw in one of his barns; and at one of the hind's houses I got oatmeal porridge made for breakfast and supper. For dinner I had bread and small beer from Duddingston village. It being my first hay harvest, and Adam being a crack mower, while I strove to keep up with him, I was bent nearly double at night when we left off work, and would have lain in the fields, rather than walk two miles, had I not got the barn to sleep in. But during the first week I was worse in the morning than at night. Gradually, however, I began to get seasoned. We did not earn over half-a-crown a day, as the grass was heavy, and knocked down with rain.

When we were done with Mr. Scott, we were hired at half-a-crown a day to mow the grass within Duddingston policies (domain or home park). This place belongs to the Marquis of Abercorn, but he seldom lives there, at least not then. But there was a fashionable party of ladies and gentlemen, and ladies and lords, staying at the house, and we were not allowed to mow near the mansion in the mornings before ten or eleven o'clock, lest the whetting of our scythes might disturb them in bed. When the day was farther advanced they used to some out, walk among the hay, and look at us. The ladies were elegant creatures, but I would have thought more of them had they not said frequently in our hearing, 'How nice it is to be a mower! what delightful exercise! how I should like to be always a-haymaking!' The innocent creatures knew no better. Adam used to say when they were gone, 'They're a wheen idle gipsies and idle loons, going about doing nothing, and living on the fat of the land; *tories* every yin o'them, ye may be sure; lying up in their feather beds there till ten o'clock o'the day. We want Sir Francis Burdett[8] at them. Odd, I'll wager Burdett would take them through hands—the *tories* that they are!'

Had Adam known how little trustworthy his political idol, Burdett, was; and had he known how wrong he was in ascribing all idleness and ill-doing to the *tories* in particular, to the gentry in general; and had he and I both understood better at that time how much working men can do for their own happiness, we might have done less work, and enjoyed the money we earned better than we did. There came to Duddingston while we worked there, a great number of people in tartan kilts and plaids, with pipers playing on their bagpipes, to celebrate the anniversary of the battle of Bannockburn. They dined in the open air, danced, drank whisky, and spent the night, and the best part of next day, in the same manner. Adam and I were amongst them, and did more harm to ourselves, than any political man against whom Burdett at any time opened his mouth, ever did to either of us. But like most young men, and like all ignorant men hearing much about political reformers and political anti-reformers, I was too ready to think that political reform was to cure all social ills. It was necessary then that reforms should be effected; it will become necessary again, and many a time; but men should look to political reforms as the means by which they can make themselves more useful and better men, not depend on them for some miracle of good fortune, which no legislation can give.

From Duddingston we proceeded to Dreghorn, near the village of Colinton, five or six miles west of Edinburgh, and joining with two men who had been working in a distillery, contracted for the mowing at that place. The grass was lighter than on Mr. Scott's farm. We mowed it for 2s. 9d. per statute acre; but what between its being lighter, and my improvement as a mower, we earned full three shillings per day each. We should have earned less, or our employer would have had to pay more per acre for us to have earned so much, had the soil been well drained and cultivated. It was strong clay land, in want of thorough drainage, on which the corn crops of the previous year had been imperfectly developed, and on which the clover and rye-grass of that year had, in places, almost perished by wet. I have been told that since then the soil has been drained and well cultured, and that the greatest of all kinds of farm crops are now obtained from it.

From that place we went, the four of us, upwards from the lowlands to the hills which form the western end of Lammermoor. At a large farm called Blinkbonnie, we had nearly bargained for a great quantity of hay to cut, but the price offered of 2s. per acre would not suit us. Going into the interior of the hilly region, we found six days' mowing at Herriot Mill, in the parish of Herriot. On leaving this place my companions bent their steps down the vale of Gala Water, intending to go into Ettrick Forest, to be in time for mowing the bog or meadow hay. Hitherto it had been all clover and rye-grass that we had mowed. The bog hay in those hilly districts is much later, the cutting of it seldom beginning sooner than the end of July, or ending sooner than August. I declined to go with them any farther. I had more reasons for separating than one, but the chief reason was that the most of our earnings was spent on whisky, which I loathed and hated. I intended by this time to return home to Branxton to the harvest, as soon as it should be ripe, and I could not think of going home without some money to give my mother, and without a new suit of Sunday clothes which I had promised myself all the preceding six months. My castle-in-the-air which I built daily at the long saw and at the mowing, the building of which mainly sustained me at the prodigious work which we performed of mowing an acre, and an acre and a half per day, while whisky mainly sustained my companions, was this—that I should go home at harvest, go to the meeting house on Sundays with my sisters, and, after an absence of eight or nine months, be seen there better dressed than I had ever been before.

Philosophers will say that the human mind should have higher motives than those indicated of myself here. True; but in sawing timber and mowing hay I gave forth too much perspiration every day to have much philosophy of a higher order within me. Nor had I any association with other thinkers to awaken it. But I shall hardly admit, even now, that it was wrong for a working man like me, earning the full wages of a man for the first time, to put some object before him, such as being superiorly dressed on a Sunday. In later years, since I have been in towns where public parks are instituted, and facilities are afforded for recreation out of doors, I see nothing in those parks and facilitated recreations more beneficial than this—that they induce working people who have the means, and who previously wasted their means in dirt and drunkenness within doors, to be clean, to be well-dressed, to care for their families being well dressed; and, above all, to care for themselves being well behaved, and to go out like honest and good men, and look the world honestly in the face.

Having parted from my other companions, I returned to Herriot, and the farmer told me that as I seemed a 'steady chiel', I might take a week at jobbing work on his farm, and the week following join his two shepherds and another man in mowing the bogs. I did so; got a shilling a day and victuals for the week of jobbing work, and one and sixpence a day and victuals for the mowing. I slept at night in a loft over the cows among oat straw, being allowed a blanket and some sacks by the farmer.

This lasted about three weeks; at which time I proposed to leave the bog mowing, and go home to East Lothian to the corn harvest. My brother had sent to me from Edinburgh, saying that the carrier, William Christison, had told him that harvest in the east country was about ready. So one Saturday afternoon, when I had got my week's wages, had taken my scythe out of the *sned*, had tied her up in neatly plaited hay-bands, had bidden the farmer, and the shepherds, their wives, the shepherd boys, and the shepherds' daughters, and the farmers' milk-maids farewell; and when I had got over the hills two miles north of Herriot, with my face towards Edinburgh, which was distant eighteen miles, I had mounted the top of a dry stone dike, and was looking at the long distance which I had to go that evening, when a laughing face just before me looked up from behind a whin bush. It was the face of my brother James. He had come from Edinburgh to meet me; had seen me coming over the hill, and lay down there to give me an agreeable surprise.

Nothing could have been more agreeable. We had a delightful, brotherly, and intellectual walk to Edinburgh together, over the eighteen miles of road, most of it down hill. We rested an hour at or near a place called Arniston, examining the ruins of a church, and the tombstones of a desolate graveyard. James has always a poetic loving-kindness for such places, and what he loves I cannot despise. We were like younger sons of *Old Mortality*, scraping the moss from obliterated letters, to read names of men and women long dead, of whom we could know nothing. But once in possession of those unknown names, we moralized on the probable characters of those who had once answered to them in days that now belonged to the dark past.

The next day but one I left Edinburgh in the morning to walk to Thriepland Hill, thirty-four miles. This I reached before dark, was pleased to find that the harvest was not yet begun, and that all at home were well, and glad to see me after an absence of eight months. And with those feelings, when family worship was over, and thanks to the Ruler of All were offered for my safe return, I went once more to sleep in the *butty house*[9] bed.

---

[8] This veteran radical was already verging on the conservatism he formally assumed in 1837.
[9] The front room.

CHAPTER VIII

1829—Much Hard Work—A Little Poaching and Some Love

WHEN the harvest was over in 1828 I continued to work on the farm, ploughing, carting, and so forth, up to Martinmas term. Wages were still low; it was difficult for labourers not already hired by the year to get employment, even at eight shillings a week. I went to the Dunse hiring markets in November; but like many other young men seeking to be hired for the ensuing half year, did not get even an offer.

On the day after the last of those hiring days I went on a visit to a place in the eastern part of the Lammermoors, at which I had heard some labourers were to be employed in draining. On my way, having to pass within half a mile of Harelawside, the place where eighteen months before, when working at the Bowshiel *hag*, I was a lodger, the thought occurred to me that I should make a call there, which doing, and telling the persons on whom I called where and at what I had been working lately—that I had been a sawyer for some months, they told me that it was fortunate I had called; for David Whitehead, the wright, who lived close by, had been saying that day, that he wanted a sawyer to help him to cut that timber which he had just got home for the new gates, which he was to erect on different farms on Renton estate. I soon introduced myself to David, and in ten minutes or less, was engaged to saw with him. His business as a country-wright was of a simple nature. Once upon a time he had employed a considerable number of hands, but had no journeymen then. He lived alone with his amiable and cheerful elderly help-mate, Kirsty. They had a dog, several cats, and an ass, and no other family. But for these they had a care as tender as they could have had for any human creatures. Indeed, they were incapable of unkindness towards anything. They took me into their house, and treated me as well as either dog, cats, or ass; and to say that, is to say a good deal. I remained with them seventeen months; but not alone all the while, as you will presently see.

Our first work was to cut the timber, most of it larch, on the sawpit.

Next we made the gates. Then we had them conveyed to the gateways on the different farms, where we put in gate-posts, and hung them. This work lasted until the end of December. I had 10s. a week with lodging, and thought myself well paid considering the difficulties of the times.

When we had put up the gates, David contracted with Sir Samuel Stirling to thin and prune the range of natural grown oak wood, on the Renton estate, which forms for several miles the north bank of the Water Eye. He required help to do this, and engaged me at 9s. per week, with lodging, *and as many potatoes for supper at night, cooked in any way I wanted them, as I could use*. This was quite as good payment as 10s. per week. We went very pleasantly to work all the winter at this wood cutting. When we rose in the morning our first business was, two hours before daylight, to get hot water to thaw the grinding stone, to have our hatchets and pruning knives ground. During this operation Kirsty had the kettle boiling for David's tea, for my oatmeal brose, and for the dog's breakfast. We reached the place of our work, distant from one to three miles, by daylight. We had each bread and butter or bread and cheese for dinner, which we ate in the woods.

David was an elder of the church establishment in the parish of Coldingham. He lived about five miles from church, with a road to go to it through moor and moss as bad as can well be imagined. It was little more than a sheep's track, and lay through that wildest corner of the moors, which Scott has described in the 'Bride of Lammermoor' as the hunting ground near 'Wolf's Craig'. No weather would keep the elder at home on Sunday; and on most Sundays, Kirsty, mounted on the ass, accompanied him. He was not a reader, and had only two leading ideas about public affairs. The first was, that the general assembly of ministers of the Church of Scotland was supreme over all other powers, whether of king or of parliament. The other was, that the law having established the church, it was the duty of everybody to go to it on the Sunday; and that it was the duty of the law to punish them if they did not go. We had many arguments on those topics, but I could not move him one whit. Neither could I alter his opinion as to taking a trout from the Water Eye, or snaring a rabbit in the woods where we were at work. He said they were forbidden by Sir Samuel, that he was a magistrate and had as much power to preserve them as if the general assembly was there present itself. We were often a whole week without seeing any person; and nobody had a charge of fishing or of game there. The landlord lived far distant. So one day being alone, I constructed a few snares of brass wire and set them. In the morning on returning to work I found one hare. At evening I took it with me in a bag in which I carried some of my tools and other things, and going out at the bottom of the wood upon the post road, met the baronet and some game-keeping and game-killing companions with him. It was the first time I had seen him, and I had seen him just as I had got the first of his hares. He inquired if I worked in the wood, and for whom, and kept me a half hour or more before him, while he enquired about the work done and about my employer; but he did not suspect what I had in my possession. I was so much alarmed, however, at the singular fact of meeting him there at the time of my first success in taking one of the hares, that I resolved not to run any more risks. I got one shilling and sixpence for it readily from a carrier who passed between Berwick and Edinburgh, which, considering that two or three each week might have been picked up and so disposed of, was tempting. But David Whitehead, with his venerable head, which though not literally white, was near it, spoke so solemnly about the law, and Kirsty intimated how ruinous it might be to them, if it were known that a person connected with them had snared a hare, that I gave up all thought of going farther in the business.

At Branxton we had been prohibited from using snares, except for rabbits at certain times. But we could use guns without let or hindrance. Our master had some first-rate fowling pieces, double and single. And when I lived with him, it was a common thing, for the men who chose, to go out and have a shot when no sportsmen were in the way. In summer evenings, when shooting was out of season, I was often sent by order to shoot rabbits, where the corn fields adjoined the meadows and the woods, to keep them within moderation, they bred so fast. Wood pigeons we also shot many of, to keep them within bounds. Thus I became a tolerably 'fair shot'.

But not only did old David deter me from seeking a rabbit or hare by his exposition of the law, and Kirsty by her more forcible appeal as to what might become of them if it were known—there was a friend, Alick F——, whom I met for the first time about this period, and with whom I soon formed an intimacy of the most agreeable kind, who gave me some new ideas about the killing of birds and beasts. He was no more than a stonemason, working for weekly wages, but he was a reader, and also a thinker. He said there was something excessively mean in snaring a hare, not only as regarded any supposed owner of the hare, but as regarded the hare itself. It was mean to put down a snare and catch it in the dark. It was below the dignity of civilized men. He ridiculed the delight which people took in shooting. I was with him one wintry day on the sea shore. It was a rocky shore; the headlands, of which St. Abb's is one, rise in majestic grandeur against the storms of the northern ocean, which ride a thousand miles on waves so high that they come as if they would go over St. Abb's. We were on the shore of a bay six miles westward, and had a wide view of the grand scenery of the storm. We became philosophic and almost poetic in our conversation. He was quarrying stones in a sheltered nook, and I had taken my gun, because it was a stormy day, to have a shot at the sea-birds, which could be more easily reached in tempestuous weather than at other times. Thus we met. In the midst of our geological speculations as to the time when, and the circumstances under which the stratum of rock was formed which he had wedged asunder, and just as we had admired the magnificence of a wave which seemed in itself to be a sea risen on end to overwhelm the land, I saw a redshank on the wing, which I thought was within shot, and snatched up the gun to shoot it. He stopped me on the instant, and said, 'Let it go! What if the hand which has more power over that ocean and these waves than you have over that gun and the shot within it, were to have as little mercy for living things? What, if you and I were redshanks, or that all this nation was as but one redshank, and the author of this storm which permits that redshank to live which you would have killed, should have lifted his arm against us?' I admitted that this argument had something in it at first sight; but that we must carry it much farther if it was admitted at all. We must go to the butcher and forbid him to kill a sheep for human food, if a redshank was not to be killed. He said it was the propensity to kill for pleasure that he found fault with, and I was obliged to admit, that it was more from a personal feeling of pleasure which took me to the sea side with the gun than the value of the birds which I might shoot; and farther, that in snaring a rabbit, it was more for the pleasure than the gain. To which he again insisted, how *mean* was the treatment of a rabbit or a hare, to set a snare for it.

I did not again go out with a gun while I associated with him, nor have I had many opportunities to do so since. But in setting down all the truth, it should be said, that his intelligent and agreeable society had quite as much to do with my seeking pleasures of a more intellectual kind than shooting at the sea side as his arguments had. And his personal society had this farther charm, that he was the brother of a certain personage who had for some months occupied the largest space in my thoughts. I had not once been in her society; nor had I attempted to speak to her. I saw her on Sundays, and knew who she was, little more. I had heard the clergyman speak of her extraordinary ability as one of his pupils. She was about my age; was, as I thought, lovely; had glanced her eyes once or twice towards the place where I sat at church, no doubt by accident; and from those glances there was created within me a new dream, sometimes a sleeping dream, but oftener a waking dream, which took up its abode in me, and expelled almost every other thought, to make room for itself. At one time it would live and grow upon the sentiments of hope, and would clothe itself in visions beautiful to behold. At others it would live on hopelessness, and would still grow and become exceedingly troublesome. My age, not yet out of nineteen, my position in the working world, only a labourer, forbade me to make any attempt to let her or any one belonging to her know what I then thought. I only hoped that there would come a time when I could with confidence offer my humble self, and pledge my live-long duty and devotion, with myself, in exchange for such a treasure. And there came a time when unlooked for events put me in such a position. I was not altogether repulsed; but I was not accepted. We parted. There was something like sorrow in her at parting; there was sorrow and mortification in me. We have never met since.

But I go too fast. Let me return to my nineteenth year, 1829, to the spring of the year when her image first dwelt within me. It was at this time that I made the acquaintance of her brothers; first, the one alluded to, then a second, third, fourth, and fifth. They were occasionally at work near to where I was employed, and we became intimate. They were all of them men above the average rate of intelligence, and many pleasant hours I had with them, conversing about books, sometimes buying books together, and frequently borrowing and lending them to read.

In the month of April, when we finished the thinning of the coppice wood, arrangements had been made for the building of a new farm house of goodly size, farm steading, with threshing mill and all farming appurtenances complete, on the farm of Harelawside. My employer, David Whitehead, obtained the contract for the timber work; engaged a skilful foreman to conduct the work, and a number of journeymen carpenters. I had the first offer of the sawing; and looked about, and found a former acquaintance, Richard Wilson, who had served his apprenticeship as a carpenter, to join me. We sent to Edinburgh for new saws and other tools; erected our sawpit, got home the logs of Memel and yellow pine from the timber merchants at Eyemouth, and went to work with great animation. David and Kirsty now removed to a more convenient house, and the whole of us, carpenters and sawyers, became lodgers with them. They were all steady young men; and the foreman, Mr. Andrew Notman, was something more; he had lived long in Edinburgh, had mixed much with mankind, and read much. He was the first to make me so acquainted with Shakespeare, as to know that in the great dramatic plays there was more than their adaptability to the stage to make them popular—there was poetry of the highest order in them; and moral instruction not inferior to the poetry. Mr. Notman was remarkable for his fine taste, and ability to execute in workmanship what his taste approved. I have lost all trace of him of late years; and nearly so of all the other young men with whom I associated there.

This year was that of Catholic emancipation, and like greater people we had our debates on the question; but we had no regular supply of newspapers, and so lost much of the parliamentary arguments. The clergymen, established and dissenting, in our district, were, however, in favour of the measure, which reconciled many to it who would have been opponents. Mr. Notman did more to make me understand the subject than any one else.

When harvest came we had more timber cut than was soon to be required. My partner in the pit and myself left it accordingly, and went to the Merse harvest. We went first to Langrigg, celebrated in the traditions of shearers for its *kemps*, or strivings on the harvest field. With most farmers the system is to prevent striving, to have the work well done. With some, but only in the Merse of Berwickshire, the system is to let the shearers go at the work and strive until they fall down, if they choose, so as they get the wheat cut down. Langrigg in those days was such a place. They usually gave a shilling or two a week for the best hands more than the market wages. Those who, like my comrade and myself, had strength and youthful agility for anything, looked out for such places—the higher wages being deemed an equivalent to the heavier work. We had 2s. 6d. per day, and victuals at that place, which was 1s. per day more than we could have obtained that year in Lothian—wages still remaining low. From Langrigg, its shearing being done, we went to Foulden West Mains. When done there, we had ten days more of harvest on the hill farm of Coxwood, in the Lammermoors, making six weeks in all. We then returned to our sawpit, and ended our work there about December.

I tried in several directions to get more timber to saw, but could not succeed. My comrade in the sawpit being a joiner, got work immediately at his trade. But having unfortunately no trade, I had once more to turn to the spade, pick, and shovel, and dig drains.

CHAPTER IX

Lost in a Bog

IT is hardly possible for the toil of a working man to be wasted more vexatiously than in digging deep drains in a marshy soil in winter; the frost thawing so as not to allow the carts to cross the soft ground with stones to fill the drains; the sides of them sliding in; the digger of them obliged, at his own expense, to clear them out again before they are filled with stones; obliged to get planks to stand upon, to keep him from sinking in bottomless moss; even with the planks, wet to the knees, from morning until night; the farmer who is to pay him holding his money unpaid until those drains are completed; they not completed until this farmer conveys stones to them; and they every day filling in afresh with new slips from the sides. Such, however, was my situation as a drainer in January, 1830, in a bog on the farm of Butterdean Mains, lying in the hollow near the hostelry locally known as 'Tammy Grant's'; now the Bank House Station of the North British Railway.

And a man working in such a bog so unprofitably to be in love, and not in a condition to tell his love; his greatest hindrance being that he is too poor to venture on presenting himself where his love would lead him!

After such days of dis-spiriting toil, I used to go once or twice a week, one week I went three times, across a moor to ——, where she lived with her parents. The distance over the moor was between three and four miles. The distance by public road was about six miles. I approached the house by the side of a wall, where was a large tree overshadowing the stack of turf fuel which belonged to the cottage. There I, time after time, sat down for several hours each time, and looked across the narrow road to the windows. Against one of them I saw the shadow of an arm, which, inside between the window and a candle, was moving to the stitches of a needle. It was the shadow of her arm; and to look at it was the object of my journey across those desolate moors so many times a week. In the cold I lay and watched this shadow, until I should have been frozen, but there was a heat of the soul too strong for frost. Once she came out to the turf stack for fuel for the next morning's use. It was at bed time; nearly ten o'clock. I could have touched her. The time had come which for months I had longed for. It was a precious moment. But I could not make use of it. I was in a dark corner when she came to lift the fuel, and knew that if I moved or spoke she would be frightened, and would run, perhaps scream. At all events, I was pleased to form a self-excuse from these considerations. But, in verity, I was unable to speak. I knew not what to say. She returned to the house. The door was fastened, the windows darkened, and I returned over the moors ashamed of myself.

But having been so near her on this occasion was only an inducement for me to go again; and to venture to the same place at the turf stack. Hearing the singing of psalms when her father was performing family worship, I stole to the window and listened, and could hear her voice singing. It was low and soft, but what melody to me! I returned over the moors that night, singing the same psalm tune all the way. And when in bed I dreamt I heard it sung, not while listening at her window, but while looking into a paradise, the abode of beings as like heavenly beings as I shall ever see in a dream again.

Next morning at breakfast, old Kirsty, my landlady, noticing the manner of my appetite, said, 'Weel, ye was away seeing her again last nicht; she must hae gi'en ye a guid answer at last; ye seem to be in cheery speerits this morning. Man, if I were you, I wadna let ony lass that ever step'd i' leather shoon put me rhae taking my meat, as ye let that yin do. Wha is she, for a' the world?'

Kirsty did not know, nor did any person know, though they came pretty near the fact in their guesses. I could not conceal from them that I was in love. The outgoing at night; the disappearance of my good appetite; and my deep melancholy (though this was in part the result of the vexatious work in the sliding drains); all those signs marked me out as one in love.

I continued to go to the window to listen to the low, soft voice; until one night, as I listened, a dog sprung upon me with a worrying ferocity which made me retreat, mindless of the melody of psalms. I kept it off at first with my stick; but, as I retreated, it followed at my heels and bit me. I turned and struck it, upon which voices of men were heard, hounding it on. Again I ran, and again it bit me. Once more I turned upon it; but it was to face several more dogs that were

75

hounded upon me by men whom I could not see. By the free use which I made of my cudgel among them, they were content now with barking. I once more ran up the hill towards the moors; and though the men followed, urging the dogs on, I escaped. When they had hounded them after me to the distance of about half a mile, they called them back, and I was left alone on the moors.

It was a moonless night, and on the moors it was misty, the fog settling so thick on the heather as to hide every mark of sheep track or bush. The alarm and hasty flight from the dogs caused me to go out of the right track, without knowing at what point I erred. After going nearly double the distance, by reckoning which should have taken me home to Kirsty's house and over several stone walls, I came upon nothing of stone wall kind to tell of my position. Standing awhile to consider, I thought the best way would be to go off at a right angle from the spot where I halted, for I knew two public roads ran parallel at the distance of about three miles. Knowing that I was somewhere between those public roads, I concluded that I must have deviated from the cross line between them, and gone either to the south or to the north, which could not be determined, the heavens above and the heather below being alike invisible. Thinking to walk straight out, without veering right or left, until I had got over a distance of three miles at least, I reckoned to reach one or other of the roads, either that in the south, near my home, or that in the north, running through the hamlet, where barking dogs had just been biting the heels of hopeless love.

I had not gone far when I came to a road, and knew it to be either the right or the wrong one; but which of them no sagacity of mine could tell. After a mile's walk on it, I came to something which I could feel to be a house. On examining it by touch, I ascertained by the porch and the railings at the window, that it was no other than the house from which the dogs had chased me away.

Afraid to linger a moment, I hastened once more to the moors, thinking I could not again mistake the direction. The thought of going six miles round the turnpike road, by the Pease bridge, and up as far as the Old Tower, which I should have to do—the Old Tower in which Scott has located the story of the hapless Lucy Ashton[10]—was such a grievous thought, and I was already so wearied, that I resolved to continue on the moors at all hazards. Besides, had I turned, there was no way to get to the Pease bridge but by passing the place of the dogs once more.

So resolving to go on and turn not, I went. But all that I could do was not sufficient to keep my organ of locality vigilant. Over and over again I bent down to feel the grass and heather with my hands, to know if I was on the grassy track which winded through the moor, and formed what was called the road. At last I could feel nothing but heather; the track of grass was lost. I was lost too. There was nothing for me now but to recur to the former plan and walk a certain distance in one direction, and again turn off at a right angle if the public road was not found. This was tried, but I was still within the prescribed distance, when I felt myself on a 'bobbing moss', which heaved up and down with me at a frightful rate. I now knew what locality I was in—full two miles from human habitation. The water beneath the thin turf was deep—who can tell how deep? But I knew it to be far more than sufficient to take me over the head if the thin turf covering broke. I also knew by hearsay, that in some places it was broken; that cattle which shepherds had allowed to go out of their sight had strayed upon it, broken the surface with their weight, sunk down, and were lost for ever. That I might avoid plunging in a moment into one of those fissures, I stood still, and moved not to the right nor left, forward nor backward. I would have tried to go backward, but was not absolutely certain if I had not turned when at first I felt the moss begin to heave; wherefore I did not know which direction was backward.

There was no hope for me but to stand still. There was a thick hoar frost, and the air was excessively cold. After a time, to restore my feet to warmth, I began to move them. The whole surface yielded, and heaved up, and again deflected, and again heaved. This told me I must not move. At last water began to run over my shoe tops. It gradually rose to my knees. Every moment I expected the turfy skin to crack and let me fall through. Every moment was like an hour. The hours were ages; I thought daylight would never come. It was like eternity; and that eternity night! Might I not be safer to move a little? I might find a surface harder with less water. I tried, though I was not sure if I moved, my limbs were almost powerless. If I moved, the water followed; for still I stood, knee-deep, with it rather gaining above the knees than otherwise, yet not gaining fast.

At last I saw the fog look whiter on one side. It was the east; and the faint twilight was above the fog. Oh, blessed east; what a light was that to me! It became more distinct, and at last it was so good a twilight as to show that furze bushes grew within twenty yards of me. Their growing place was dry land I knew, and I spread myself down on hands and knees, though almost over the shoulders in water, to creep to that dry land, thinking that if I came to a fissure, I should be less likely to fall through lengthways than I would if standing upright on foot. I got out in safety; made the best of my way home, ashamed to look old Kirsty in the face.

From digging drains in the marsh, where so much time was lost by the premature closing of them, I went, in connexion with two other men, to a higher district on the same farm of Butterdean Mains. When the work was apparently two-thirds done there, the two men said they had made arrangements to go to Australia as shepherds, and that, if I would allow them to draw half the money for the whole contract, I would have only one-third of the work to do, and would get as much money as they. To this I readily consented, and they went to Australia. The remainder of the work, however, was nearly all bottoms of deep drains, very hard; and in one part it was to cut over a rising ground, to let the water escape from a marsh into a rivulet below. Here I found whinstone rock. It had to be bored and blasted with gunpowder, and that at the price per rood of cutting through clay or gravel. I bored, hammered, blasted, hammered again, began early, worked late, but still made little progress. It was an inexpressible trouble—worse almost than hopeless love. I could not get a farthing of payment for the work which was done until this was finished. It was done at last, and in reckoning my time, the whole of that winter's work in draining averaged about twopence-halfpenny per day. Mr. Logan, the farmer, would not make the smallest allowance for unseen difficulties. He only said that it showed me to be the greater fool, that I permitted the two men to go to Australia before the work was finished.

It was now April, 1830. A new harbour was begun to be built at the Cove Shore, and labourers were wanted there. I went to it and was engaged, first at 9s. a week. The contractor had some men at 10s. and a picked gang of hands known to him at 11s. He heard that I had been working as a sawyer, and perhaps thought me not likely to be a rough and ready labourer for work wet or dry—in the sea or out of it. Moreover, I looked ill in health, and was actually ill. Mind and body had been both overworn, and I did not eat the food in three days which was necessary for one day. But I had not been a fortnight there, when I stepped all at once into the front rank, into favour, and into 11s. a week. The foundation of the quay head was attempted to be laid at the lowest ebbs of the spring tides. The hands could only work about two hours at each of three of four ebb tides, once in fourteen days. Strong boxes were sunk to work in; the water being baled out, the sand and silt thrown out, and the rock beneath cut into form for receiving the lower course of stones. Only two shovels throwing out the sand could work at once; those who did work in the box were crack hands, and took it by turns. Several tides had been lost and no stone laid. One day Mr. Wilson, the contractor, was urging the men in the box to exert themselves and get the sand out, that he might not lose all the spring tides. One of them grumbled and muttered about their doing more than they were paid for. I was as ready then, and doubtless am still, to look for adequate payment for work performed as any one. But there are times when one's sense of right and energies carry them above thoughts of payment. This was such a time with me. I sprung over the side of the box, took the shovel from one of the men who was handling it rather awkwardly, and commanded him, with something like a look of fierceness, to make way for me. He seemed to hesitate; upon which, in the impulse of the moment, I seized him in my arms and tumbled him over the side into the water, three or four feet deep; some of those on shore pulled him out. Seeing this, Arthur Forsyth, one of the masons, who, like the contractor, was impatiently awaiting the clearance of the foundation to get a stone laid, sprung into the box with me from a ledge of rock, and we jointly bundled the other man out. We had both energy and strength, but, what was of as great service, we both knew the art of working expeditiously with tools in a narrow space, without being a hindrance to each other. In a space of time incredibly short, we threw out several tons of sand; got to work with short heavy picks upon the slaty rock below; had the bed of a large stone cut out, and the stone laid in its place—where it lies to this day—before the tide had risen half way up the outside of our temporary coffer-dam—the box.

A boat came and took us and the tools on shore. On stepping upon the rock, Mr. Wilson said to me, 'Well done, you are the man for me.' He ordered James Hamilton, the time-keeper, to put me on the highest scale of wages. I continued at that department of the works, often immersed to the middle in the sea water, until all the foundations were laid. Within a few days of the first immersion, I was completely recovered from my stomach disorder; and was restored to the most robust and cheerful health. Night time and day time, when the ebb

79

tides served, I worked, chiefly with the fishermen as associates (some of whom had once been lads at school with me, as previously stated); and each day of that toil which some people would have thought to be, or felt to be, killing toil, only added to my strength. The fishermen had been used from babyhood to dabble in the sea, and thought nothing of it.

But with the restoration to health and the increase of strength, that mysterious disorder of the affections which had troubled me so much during the winter did not become less. I did not yet take courage and run the hazard of a repulse, by seeking an interview with her, and making a confession. But I did worse. And now, my child, I have something to write of, to which I crave your special regard. It is not my design in these memoirs to overlay them with good advices. If young men could be made to comprehend human life in its practice before they have learned the truth, at the great expense of the most valuable years of their lives, it would be well. This can be effected better by such a circumstance as I am now about to relate, than by any proverb, or abstract maxim of good advice.

I had not the privilege of going into her society. But I had now the daily satisfaction of associating with one or more of her nearest relatives, and with two or three other relatives bearing the same name. To me there was a charm about every one who bore that name. In the society of those most nearly related to her I spent much time. Never once was she spoken of by them to me, and never by me to them. But it happened at times that in talking among themselves they mentioned her name. The sound of it gave me a sensation like some sweet note of new music. With one of them more especially, written of in the last chapter, I associated much; much for the sake of his own intelligent conversation; but much, also, though perhaps unknown to him, because his eyes, evening and morning, had looked upon his sister—had seen her in the family home, where I had never seen her. Our conversation was often of books, of poetry and philosophy. But the poetry and philosophy had sometimes the flavour of whisky. I abhorred that deceitful enemy so far as its bare self was concerned. But at pay days it was hardly possible for the most abstemious and resolute to escape the expenditure of some money on drink. We had a motley assemblage of masons, quarrymen, and labourers, from nearly all parts of Scotland. But if the strangers were disposed to corrupt the natives, it is just as true that the natives were willing to be corrupted. Drink at each pay day, and occasionally between pay days, was almost unavoidable. But if avoidable, I hardly remember one now who sought to avoid it. The most that my intelligent associate and myself did was to make choice of a few of those who could enjoy intellectual conversation, and retire to some private place, where we sung songs, quoted poetry, delivered home-made verses, and spent more hours of our time than enough. Neither our drinking nor expenditure were excessive, taken by measure; but our hilarity was often loud enough. We began to be remarked and talked of. The interchange of thoughts with one who, in most things, thought so nearly alike with myself, and who was a member of a family circle which seemed to me the central circle of the universe—with a star within it, was a charm not to be cast away, but to be retained for ever; if for ever I could retain it. I would accompany him almost to his home, several miles from mine. I dared not go farther than just within sight of the family cottage; but I did go within sight of it often, for the sake of seeing it. I would suggest to this member of the family, and even to others more distantly related, to go with me and sit down over a bottle of ale, though for myself I loathed the drink, merely that I might perchance hear her spoken of; or, at the least, enjoy the sweet privilege of holding converse with, and making myself agreeable to those who saw her every day, and were her nearest and dearest connections.

But need I tell the result? Instead of improving my position by making myself respected by the more domestic members of the family, I was looked upon as a doubtful acquaintance who led the brothers astray, or as one who, if not leading them astray, was going astray with them.

At hay time this year, 1830, I left the Cove Shore with three other men, and mowed at Thorntonloch, Branxton, and Pathhead. We had no binding engagement with Mr. Wilson, at the shore, but my conscience was hardly at rest for a long while after, for having left him at that critical time, when he required all his best hands, and more than he could obtain. We returned to him when hay mowing was over. The others left him again at harvest, but I remained.

When mowing the hay, we joined with us George Skeldon, who was our precentor at church. I had learned some church music, and we sung together at resting hours. George suggested that I should the next Sunday take his place in the desk, and be precentor for the day. My ambition lay in that direction, though it is questionable if I had the ability, or the necessary confidence. I tried—got on pretty well, until the last psalm; on beginning to sing over the first measure in solo, as is customary there, my voice quivered, hands shook, and eyes became blind. On rising to sing I had caught a glimpse of *her* sitting in the gallery, and looking intently down upon me. I stopped. One of the elders sitting close at hand took up the tune which I had been attempting, and carried it on, everybody singing as if nothing had happened. But I was mortified beyond my power to tell. To have 'stickit' the tune before all the congregation was unhappy, but to have done so before *her* was agony.

I went home and tumbled into bed without taking dinner, and never showed my face again until next morning.

If you imagine me carrying heavy stones upon a barrow, six men to the barrow; driving wedges into the rock by the swinging blows of an enormous hammer; upturning the wedged rock with iron levers, each of which were as much as two men could lift: if you imagine me in my lodgings at the Cove, occupying the same small apartment in the same small house, with James Hamilton, chief quarryman and time keeper; James at night repairing shoes, sometimes his own, sometimes mine, while I read to him from the *Casquet of Literary Gems*, a delightful publication which I then received in monthly parts: if farther, you imagine us working sometimes in the night, sometimes in the day, as the tides might serve, pulling out to sea in boats during the day when not working—you will see pretty nearly what my life was at the Cove Shore in 1830.

In the winter my friend Alick, already alluded to, heard of the library of a deceased gentleman, Mr. Thomas Burton, to be sold. We bought it jointly; picked out the books we thought the most choice; sold the rest; and then put our own into two equal divisions, and drew cuts for them. We could have agreed to divide them without drawing cuts, had it not been for *Don Quixote*; both of us wanted the Don. So we agreed to put him into one of the lots, and chance him; that lot fell to Alick.

Some terrible shipwrecks occur on that rocky coast. In the winter of 1830, while we were at work there, a brig was driven within sixty yards of the shore at Bilsdean Burnfoot, where she was speedily dashed to pieces, with nine men on board. The pointed rocks, and deep fissures, rendered our efforts to save them doubly hazardous; but we got them all on shore, Arthur Forsyth being conspicuously daring. The bystanders were pleased to pay me a similar compliment. I refer to it now to say that so far as my knowledge of such services goes, they result so much from an impulse of the feelings, that I was not then aware, until the men were all saved, of being engaged in anything to attract notice.

I must now hasten to other scenes.

[10] The heroine of *The Bride of Lammermoor*.

CHAPTER X

1830—Work in a Stone Quarry—Edinburgh Reform Riots in 1831

A T the close of the last chapter, it was said I must hasten to other scenes. I am hastening. Yet this chapter is still to tell of scenes not much different from those in the last: it is still a chapter of picks and quarry-hammers—of wheel-barrows, spades, and shovels. I am about to leave the Cove Shore, and go to a garden nursery at Edinburgh. But before I go, let me tell some events which occurred while I was still at the works of the Cove Shore. One bleak day in November, 1830, the wind strong from the north, and the sea rolling heavily upon the rocks at the Pan Doocot (dovecot), where twenty or more of us were quarrying blocks of stone to be conveyed to the Cove Shore, two miles distant, by sea, a little boy came and stood behind us for a time, shivering in the cold. He said nothing; and one of the men at last asked what he wanted. He replied that he wanted me, mentioning my name, but he did not know which was I. Mary Lowe had sent him down from Linkheads, he said, with a newspaper, for us to read something that was in it: he was to take it back again with him when we had read it. They had all read it at Mary Lowe's, at Linkheads, and they were mostly all 'fou' already, they were so glad of the news.

Hearing this, we agreed to get under shelter of the ruins of the Pan Doocot at once, and see what the news could possibly be which the visitors at Mary Lowe's hostelry were already getting 'fou' about. On opening the paper, there were in bold letters, on the top of a column, these words, or nearly these, 'The tories driven from power at last!— Glorious triumph of the people!—Henry Brougham, Lord High Chancellor of England; Earl Grey, prime minister!'

Those of us who knew least of politics knew enough to understand the importance of this announcement. We took off our hats and caps, and loud above the north wind, and the roaring sea, shouted 'Henry Brougham for ever!' At that time we knew little of Earl Grey. His career as an opponent of the tories was before our time. His career as a minister was only then beginning.

We were not unprepared to hear such news as this, as a previous newspaper informed us that Sir Henry Parnell had made a motion for inquiry into the expenditure of the civil list; that the government of which the Duke of Wellington was prime minister had opposed him, were defeated, and had resigned; and that Earl Grey, a reformer, had been summoned to form a new government. I had charged Mary Lowe to send us a newspaper to the Pan Doocot quarry as soon as one could be got, to let us know the result. We read over the list of the new ministry. Some of the names were unknown to us, and some familiar names that *we* thought should have been there were not there, the name of Hume especially. We one and all thought it wrong that Joseph Hume should not be a member of the new government. We were ignorant of party connections and differences—ignorant of the atomic nature of some politicians, of the gregarious nature of others.

At another time we got a paper, and read Earl Grey's declarations that the principles of his government would be Peace, Retrenchment, and Reform. Joseph Douglass, a labourer, was the only man among us who found fault with that declaration. He objected to the word 'peace'. He said Britain had never had a prosperous day since there was peace. War was the thing for the country, and especially for such a country as this, which had so many war-ships that it could lick all the world. War was the thing to make good wages. Two or three of the fishermen who were beside us knew otherwise, and called Joseph a blockhead, and asked him if he would like to see the press-gang at them and their families again, as it used to come in the time of war, and force them away from home and family, put them in irons if they did not go willingly, and carry them in carts to man the ships of war. Joseph replied that he was not afraid of war; if the king wanted men that minute, he would go on board a man-of-war, rather than the French should not be well licked again. One of the fishers in rejoinder said he might first learn to take his wheelbarrow on *board* of that plank in the quarry without stumbling off ten times every day as he did. Joseph was rather blind, and used to stumble off the plank. Yet no ridicule would put him down; his voice was still for war. But I have met people since that time, who should have understood such a question much better than poor Joseph could do, who were as politically stupid upon it as he was personally ignorant.

Such was the place and manner of our reception of the news of the tories being out of office, and of the whigs being in.

During the winter I continued at the Pan Doocot quarry. It was between two and three miles from the Cove Shore, and about one mile from Thriepland Hill. This was convenient, and I now lodged at home. A number of masons were hewing the blocks of stone, and each hewer had a labourer allotted to him to do the rougher work upon the stone with a short pick, technically to 'scutch' it. The masons were intolerable tyrants to their labourers. I was in the quarry, cutting the blocks from the rock when the tide was out: and when the tide was in, I went and scutched with some of the hewers, chiefly with my friend Alick. One day, when we had been reading in the newspapers a great deal about the tyranny of the tories, and the tyranny of the aristocracy in general, and some of the hewers had been, as usual, wordy and loud in denouncing all tyrants, and exclaiming, 'Down with them for ever!' one of them took up a long wooden straight-edge, and struck a labourer with the sharp edge of it over the shoulders. Throwing down my pick, I turned round and told him that so long as I was about the works I would not see a labourer struck in that manner without questioning the mason's pretended right to domineer over labourers. 'You exclaim against tyranny,' I continued, 'and you yourselves are tyrants, if anybody is.' The hewer answered, that I had no business to interfere; that he had not struck me. 'No,' said I, 'or *you* would have been in the sea by this time. But I have seen labourers, who dared not speak for themselves, knocked about by you and by many others; and by every mason about those works I have seen labourers ordered to do things, and compelled to do them, which no working man should order another to do; far less have the power to compel him to do. And, I tell you, it shall not be done.'

The labourers gathered around me; the masons conferred together. One of them said, speaking for the rest, that he must put a stop to this; the privileges of masons were not to be questioned by labourers, and I must either submit to that reproof or punishment which they thought fit to inflict, or leave the works; if not, *they* must all leave the works. The punishment hinted at, was to submit to be held over one of the blocks of stone, face downward, the feet held down on one side, the head and arms held down on the other side, while the mason *apprentices* would whack the offenders with their leather aprons knotted hard. I said that, so far from submitting to reproof or punishment, I would carry my opposition a great deal farther than I had done. They had all talked about parliamentary reform; we had all joined in the cry for reform, and denounced the exclusive privileges of the anti-reformers, but I would begin reform where we then stood. I would demand, and I then demanded, that if a hewer wanted his stone turned over, and called labourers together to do it, they should not put hands to it unless he assisted; that if a hewer struck a labourer at his work, none of the labourers should do anything thereafter, of any nature whatever, for that hewer. (The masons laughed.) 'And farther,' said I, 'the masons shall not be entitled to the choice of any room they choose, if we go into a public-house to be paid, to the exclusion of the labourers; nor, if there be only one room in the house, shall the labourers be sent outside the door to give the room to the masons, as has been the case. In everything we shall be your equals, except in wages; that we have no right to expect.' The masons, on hearing these conditions, set up a shout of derisive laughter. It was against the laws of their body to hear their privileges discussed by a labourer; they could not suffer it, they said, and I must instantly submit to punishment for my contumacy. I told them that I was a quarry man, and not a mason's labourer; that as such they had no power over me. They scouted this plea, and said that wherever masons were at work, they were superior, and their privileges were not to be questioned. I asked if the act of a mason striking a labourer with a rule was not to be questioned. They said, by their own body it might, upon a complaint from the labourer; but in this case the labourer was insolent to the mason, and the latter had a right to strike him. They demanded that I should at once cease to argue the question, and submit, before it was too late, to whatever punishment they chose to inflict. Upon hearing this, I put myself in a defensive attitude, and said, 'Let me see who shall first lay hands on me?' No one approaching, I continued, 'We have been reading in the newspaper discussions about reform, and have been told how much is to be gained by even one person sometimes making a resolute stand against oppressive power. We have only this day seen in the papers a warning to the aristocracy and the anti-reformers, that another John Hampden may arise. Come on, he who dares! I shall be Hampden to the tyrannies of masons!'

None of them offered to lay hands on me; one said, they had better let the affair rest where it was, as there would only be a fight about it, and several others assented; and so we resumed our work.

Had it been in summer, when building was going on, they would have either dismissed me from the works, or have struck and refused to work themselves. It was only about the end of January, and they could not afford to do more than threaten me.

On resuming work at Alick's stone, he and I discussed the matter privately. He admitted that for a mason to chastise his labourer was wrong; but adhered to the abstract principle that masons, having trade privileges, were bound to maintain them, without submitting to have them discussed by any other body of men, not even by labourers who might be subject to the injustice of those privileges. He could see no analogy between the question of the labourers rising against the exclusive privileges of stonemasons, and that of the unenfranchised classes of the community rising against the exclusive privileges of the boroughmongers. He said building could never be carried on, if labourers were to have equal rights with masons. And, finally, that I had made myself look exceedingly ridiculous in setting myself up as an opponent of usages and trade regulations which nobody had ever before presumed to question. I maintained that stonemasons had no excuse in calling for the reform of exclusive privileges of the landed gentry and aristocracy, until they abolished their own exclusiveness and tyranny.

About this time I began to reflect gravely on the life that was before me. I had learned no trade. I had declined to go to my brother the forester, to follow his profession, because I thought of staying at home to be a ploughman. I had not always succeeded in getting hired as a ploughman, and had become a labourer at any kind of work that presented itself. Was I to continue, and do nothing better? I called to mind that my brother had been a working hedger and ditcher until he was older than I; that he educated himself for a situation above that of a working man; but that I had heard him say, that had he been a year or two in a nursery at his outset, to have learned the practice of arboriculture, he would have found it beneficial.

I resolved to try what I could do for myself in that respect. Going to Edinburgh, I sought and obtained employment at the nursery of Messrs. James Dickson and Sons, Inverleith Row. I entered the grounds about the beginning of February, 1831. My first work there was trenching and digging the beds for the seed of trees and shrubs to be sown in March, wheeling manure through the long, narrow alleys, and so forth. My wages were six shillings a week, and no more, in consideration that I was to have instruction for the labour performed. I had lodgings in the bothy within the grounds. Five other men, professional gardeners, were in the bothy; four of whom slept in a small room, which, though small, was not so uncomfortable as the place where I and the other slept. Our bed was a narrow space within a recess in the kitchen compartment of the bothy. It was hardly wide enough to have held our two coffins had we been dead; and had we been coffined alive, we could have hardly been in worse confinement than when in bed. The kitchen fire, at which we cooked our victuals, was within two feet of the bed; and a thin wall was all that separated our heads from the stove pipes in the greenhouse. We had no ventilation; and, when summer came, the place was as bad as any steerage berth I have ever occupied on board a ship, and I have been one of four hundred and fifty persons between decks. Outside the bothy, all was flowery, green, and ornamental. Visitors came often, and admired always; yet behind the bricks in that floral paradise, the greenhouse, there was our sleeping place, as odiously unhealthy as it has ever been my misfortune to know a sleeping place to be.

Two of the gardeners had, like me, 6s. a week; one had 6s. 6d.; the other three had 7s. One of them, Mr. F——, is now a gardener and land steward, standing alike distinguished for intellectual and professional excellence. There were twenty or thirty other young men, who lodged without the grounds, working in the nursery at the inferior wages of 8s. a week, in the hope of getting a situation through the interest of the employers. A few were master gardeners out of place, submitting to work for 9s. a week, in the hope of getting other situations as masters. A few were regular hands, continued from year to year at 9s. a week—men who had broken down in reputation as gardeners, and who had no chance of other situations, though not without hope. All these, save the six in the bothy, lodged and boarded themselves without the grounds.

Thus the best gardening ability of well-educated young men who had served apprenticeships and had studied botany, and of master gardeners who had been in good situations, was secured for the nursery business considerably below the pay of street scavengers. The men had some hope that they might, by serving a few months there, or even a year or two years, obtain appointments to good places; to journeyman's places in the nobility's gardens, if their ambition or abilities ranged no higher; to the places of foremen, if they sought that much and no more; or to the places of masters, if they looked so high. The gentry and nobility were then, and still are, in the habit of applying to nurserymen for master gardeners; and the master gardeners apply to them for foremen and journeymen. This is done in the English nurseries as well as in the Scotch. But in England the nurserymen do not cultivate their grounds by employing men at half-wages, as they do in Scotland, making the other half of the wages be the reversionary interest of a place, not unfrequently the promise of a place. Of broken hopes, or of hearts sick with hope deferred, you shall hardly reckon so many in all the world, on the same limited surface of earth, as in the grounds of the Scotch nurseryman.

To me individually, the employers (father and sons) were just, and even kind. When I was about to leave them, at the end of eight months, the elder Mr. Dickson gave me a written testimonial of character that almost surprised me. I had heard him accused of seldom saying as much of men as they deserved, in his written testimonials. Of me he wrote that I was steady, indefatigable in study, always at hand when wanted, and ever willing and obedient. I was aware that he could not say anything to the contrary; yet I hardly expected him to say so much. Possibly I was indebted to the good reports of the foreman, Mr. William Howden.

Two months, at least, of my stay there were taken up with building. During the winter, main drains, or conduits, deep and wide, had been dug out, and they still stood open in spring, to be built and covered in at leisure in summer. Mr. Howden one day said that a mason must be sent for to flag the bottoms, build the sides, and cover them in. I rejoined that I could do it well enough. He smiled, and asked if I had been a mason; to which I replied no, but I could do all the building he required. He said I might try; and having tried, I was allowed to go on until the whole were finished. There was such a thought in my head as this, I shall not deny, that the wages of masons being 20s. per week, while my wages were but 6s. a week, the employers might possibly add something to mine; but, as it appeared, such a thought did not occur to them.

We lived meagrely in the bothy; oatmeal porridge of small measure and strength in the mornings, with 'sour dook', a kind of rank buttermilk peculiar to Edinburgh; potatoes and salt, occasionally a herring, for dinner; and 'sour dook' and oatmeal for supper. We never had butcher's meat, and seldom any bread. To have had even enough of this food it would have required all my wages. But I confined myself to 4s., occasionally 3s. 6d., per week for food. The remainder I expended on books, stationery, newspapers, and postage of letters.

Postage was a heavy tax at that time to persons like me, who took pleasure in writing letters. My washing was sent to Thriepland Hill by the carrier. I never, for so many months at any other time of my life, suffered so much from hunger and philosophy as then. I devoted much time, frequently sitting up half the night, or rising at day-break in the summer mornings, to reading, writing, arithmetic, and other studies; and an expenditure for books and stationery could not be dispensed with. Nor could newspapers be omitted at that time. The Reform Bill had been laid before parliament, and the public anxiety was excited by the debates, to an extent beyond the power of any one to believe who did not live then. Three of the men in the bothy cared nothing for newspapers, at least, they did not choose to pay for them. But the other three, of whom I was one, joined funds together, and got the *Caledonian Mercury* on the second day after publication, for half price. It came out three times a week, and gave the debates at considerable length, the leading speeches at full length. It was the 7th or 8th day of March before we got the report of the great speech of Lord John Russell on the 1st of March. I was selected to read it in the bothy, and as many men as the small place could hold were packed together to hear it.

The bill was read a first time without a division, after an animated debate which lasted seven days. On the motion for the second reading the debate lasted two days. The speeches were perused with intense interest everywhere, even in such places so socially remote as our bothy, and by persons who, like us, ate less than enough of oatmeal porridge and 'sour dook' that we might get the newspapers.

On the 22nd of March the second reading was carried by a majority of *one*, the votes *for the bill* being 302, *against the bill* 301. On the 18th of April, on the motion that the bill be committed, General Gascoyne moved an amendment that the number of members ought not to be diminished, which was carried by 299 to 291, giving a majority against the reform ministry of eight. Three days after this, the ministers were again defeated by 164 to 142, upon a question of adjournment which postponed the voting of supplies. The ministers tendered their resignations to the king, which his majesty would not accept. They were desired to proceed and carry the Reform Bill as best they could, but not to abandon it. They then advised the dissolution of parliament, to which the king readily gave assent, and parliament was instantly dissolved.

Never did the act of a soverign of England encircle the throne with such popular enthusiasm as this act of King William IV. The bill was looked upon as the king's own measure. The country was divided into two parties, the anti-reformers, few in number, though politically powerful; and the reformers, including the vast majority of the population. All the different classes of parliamentary reformers united at the elections, and the cry was, 'The bill, the whole bill, and nothing but the bill!' The anti-reformers were signally defeated in England and Ireland, though in most cases successful in Scotland. Of eighty-two county members in England, all were pledged to support the bill except six, returned for Westmoreland, Bucks, Shropshire, Huntingdon, and Monmouth.

At Edinburgh there were only thirty-three electors, the self-nominated town council. They were entitled to return one member. The candidates were a young man named Robert Adam Dundas, now known as Robert Adam Christopher, one of the members for Lincolnshire; and Francis Jeffrey, Lord Advocate of Scotland, an eminent lawyer and orator, and distinguished as a literary essayist and reviewer. Four-fifths of the entire male inhabitants of Edinburgh above twenty years of age petitioned the council to elect Mr. Jeffrey; so did the members of the Merchant Chamber, and nearly every other public body. They, however, elected Mr. Dundas. The first petition I ever signed was to the Edinburgh town council in favour of Francis Jeffrey.

Terrible riots ensued, which were in fact only a continuance of the riots which occurred at the illumination of the town on receipt of the news that the second reading of the bill was carried by a majority of *one*. I was present at the first of those riots.

The majority of *one* for the second reading of the Reform Bill was celebrated throughout the kingdom by a mixture of illumination and darkness, lighted windows and broken glass, bell-ringing and prohibitions of bell-ringing—by rejoicing and rioting, strange to behold, and still more strange to think upon. There abounded in all extravagance the liberal joy that the reformers were triumphant, associated with the most resolute tyranny to compel the anti-reformers to put on signs of rejoicing when they felt no joy. In Edinburgh the Lord Provost, head of the city magistracy, and the other members of the anti-reform corporation, were solicited by the inhabitants to proclaim a general illumination. They refused: but seeing, as evening came on, the general preparations for it, and the threatening aspect of the street mobs, they assented that the town should be lighted, and proclaimed accordingly. To many householders, who were willing to be guided by them, and by them only, the published authority came too late. They knew nothing of it, and remained in darkness. Others who were deep in political grief at hearing of the majority of *one* against rotten boroughs, resolved to keep their houses in gloom, and to sit within and mourn. Unfortunately for those of darkness and sorrow who lived in Heriot Row and Abercromby Place (spacious lines of first-class houses fronting to the Macadamized road-way newly laid with loose stones, and to the Queen-street Gardens, with their iron railing), the Lord Provost, an unwilling man to light his windows, lived there. Stones were thrown and his glass was broken. The sound of crashing glass and the facility of getting missiles to throw whetted the appetite of the ten thousand headed mob—a little taste of window breaking to it, being not unlike a little taste of worrying to the wild beast—and so to the work of destruction the mob rolled like a sea, and roared like storms meeting upon rocks and seas. It proclaimed itself the enemy of anti-reformers and of glass. Like tides about Cape Horn where contrary winds meet tides, as banded constables meet mobs to beat them back, this human sea, storm risen, rounded the Royal Circus, Moray-place, Queen-street, Charlotte and St. Andrew's Squares, through the long streets which join the eastern and western boundaries of the New Town together; and with wrath where it flowed and wreck where it ebbed, bore upon its surf the sea-weed that knew not whither it was carried.

I was a piece of its sea-weed. I was now for the first time tossed upon the waves of a popular commotion. At the beginning there was a pleasing sensation of newness. Even the first sound of breaking glass was not unmusical. Combativeness and destructiveness were charmed. But, as dash went the stones, smash fell the glass, and crash came the window frames—dash, smash, crash, from nine o'clock to near midnight, reflection arose and asked seriously and severely what this meant; was it reform? was it popular liberty?

Many thousands of others who were there must have asked themselves the same questions; yet still the cry was, 'Up with reform light, down with tory darkness!' And unilluminated tories, masters and servants, male and female, aged and youthful; even the infant tories in their mothers' arms came to the windows, holding candles, all they had in their houses, twinkling feebly on the face of night, to let the mob see that toryism was smiling, was joyful; happy, very happy, at the advent of reform, and the majority of *one*. But those signs of truce came too late. Reform would hold no truce until anti-reform windows were broken.

The tory newspapers proclaimed this outrage to be the first fruits of reform. And when, a few days after, at the election, another mob threatened to throw the Lord Provost over the North Bridge, and pursued him with a purpose of mischief until he took refuge in a shop in Leith-street, from which he was carried away, so the story went, barrelled up in a hogshead; they promised the country in general, and the city of Edinburgh in particular, a continuance and extension of such riots at all future elections. The reform newspapers were content to say that the riots reflected no discredit on reformers, the rioters were only 'the *blackguards* of the town'.

In subsequent years I have often reflected upon this word 'blackguard', as applied to political glass-breakers. Whatever unsolved problems we might suggest in social and political philosophy about the term, I believe that there is now one problem solved by experience, which was hidden in futurity then—namely, that the greater the number of men enfranchised, the smaller is the number of 'blackguards'.

It was in the month of May or June, in that year, 1831, while in the nursery at Inverleith, that I made the first attempt to get sentiments of my own writing put in print. The task cost me more than the half of each of three nights. It was a letter to one of the Edinburgh newspapers, and was written, and re-written, and again amended. On the day after it was finished to my satisfaction, I, at the breakfast hour, hastened to swallow my porridge in as few minutes as possible, which having accomplished in a space of time wonderfully short, I put on my bonnet and ran off, up Inverleith road, through Cannon Mills, up Broughton-street, and so into Edinburgh, a distance of about two miles. Arrived at the editorial letter-box, I took the letter from my pocket, and dropped it in as if I had been doing a thing that had guilt in it. A glance down the dark passage of the receptacle proved that the letter was gone out of sight deeper than I could see, and then, as if the editor might be lying at the bottom and looking up at me, I blushed

94

and turned away. As soon as I had walked a distance that might look business-like, I broke into a running pace, and soon reached the nursery. As I passed people on the streets, I fancied they looked as if they knew that I had been putting a letter into the box of a newspaper editor, and that he was shaking his head at it by this time. Still I thought it would be in print next Saturday.

Next Saturday came, and with it more impatience than I could easily control. When it was evening, and the wages were paid, and all the sweeping of the walks was done, which usually fell to me to do on Saturdays, I once more swallowed my porridge in an exceedingly small number of minutes, and set out for Edinburgh to buy the newspaper to which I had sent my letter. I paid for it in the office, got outside, and opening it slowly, gradually, anxiously, did not see those lines of print upon which so much expectation and the sum of sevenpence had been expended. Seven pence was the price of newspapers in those days, and was too large a subtraction for me to make from my wages of 6s. a week. But it was made, and the return I got for it was the following lesson from the editor—a lesson which I subsequently profited by, and which most fresh hands at newspaper letter writing should endeavour to improve from: '*A Constant Reader* is informed that we have only had time to read as much of his *long letter* as proved that it was not fitted for our columns. *The subject has already been exhausted.* We do not know if our correspondent's composition required correction; but if it did, *he is the only person whom we know who should correct it.*'

I have here put the words in *italics*, which should convey the lesson to others as it was given to me. A long letter upon an exhausted subject (it was the Reform Bill), by a writer who had no more originality than to call himself '*A Constant Reader*', and to ask pardon for the errors of a first attempt, was an infliction which editors do not willingly endure; it is one which they should not have to complain of.

About a month after this, I read a paragraph in a newspaper about the kirk session and the poor of the town of Dunbar. Knowing something of the kirk sessions, and of the poor of that and other parishes near it, I took pen and paper and wrote facts without any attempt at fine composition, and without study, except the grammatical care of making the facts intelligible. I sent them to the editor for his private information, that he might refer to them if he thought fit; but said nothing of having been a rejected correspondent previously. Yet this letter was at once inserted, the editor saying, in a commentary, that though it came to him for private perusal, it was too important to be withheld from the public. This was my first appearance in print; and the letter was published because it contained information which was new; the other was not published, because it contained no information that was new. Since then I have always studied to put something in my newspaper correspondence which readers were not likely to have known before; and abiding by that rule have been, upon the whole, successful.

Having here incidentally mentioned the Scottish kirk sessions, which, up to the year 1845 were charged with the care of the poor, and who up to that time, until the legislature interfered, most grossly neglected, or wilfully abused their charge, I may take a step—a long step—in advance, for a few minutes—no less a step than the measure of thirteen years. I had reached at that time what is considered the highest branch of newspaper literature. A certain portion of the leading articles of one of the principal daily papers was allotted to my pen.

The subject of the Scottish poor, and the kirk sessions, who should have cared for the poor, but did not, had grown out of the miniature dimensions which rendered it almost an invisible question to politicians thirteen years before, and was now so great, so loud-voiced, and im-portunate, that they were constrained to turn and face it, and grapple with its necessities, and set its wrongs right. This subject, which first led me into print at a time when I had no privilege but to sympathize with the infirm poor, and could only resolve that if ever the opportunity should occur I would use it to vindicate humanity in their behalf, came to me again—or rather I was drawn to it again—when in the daily practice of meeting members of parliament and of writing for 'leading columns'; and I have the conscientious satisfaction of believing, that through those various conduits of argumentative influence I assisted in removing from the minds of economists in England the unhappy opinion, that the old Scottish poor-law was consistent with national or political economy: and the further and higher satisfaction of believ-ing, that I assisted in removing from old Scotland her deepest disgrace —the starvation of her aged and infirm poor. I only regret that the reform did not go a few steps further, to save the inhabitants from being driven into the towns when they are old.

As the wages of 6s. gave me nothing to buy clothes, after victualling myself for seven days and procuring such books, stationery, and other things that were necessary for the tasks of study which I had set before me, I asked leave to go from the nursery, at the beginning of August, to the Berwickshire harvest; obtained leave for a month, and with six other men, three of them gardeners, two sawyers, and one a carpenter, left Edinburgh on the 3rd of August to go to St. James's fair, which is held on the 5th at Kelso, forty miles from Edinburgh. At that fair shearers are hired for the harvest by the farmers of the shires of Roxburgh and Berwick, should the corn be ripe so soon. I had, during three or four weeks, put myself on the lowest possible expenditure for food, and ceased to buy anything of book or newspaper kind, to have a few shillings saved to take me into the country to look for harvest work. None of the seven had more than a few shillings. We had not gone more than five miles from Edinburgh when a circumstance occurred which let each know the amount of the money possessed by the rest, and that, in the whole, we had set out with funds amounting to thirty shillings.

Two of the men were some hundred yards in advance of the rest, and at the turning of a road were attracted by seeing a gang of thimble-riggers with a board, a thimble, and a pea, sitting at play; two men who looked like shearers, and who said they were going to Kelso fair like us, were risking their money and winning. Another man, habited as a shepherd with his dog at his feet, and who seemed to be a stranger to these two and to the thimblers, stood and spoke sagely against all gambling, and wondered how men could be so silly as risk their money. Yet, in a short while, as if charmed with the winnings of the other two, he tried also and was likewise a winner. I reached the spot just as my friend John Tait, the sawyer, was about to risk half-a-crown. I counselled John not to risk his money; but he made the venture and lost. Another of our men tried with half-a-crown and likewise lost. I told him that he lifted the wrong thimble, and that if it had been my stake I should have lifted one of the others. The thimble-rigger without touching the remaining two, so far as I could see, asked which one I should have lifted had it been my play; to which I replied by taking up one, and there, sure enough, under it was the pea. I was urged to go on and try my fortune, and believing that I was now sharp enough to detect the transitions of this mysterious pea, I put down half-a-crown, lifted, and, lo! I was a winner. But in trying again I lost, and so on once more, and once again, until I had no money, having entirely neglected for my own guidance the warning I had given to John Tait. John again risked his money, and so did each man of our band until every sixpence was gone. Suspecting that there was a trick by which the pea was removed and not left under any of the three thimbles, except when we were allowed to win, and that then three peas were used to make such a beginner as I sure of winning, some of us snatched up the three thimbles at once, and all were blanks. We complained of their cheating us and said they must give us back our money. But now we found that the shepherd with the cudgel and dog and the two men with reaping hooks were part of the thimble gang. We insisted on having our money returned. Whereupon, at a signal from some of those who stood guard over him, the man who worked the pea and thimbles and held the money rose from his seat and ran off; the others with their cudgels and reaping hooks looking us fiercely in the face, as if daring us to dispute his motions. We had all sticks in our hands. The turnpike road also on which we stood was newly laid with broken stones, and afforded missiles to any amount; and though they were seven rough-like fellows, besides the one who was away with the money, we also were seven. John Tait was the first to flourish his cudgel, and call us to the onset to give them battle and get back our money. It fell to me to encounter a man who had one of those sharp weapons called a scythe hook, which might have cut off my head—which, at the least, would have been used to wound me, had not a rather formidable staff which I carried, parried his intended cuts, and ultimately knocked the weapon out of his hands. On being disarmed he retreated as his comrades had done, and took to the loose stones, by which we should have had indifferent heads to go to Kelso fair with, had we not rushed in upon them, sticks in hand, at what, in military tactics, would be called the 'charge'. They were routed by this charge, and went off at racing speed in two divisions, in different directions, four of our men pursuing four of them, while three of us, Tait, Walker, and myself set off, also at racing speed, in the direction which the man had gone with the money. In our absence the other seven thimblers re-united and gave battle to our four men, who, in their turn getting the worst of the affray, retreated after us. We reached a small public-house which stood alone by the side of the road, and could see far enough towards Edinburgh to observe that the man with the money was not upon the road. We felt assured that he was in the house; and going in, I thought to be a good general, and so locked the outer door to prevent his escape while we searched in the different apartments. The landlady came hastily and implored us not to make a disturbance, for she had a daughter at the point of death lying in the bedroom. She said no man had come within the door. Filled suddenly with pity, and almost with remorse for coming thus roughly, and as it seemed unjustifiably, into the afflicted woman's house, we begged pardon of her, and said we would not further disturb the death-bed of her daughter. Not to make more noise upon the ears of the sick one, I moved quietly to the door to open it, but saw, as the key was about to be put into the lock, that eyes were looking through the keyhole. They did not see me, the passage where I stood being dark. I listened; and heard one man tell another that the man and the money were inside, and also that the old woman was all right for them; she would save him if she could. On Walker and Tait hearing this from me, they rushed instantly to the bedroom in which the dying daughter was alleged to be, and there lay under the bedclothes, dressed in a woman's night-cap and bed-gown, with face rubbed over with chalk to make it deathlike, the man with the board, the thimbles, the peas, and the money, and no sick woman at all. He offered us any amount of cash out of what he had, or all which he had, to save him from harm and let him escape. The landlady prayed to us not to say anything about her, else she would lose her licnece, and urged that she knew nothing about the thimblers, and had only out of pity for the stranger, not knowing who he was, tried to protect him.

This to us was well enough so far as it went; but the question was now, how were we to get out of the house, and fight our way through the seven thimblers outside? We could neither see nor hear of our four men without, and it was evident that they dared not approach the house. I thought it best to make friends with the man within, by taking only half the money we had lost, though he had offered us several pounds more than our own—all he had. My two comrades were resolute to the contrary, and would not take less than the whole of our own money at least. Meanwhile a scene was performing without which we did not know of. A number of the Gilmerton coal carters had been attracted by the conflict of charges, retreats, and counter-charges, as seen from a distance, and had come to see what the affray was. The thimblers without the house offered them money in hand, and as much whisky in reversion, as they could drink to help them. The carters said no, they would rather help to give them a thrashing; and they would do so if they only knew which were thimblers and which not. Upon this the pretended shearers and the shepherd assumed to be the men who had been cheated out of their money, and pointed to our men as the accomplices of the thimble-riggers. The carters accordingly turned upon our unfortunate comrades with their whips, flogged them, and gave them chase. They soon discovered their mistake, however, and returned upon the real sharpers, who fled to the fields. Seeing the times to have turned in our favour, I opened the door. Our prisoner with the peas and the money gave the carters ten shillings to be allowed to escape. We got the thirty shillings we had lost; and though some of those present would have taken more, the majority decided that it would not be honest or honourable to take more than our own. So we started on our journey, and saw the thimblers no more. Nor have I from that day to this risked another half-crown, nor so much as sixpence, at gambling. We had a narrow escape. As it was, blood was shed, and the affray more than once looked as like one in which lives would be lost, as a conflict, which had no mortal results, could look.

We proceeded to the Lammermoors, over Soutra Hill, walking quickly lest re-enforcements of thimble-riggers should pursue us. It was now late in the day. When the hour of sunset came, some of our band were so foot sore that they could not walk farther that evening. Seeing a farm-house and barns on the side of a hill, half a mile above the road on which we were, I went up to it while the others rested, and asked if the farmer would allow us to sleep in his barn all night. He demurred on hearing that there were seven of us: but his wife interrupted his demurrage by saying, 'Hoot aye, let them have the barn; they're going to shear somebody's corn. What would ye say when our corn is ripe if nobody came to hire themselves to shear it?' Hearing this, the farmer sent a messenger to the roadside for the other men, that I might not have the fatigue of going for them, and returning up hill.

When we had stretched down on the straw in the barn, he and his wife, his daughter, and one of the milkmaids came and surveyed us. The old man said he hoped we were all religious lads, and his wife said, 'Hoot aye, they're decent young men, dinna fear,' to which the daughter added. 'They're *weys-like* (respectable) young lads.' Upon this the maid was sent to prepare a supper of milk porridge for us. When it was brought to the barn the farmer came again to see that we asked a blessing to it. We told him we were thankful for the kindness of him and the mistress, for providing so well for strangers like us. But he checked us and said, 'No, not unto us, not unto us, but unto God give thanks.'

We slept in the straw soundly, and next morning went on our way filled with gratitude, and with milk and barley bannocks. I have never seen those good people since, nor do I remember their names; but through all the changing scenery of intervening years I still see their farm fields and their benevolent faces so distinctly before me as to know them again should we ever come together. The place was a few miles from the small burgh town of Lauder.

We went out of the direct road to Kelso, when approaching the early farm districts, to look for shearing, thinking we might get hired before going to the fair. But the harvest was nowhere ready. At sunset we were at the farm of Sandy Knowe, upon which the early years of Sir Walter Scott were spent, in the society of those who nourished his natural talent for romantic story-telling. And Smailholm Tower, a ruined castle, beautified by his poetry, was before us. We tarried by the ruin to rest and speak of poetry and romance; of Scott, and of Scottish border history, until the sun was down, and the illumined west had become like Smailholm Tower, the grey remnant of a day, passing and gone, gone for ever. Kelso was yet several miles from us, and by the duration of our day's journey lengthened by divergences in search of ripe corn to shear, we were all tired. Encouraged by the kind treatment which we had received from the farmer beyond Lauder, we proceeded to the farm house of Sandy Knowe to ask leave to sleep in the barn. But they would not allow us to get within doors. Leaving the inhospitable place, we found a dry sandpit, and resolved to make our bed among the sand until daylight in the morning. But the farmer and some of his men came down, and said if we did not go away they would set their dogs upon us. They led two ferocious hounds, and two or three loose dogs growled so savagely that we did not hesitate to retire. We again passed the ruins of Smailholm Tower, and thinking it would be poetical to sleep there all night, as well as convenient, we entered to see if among the stony wreck we could make a bed. But the men with the stony hearts and the growling dogs came upon us again, and we had no help for it but to trudge off to Kelso.

We could get no lodgings there, every place being filled with cattle dealers and other strangers already arrived for to-morrow's fair. Thoroughly worn out, we lay down on the causeway of a narrow street where there seemed to be the least traffic, and the least danger of being run, ridden, or driven over, in our sleep. Some of us were already asleep, when a weaver and his wife, opposite to whose humble cottage door we lay, came out, and said they could not go to bed, nor rest if they were in bed, with the thought of fellow creatures lying in the street. They had a large family of children, a small house, and were only poor persons, they said: still, if we would go inside they would at least give us the shelter of a roof and a fire to sit by. We went in. The weaver and some of his children made a bed for themselves beneath the loom; his wife and the other children went to a bed in the loft, and four of us lay crossways on the bed which they had vacated in the kitchen. The other three stretched themselves on the clothes-chests and the chairs. In the morning, one of us went out and bought tea, sugar, and bread, for breakfast, while the kind woman got us water and a tub to bathe our blistered feet; and the weaver gave his shaving razors to those who needed shaving, and took his other razor, which was past shaving, and pared such of our feet as had bruises; and took a darning needle and worsted and drew it through the blisters, leaving a worsted thread in the blisters—the best possible cure for them. When we had breakfasted, and were all bathed, doctored, and refreshed, the good woman, her heart overflowing with motherly generosity, said, 'No; we must not offer to pay her; no, we must not speak of thanks even; we were, no doubt, some mother's bairns; she had bairns of her own, and the wide world was before them yet; it would be an awfu' thought for her to think it possible that they might ever be without a roof to sleep under; oh, no; we must not speak about paying her; she had done nothing, nor the gudeman had done nothing but their duty, their Christian duty, whulk was incumbent on them to perform to their fellow-creatures.'

On getting across the Tweed, from the town to the green, where the fair is held, we saw, and lingered admiringly to look upon, that rich scenery of meadows, woodlands, ripening corn fields, and hills beyond the corn fields encircling in the folds of the sparkling Tweed Roxburgh's ducal mansion, the Fleurs, and the near neighbour of the Fleurs, beautiful Kelso.

None of the farmers would hire us for immediate work; they said harvest would not begin until after ten days. Several offered to engage us conditionally to come to them at the end of that time; but Walker and I were of opinion that if we travelled into the Merse of Berwickshire, we should find ripe corn sooner than on the farms where conditional engagements were offered in Roxburghshire. The other five thought not. So we two separated from them, and reached Greenlaw, the county town of Berwickshire, that evening. There I found Mr.

Notman, who was foreman of the house carpenters, when I sawed the timber for them at the new building at Harelawside. Bob Gillies, Allan Moffat, and Hugh Moffat, were also there. Glad hearted and merry were we to meet again. There was a new county hall and other extensive buildings in process of erection. Mr. Notman offered to get me employment at once until the harvest began, which I would have accepted, but intelligence came to Greenlaw (pronounced *Grinly*), that Thomson of Bogend, near Dunse, was about to begin to shear, and that he wanted hands; so we went there.

CHAPTER XI

I Take the Shilling

O<small>N</small> the harvest fields of the farm of Bogend, the 'kemping', the slashing down of the ripe corn, the mad strife of the shearers, and the instigation of the master and the grieve to make the shearers go more madly, were famed as being without parallel even in the Merse of Berwickshire. In any one day, the shearers hacked down—their work could not be called shearing—three times as much corn, at least, as the same number would do, or be allowed to do, in the Lothians. The payment was, per day, from 3s. to 3s. 6d.—nearly double the wages of the Lothians, and the food was better. In Lothian the oatmeal porridge sent to the harvest fields for breakfast is seldom well boiled, the larger quantity of meal used rendering it so thick that to attempt to boil it well would burn it, and any cook or porridge-maker who sends the breakfast burned or singed ('singit parritch') to the field, is a very bad cook indeed, whom the shearers soon declare against. To send out *thin* porridge, without the large quantity of meal, would be to offend the appetites of the Lothian ploughmen, and not less so the appetites of the Irish shearers, who are employed in great numbers at the Lothian harvest. The milk is also *thick*, inasmuch as it is, or was, stored up for harvest use, and salted, during several weeks before harvest began. I have heard that this abominable milk is not now tolerated, and that the shearers are seldom offered it when it is longer kept than four-and-twenty hours.

In Berwickshire the custom was always to give the milk taken from the cows in the morning to the shearers in the evening; and that milked in the evening was given to them in the morning. The cream was removed, and it became skimmed milk; yet it was called 'sweet milk' by us, to distinguish it from the sour or 'lapperd' milk of Lothian. If a dispute should arise between a Merse and a Lothian man, no matter what the origin of it might be—perhaps the confession of faith, or the established church—it is extremely probable that, before they end, the Merse man taunts him of Lothian with being content to 'sup sour milk to his parritch'; and the retort of the Lothian man is, that the hinds in the Merse are content to be worked like brute beasts, that the masters ride after them at the plough, and 'crack a whip' over their heads, and lash the horses until they trot in the plough, with the hinds trotting and hobbling after them. The hind of Lothian adds that no master dares do that to him or his horses. If the Merse man denies that he is driven like a brute beast, or even like a slave, the other asks him why it is that he, year by year, changes his master; that he is always shifting from one to another, while the Lothian man often remains twenty years or a lifetime with the same master.

This difference between the habits of the *hinds* (so called because they are *hired*) in those two counties is more than the Merse man can explain. The Tweed river separates the Merse from Northumberland; yet the Scotch system of working and hiring on the one side and the English system on the other are almost identical. A rivulet which one can step over dry-shod separates the county of Berwick, in which the Merse is situated, from that of Haddington, called East Lothian, with a few miles of moorland on the rivulet sides; yet the style of working, and many of the domestic customs and social habits are as different as if the Merse and Lothian were separated by mountains measuring hundreds of miles.

If the mother of a Merse ploughman hears that her son is courting a Lothian lass, she asks him in dismay, how, if he marries that lass, he expects to get his *scones baked*? If he says, 'Mother, she can bake a scone as weel as a Merse lass,' the mother asks if she can 'plot the bowyes'. If he replies that she can 'plot the bowyes, and rheam the rheam, as sweet as was ever rheamed rhae milk i' the Merse' (plot— *scald*; bowyes—*milk vessels*; rheam—*cream*; rhae—*from*), his mother probably asks no more questions, but consents to have the Lothian lass for a daughter-in-law. She takes it as almost a certainty that this daughter-in-law will have a good 'providin'.' As the hinds live much longer in one service, and have better 'gains' in Lothian than in Berwickshire, in which last, by moving much about, they verify the saying that 'a rolling stone gathers no moss', they of Lothian usually give their daughters a better providing at marriage.

As indicating some other peculiarities of the maids of the Merse and of Lothian, I may report what their respective admirers may be heard saying of them. He from the Lothian side of the small rivulet before mentioned is told once more that he cannot get a lass for his wife in

Lothian who can bake a scone. He rejoins, that he cannot get one who, can 'fill muck at the midden, and drive the muck carts, as they do in the Merse; they never,' he says, 'gar women drive carts in Loudan.' And he says the truth. The Merse man next takes up what he calls the Loudan *tone*: he says, 'In Loudan the women are so slow at their work, and have such a long tone to their words, that when they speak they stop their work until the *tone* comes to an end, and in that time a Merse woman would work round about them.' The apologist of the merits and manners of the lasses of Lothian cannot suffer this to be the last word; he retorts smartly, and without a very long tone, that 'if the women o' Loudan dinna cut their words so short as they do i' the Merse, neither do they cut their claes so short; gin the lasses o' the Merse would eik the Loudan *tone* to their short goons, their short goons would *set* them the better, and maybe the lads would like them naething the waur.'

Should these disputants be shearing with the Merse women within hearing, as is most probable, the 'Loudan louts', as they are ill-naturedly called, may reckon on a *kemp* which shall stretch their skin before they get to the end of the field. Their best agility and strength, and their worst and fastest work cannot cope with these women as shearers. The men have not yet been born who are their matches at a kemp. They will be first at the land end if they should slash the corn down, and trample over it without laying it in the bands for the band-sters to tie in sheaves. They must, and will reach the land end first. The Lothian shearers, let them do their best, must only follow. When the latter do reach the land end, they will be taunted by the others, and told that they must 'sup another bow o' meal, afore they kemp again wi' the lasses o' the Merse, or cast up to them about their short goons!'

Besides the higher wages and the fresher milk to be used with the breakfast and supper porridge, the shearers in Berwickshire get a larger loaf of bread for dinner; the choppin[11] (nearly an imperial quart) of small beer, which, with the bread, is the harvest dinner, is similarly weak in both counties. In Lothian, the farmer contracts with a baker for the harvest bread, and specifies what weight the loaves are to be—about fourteen ounces. In Berwickshire the law is enforced, which ordains that each shearer's loaf shall not be less than sixteen ounces. The Lothian bakers have no advantage, as their contract prices agree with the weight of bread. Nor have the farmers any advantage from the light bread, for the additional two ounces is more than earned by the additional work done in any one hour of the day in Berwickshire.

To us who went from Lothian to the Merse, the higher wages was always the ruling cause of our migration, and no amount of work, not even the fame of the endless kemping of Bogend deterred us. But we got enough of Bogend at the beginning of harvest, 1831. My comrade, William Walker, was already affected by a consumptive disease, of which he soon after died. He had as brave a heart for work as any on the field, and was as good a shearer, but had not strength. I was a bandster to six shearers; and the crop was barley, of great bulk, the straw broken down by storms, dry and brittle, the bands made of it so bad that they would hardly hold a sheaf together; none of them made with care, the strife of kemping being incessant. I was not farther beat than the other bandsters, but I was beat, and could not keep to the heels of my six shearers; no, not with exertions the most excessive. Walker could not remain, and I was quite willing to go with him somewhere else. It was Dunse market day, and we went there. As we entered the town, the farmer of Dyket Head looked at us; said we were 'likely chiels'; asked me if I could fork in the field, or drive and load a cart, as well as shear or bind, and upon my undertaking to do anything in shearing, binding, forking, cart loading, or driving, that he might require, he hired us at 18s. per week, with board and lodging, for the harvest. We were with him a month; at the end of which time I returned to Edinburgh.

My leave of absence had been only for a month, and I had extended it to five weeks. But this did not affect my interests at the nursery, as I had made up my mind to take work at any labouring drudgery, street sweeping itself, if I could get 10s. or 12s. a week for it, rather than go again to the nursery at 6s. a week. I called on Mr. Dickson, and told him that I could not stay longer, as I would soon wear myself out of clothes, and have no money to renew them, if I did not seek work elsewhere. He expressed regret that I had no one to assist me to remain and prosecute my arboricultural studies. He said he feared that I was making a sacrifice of myself. But as I had given him the highest satisfaction, he would write a testimonial to that effect, and it might introduce me somewhere else. He then gave that certificate of steadiness, industry, readiness at all times, devotion to study and so forth, which I mentioned in a previous chapter. I thanked him, and walked upwards to Edinburgh, to me a very uphill journey, for I knew not where my next work was to be, and I had already expended all my harvest wages, save a few shillings, on articles of clothing. I tried the sawyers, but could not succeed in getting work among them. Edinburgh had not yet, in 1831, begun to build in the foundations dug out before the breakage of credit in 1825; it had not finished its half-built streets, squares, or crescents; it had not begun to inhabit many of its new houses; in short, it had over-built itself, and there was but little employment for men in the building trade, and none for new sawyers like me. I tried the market gardeners, but it was not the season of the year for them to take new hands. A young gardener from Chirnside, in Berwickshire, named Darling, and a companion, also a gardener, had come to the nursery to work a year or two, for the chance of getting situations as journeymen in some nobleman's establishment, but seeing the melancholy prospect before them, they went out at the dinner hour of their first day there, went direct to the High-street of Edinburgh, found a recruiting party of the Scots Greys, and enlisted as soldiers. The sight of the bothy suggested that they might be better lodged, paid, and fed in a barrack-room, while it was hardly possible for them to be worse lodged than there. William Niven, who had been my companion in the bothy, was the first to tell me about Darling and the other, and that he had a mind to enlist also. I remarked that it was singular that so many east country men were enlisting, and all going to the Scots Greys; that Walker and I had seen two Berwickshire ploughmen enlist for the Greys while we were at the harvest; and that James Grieve, who had been a fellow labourer with me at the Cove Shore, also a fellow-mower at the hay—formerly a schoolfellow at Birnyknowes School, and thrashed there by the schoolmaster, like myself—that he had enlisted into the Greys; that Dan M'Gibbon, also a labourer at the Cove, and young Douglass, who wore petticoats when I went to school, and had rushed to the size of a man like a mushroom —that all of these had gone direct from the Cove Shore to the Greys. And while we were walking about and talking of this, a person who knew me came and told us that Walker, who had been at the harvest with me, and had returned to Edinburgh only a few days before, had that very day enlisted as a soldier into the Scots Greys. Niven said, 'Let us go too'; but I shook my head, and replied, that I felt I had some other duty to do in the world, or destiny to fulfil, than the duty or destiny of a soldier. He asked if I could tell what that duty or destiny was—if so, why did I not begin the work? I confessed myself at a loss to tell what I was to do, still I was not satisfied to try soldiering—the term of engagement was too long, it was irrevocable when once entered upon. 'Besides,' said I, 'the Royal Artillery would be my choice rather than the Scots Greys, were I to enlist as a soldier; for there, the chances of advancement and the pay are superior'. He said he did not care which corps he went into; he would follow me. We walked towards Leith, and going to the Fort, had a look at the artillerymen who form its garrison. I shook my head, and said he had better return to the nursery, and I would go to the country, where I might possibly get work at draining farm land, road making, quarrying stones, or at something else which should at least enable me to get enough of brose and sour milk, a book now and then to read, and clothes to wear—none of which I could obtain to the fullness of my requirements, in the nursery. I could have returned to the work of harbour building, at 11s. a-week, not at the Cove, that harbour was finished, but at Coldingham, twelve miles farther east, where another fishery harbour was begun to be built by government, as that at the Cove had been. But on leaving that kind of work before, I had promised myself never to return to it. There were some agreeable and intelligent men employed at it, but the greater part were the very *débris* of civilized mankind, gathered from each quarter of the Scottish and north of England compass. We had stone-masons at the Cove who had come from Edinburgh, Glasgow, Dundee, Berwick, and Newcastle, some of whom were literally without a shirt, and without tools, when they came; who borrowed tools, borrowed shirts, earned 18s. a week, and drank it all in whisky, week after week, for months together, except what was laid out for them in oatmeal for food, when they could not get whisky. We had quarry men and labourers of the same stamp, with whom it was impossible to work without wasting some part of our wages in whisky. This led those young men already named to leave the works to be soldiers; other employment could not be obtained, and any change seemed better than that killing toil at the shore, the payment of which was but the means of getting more drink, and more drink the means of sinking deeper in self-despisement. It had induced me to seek another industrial sphere; and still, though not able to remain in that other, it deterred me from returning to it.

While still uncertain where to go to look for employment, some one told me of a public library and reading-room, which were in process of formation for the use of working men, and that it was possible that

I might obtain the situation of librarian. This was a grand idea. It seemed to be the 'open Sesame' of all the world; that it needed only to be pronounced, and all would be accomplished—the world's doors would fly open. Alack! when I tried it, the raw looking 'Lothian lout' was rather an object of derision to those town-bred artizans who were collecting from the public the elements of the public library, than their fellow-equal, with intellectual sympathies like their own. I was pronounced to have formed a very absurd opinion of what a librarian should be, when I thought that a person of my *class* could fulfil its duties.

If you would observe, and study, and philosophize upon those social distinctions which the superior classes raise up and maintain, to the exclusion of the inferior, look not for them only in such gulphs as lie between the bishop and the curate, between the lord and the tenant farmer, between the merchant who sells wholesale a gross of goods at a time, and the shopkeeper who sells by retail—one article from the gross at a time. Look for them also between the artizan who has long tails to his coat, and the humbler labourer who has short tails to his coat; between the engine-maker, who is a free member of his trade, and the blacksmith, who has not been apprenticed to engine-making. The curate may rise to be a bishop, the merchant may become a lord, and the shopkeeper who sells by retail—one article out of the gross at a time, may rise to the dignity of selling wholesale—the whole gross at a time; and all of them, the new bishop, the new lord, and the new merchant, shall be admitted freely into the new positions which their talents or good fortune have raised them to; but the labourer who has only short tails to his coat, shall not be admitted on an equality with the artizan who has long tails to his coat; nor shall the mechanic who is a free member of his trade, admit the blacksmith to an equality with him, either socially or professionally. No matter how high the ability of the blacksmith may be, nor how willing the master-mechanic may be to promote him and make use of his superior abilities, he is doomed to remain a blacksmith; he cannot pass the boundary which rigorously excludes him from rising above the level of the blacksmith class.

Perhaps in the economy of nature there is nothing lost ultimately by such infringements of individual liberty, through class exclusiveness. Whether it be merchants restraining other traders from trading in their currents of commerce, as they once did, or mechanics restricting the number of apprentices who seek to enter their trade, absolutely prohibiting men from working at it who have not formally been apprenticed, as they still do—nature vindicates *her* privileges against them all. The excluded individual, or number of individuals, become more inventive because of their exclusion. Nearly all those adventures in foreign commerce which have grown to the magnitude and solidity of national institutions, originated in some repression of thought or enterprise in persons excluded from ordinary commerce by others who possessed the power and the will of monopolists. And very many—by far the greater number—of the inventions in the industrial sciences which have created our gigantic manufactures, were the offspring of men not professionally entitled to invent. Those inventors who originated most of the mechanical trades would now, were they to live again, be excluded from working at their own inventions, even though they came with the inventive genius to improve them, which they possessed when originating them. It is the disposition of all human societies to be exclusive; and nature, in dealing with them for her own vindication, seems to be impelled to give the excluded and proscribed a new sphere of action. This benevolence of nature leads her into divergent courses; but each divergency, from that twilight time of society when the first fragments of history are seen emerging from darkness, has resulted so unquestionably in giving a new epoch to advancing civilization, that one is almost constrained to believe that the antagonism of classes, of parties, of principles, or of trade privileges, is requisite to give progress to improvement, and force to progress.

But the distance between the separated classes of society, and the distance between the opponent ranks of industry, are reduced as intercourse is enlarged. The locomotive does more than subdue the space between town and town—it lessens the space between man and man; and gives them newer thoughts the closer that they come together. While it is yet the sleeping time of night, its brother steam-engine, at the printing press, labours as if each piston stroke was an impulse of its great heart to enlarge the minds of the human millions, for whom, while the sun is but rising, the locomotive shall carry away to all points of the geographic compass, through all sections of the social scale, the knowledge which the press has multiplied in the night.

Each new subjugator of time and geographic distance, be it steam, strong enough to mingle the population of cities and shires in one corporeal admixture; or electricity, fleet enough to snatch up a thought, leave it a hundred miles away, and return for another ere the birth-time of the next be over—each is a subjugator of enmities and social distances. Were I again the 'Lothian lout' I was in 1831, going in my 'thick shoon', trowsers of corduroy, coat of fustian, and bonnet of blue, with a sun-tanned face under the bonnet of blue, perhaps the artizans with coats of broad cloth, and tails to their coats, might no longer take the measure of *mind* by the measure of the coat tail, but admit that *mind* may have an abiding place under fustian, with thick shoon below it and a blue bonnet above.

Though I failed to become a librarian, or to be admitted as an intellectual co-equal with men who could earn three, or four, or five times the wages which I had been earning, the attempt introduced me to another kind of employment, which, though not directly, was in some degree related to literature. Any employment which led me, or produced wages enough for me to lead myself into a connection with books, seemed at this time the most preferable of all others. On being offered an engagement, though temporary, to travel and obtain subscribers to a weekly paper, I eagerly accepted the engagement; though, truth to tell, I possessed then, as I still do, but little of that talent requisite to success in addressing the world to its face, and talking it into a belief that it should become a subscriber. I travelled several weeks, and, though assiduously eager, was but indifferently successful. The country people needed to be associated in clubs to become subscribers to a paper; and the labour of getting as many together as would make such a club was tedious and expensive. I had also the duty of collecting outstanding accounts; which, like the task of persuading those who were not readers to become readers, was tedious—it was the task of persuading those who had read without paying, to pay and go on reading again.

Still, through the liberality of those who entrusted me with the task, and my increasing experience, I was making progress; hardly securing a present advantage, but opening, as I thought, wide and sunny prospects for the future, when one morning I awoke and there was no sunny prospect for the future; all was present darkness, and I lay in a pit so deep that I saw no light and no variety upon its gloom, but the horrid shapes which rose, sunk, rose again, and whirled in a fevered dream. I had gone among those very persons, the least worthy of them, who ten months before were deemed unsuitable associates to work with; and within a few days after, meeting them at a neighbouring fair, was flattered into the belief that I was now in a position so much superior to theirs, that it would only be *manly* in me to treat them, and so forth.

From other acquaintances who were merry because it was the fair day, merrier still at seeing me and singing 'Should auld acquaintance be forgot', orders came freely for my paper. Everybody in that neighbourhood was to read it, and make everybody beyond them read it. And thus, with a present time around me all satisfaction, and a future time before me all hopefulness, passed the fair *day*. The fair *night* also passed away; but it rolled over me like a stormy sea, in the stormy society of that section of old acquaintances first-named, and not to be named again.

I was stricken to the earth; not only so metaphorically, but physically, veritably, and left moneyless; and ah! heavier calamity, hopeless and ashamed; abhorring to look upon myself, and ashamed to look upon the world. All the music of old songs and the joyous voices had now ceased; all but the yesterday's echo of one voice, that of my good friend Mr. Hugh Brown (now of Dunbar, then of Innerwick). When more than a day and another night had passed, I still heard the echo of his good counsel, given as he parted from me on the fair day—'Take my advice, leave them; they're nae better than they should be.' Up to this time, in corresponding with my excellent friend (and to this time I do correspond with him), I hardly ever write his name, or look upon it when it is written, or speak it, or listen to it when it is spoken, but the echo of that friendly counsel, and the form and image of that disastrous time, come back upon me—'Take my advice, leave them; they're nae better than they should be.'

What availed it now that I could carry my mind back to the time when, at the stone quarries, I had singly stood up in defence of the rights of labourers against the masons, and that the same subject having arisen during the night of the fair, was discussed in a friendly manner at first, in a manner not of my choosing at the last; that men present, whom I had not known before, asserted that had they, as masons, been at work when I, as a labourer, called their privileges in question, they would have vindicated their privileges upon my body; and that, being now defied, they proceeded to do so now? What availed it to me that I had originally the best side of the dispute? I had the wrong side at last, for it was the weakest side, when that was to be estimated only by the amount of physical strength which I could bring to bear upon it, and that after midnight, in a motley company—many of them strangers, some of them, as it resulted, but too eager to bring the dispute to a personal conflict to facilitate the design of robbing me. All those fragmentary recollections availed me nothing. I knew not at what moment the money was taken from me, nor by whom; I only knew that it was all gone; that its loss was more than I had then the means of replacing; that I had been buffeted, was bruised, and that every failing effort to obtain a glimpse of hope, only showed despair in a new and more hideous form.

During several days and nights I wandered through the country, my face westwards towards Edinburgh, but my feet moving slowly thither; moneyless all the while; most of the time unrefreshed by food or sleep. During one hour I would plan how to go out of the country, and return not, nor let any being know where I had gone, save that Being from whom I could not hide myself; but again came the assurance that to do so would be to leave behind me the belief, and with it enough of probability for it to grow upon and have an enduring existence, that I had disappeared because there was money in my possession which was not my own, not that I had gone away because that money was lost. And in this black prison of despair which arose on each side, walling me in, as it then appeared to do, from all hope, there came a new thought, and with it relief, because it was new—the thought expanding to an action, the action written on the black wall, the writing dancing before my eyes—that I should—what? if I could not break the prison of despair, I should end the imprisonment! But again—no, that would not be the *end*; I had not been so mysteriously made, to be thus *ended*.

But a week of such wandering and very *low diet* brought some light upon the gloom. I know not whether it was a chance of good or ill, but a remarkable chance it was, that brought William Niven and me again together. I sought not him; nor sought he me. We met in the vicinity of Edinburgh. His friends, who sent a small monthly remittance of cash from Dublin to maintain him in the bothy, in addition to the wages he received there, had refused his request to augment the allowance, and he was resolved to stay no longer in the nursery. This resolution arose chiefly from a suspicion, well founded, as it turned out, that he had always been deceived as to who and what his parents were; and that they were in a condition far superior to confining him to the allowance of twenty shillings a month to help his six shillings a week in the nursery, or even to enforce upon him the humble profession of a gardener. He was now resolved to be a soldier. He told me all his troubles, and I told him mine. I gave my papers and accounts to the gentlemen who had employed me, and had an interview with them. It was not long until I was enabled to send them the money I had lost, with what I conceived to be good interest honestly due to them. But they returned the interest, and took nothing but that which I should have paid them had no mishaps occurred. The depth of the degradation and suffering which I endured after losing their property, was followed by a pleasing satisfaction, not proportionately high, yet pleasingly elevated, when I had repaid it to them. I could not feel a sense of satisfaction proportionate to the former misery, for there was still, in the very act of repaying that money, and in the recollection that it was paid, a sense of humiliation, arising from the thought of its having been lost in such a manner.

When I met with William Niven on this occasion, we remained together for several days, and much to his satisfaction, I at last agreed to go with him to have 'just a conversation, if nothing more', with Corporal A—— of the recruiting party of the 2nd, or Royal North British Dragoons, the regiment popularly known as the Scots Greys. I had, however, fully made up my mind to more than a conversation with the corporal; indeed, the only hesitation I had felt about enlisting as a soldier, was as to the regiment I should choose. In Scotland, young men smitten with military ambition, and gifted with not less than five feet ten inches of upright bulk, talk vauntingly of the grey horses, their long white tails, the scarlet coats, the long swords, the high bear-skin caps and the plumes of white feathers encircling them in front, the blue over-alls with the broad yellow stripes on the outside, the boots and spurs, the carbines slung at the saddle side, the holster pipes and the pistols, the shoulder belts and pouches with ammunition, and, in the wet or the wintry wind, the long scarlet cloaks flowing from the riders' necks to their knees, and backward on the grey chargers, whose white tails wave with them behind—of these they talk proudly, and depicture in their inward vision the figures of themselves thus accoutred and mounted, the grey chargers pawing the earth beneath them, snuff-ing the battle from afar, the trumpets sounding, the squadrons charging, Napoleon's columns broken by the charge, *their* charge, with Napoleon exiled, and Europe at peace! Tell the young Scotchman who recites the glories of his favourite Greys while he rests on the harvest field with listening shearers all around, or when he listens in the charmed crowd in the village smithy to the veteran who is village smith now, but who was a farrier in the regiment once, that the Greys did *not* do the whole of Waterloo; that they did *not* win all nor any of 'Lord Wallinton's' battles in the Peninsular War, inasmuch as they were not in the Peninsula; that the Highland regiments were not the regiments '*always* in front of Wallinton's battles'; tell the young Scotchman, or the old one either, the historical truth, that the 42nd Highlanders were not slain at Quatre Bras, on the 16th of June, through their impetuous bravery, but through the irregularity of their movements, whereby, in forming square to receive cavalry, two companies were shut out and *skivered* by Marshal Ney and the French dragoons; tell him that more reports were circulated in newspapers during the war, setting forth the superior achievements of the Scotch regiments—those reports still existing in tradition—through the Scotch soldiers being *nearly all able to write* letters home to their friends, while very few of the English or Irish soldiers could write home to their friends, there being no parochial schools in England or Ireland as there are in Scotland; tell the young Scotchman at the smithy-door all or any of these things, especially the last, that it was the *writing* quite as much as the *fighting* of the Scotch regiments which distinguished them, and he will tell you that you are no Scotchman; that you are not worthy of having such regiments as the 'Heelant Watch' (42nd), or the 'Gallant Greys'.

At that epoch of my life to which I have now brought you, I had read enough of modern history to know that Englishmen and Irishmen were as much respected in the army as Scotchmen; and I had heard enough from old soldiers to be convinced that having a fair education in writing and account-keeping I would have a much better chance of promotion in a regiment of English or Irish, where there were few men who could write, than in an exclusively Scottish regiment, where almost every man was a writer or accountant. Still there was the charm of the Greys being Scottish, with their fame for deeds of gallantry. An entire troop of them, shortly before Waterloo, had been raised from among the farming men in my native parish, and parishes adjoining, by the late Sir James Hall, of Dunglass, for —— ——, and though the —— thought fit to 'sell out' when the regiment was marching to Waterloo, the men from our parish did not 'fall out' with him, but marched to the battle; many to be killed, more to be wounded, all to be honoured by sharing in the great finish to Napoleon's wars, which, before, seemed as if they would have no end, and nations no peace;

mankind no time to do aught but slay one another. Moreover, the doubtful reputation of the captain who marched with them until he smelt the battle from afar, was more than atoned for in the family by the reproaches which his mother poured upon him on his return home, and by his heroic sister, Lady De Lancey, who, first, like a bird upon the wing, its mate in danger, hovered on the edges of the field until hearing that Sir William De Lancey, her husband, had fallen mortally wounded, she penetrated to the very centre of the battle ground to find him. In the midst of that terrible carnage she remained with him for many hours, binding up his deadly wounds with her own clothing, torn from her body; trodden upon by the hoofs of the charging cuirass-iersof France, and again by the hoofs, not softer than theirs, of the coun-tercharging cavalry of England; covering his body when there was no life in it, with her own, which had but little life; watching by it during the whole of the appalling night which followed, that it might not be lost; or, nobler homage to her name, because no sense of danger, suffering, or terror, could repress in her the devotion of wife and woman.

William Niven had seen the Greys in Dublin, and having a natural disposition to be charmed with the picturesque, was charmed with them. He knew where, in Edinburgh High-street, to inquire for the corporal; and having inquired, we found him in his lodgings, up a very great many pairs of stairs, I do not know how many, stretched in his military cloak, on his bed. He said he was glad to see anybody upstairs in his little place now that the regimental order had come out against moustachios; for since he had been ordered to shave his off, his wife had sat moping at the fireside, refusing all consolation to herself and all peace to him. 'I ha'e had a weary life o't,' he said, plaintively, 'since the order came out to shave the upper lip. She grat there—I'm sure she grat as if her heart would ha'e broken, when she saw me the first day withoot the moustachios.'

Having listened to this, and heard a confirmation of it from the lady herself, as also a hint that the corporal had been lying in bed half the day, when he should have been out looking for recruits, for each of whom he had a payment of 10s., we told him that we had come looking for him to offer ourselves as recruits. He looked at us for a few moments, and said if we 'meant it' he saw nothing about us to object to; and as neither seemed to have any beard from which moustachios could grow, he could only congratulate us on the order that had come out against them, as we should not have to be at the expense of getting burned corks to blacken our upper lips, to make us look uniform with those who wore hair. The order, however, was soon after rescinded; and hair upon the upper lip for those who had it, burned cork upon the skin for those who had no hair, were once more the regimental order.

We assured the corporal that we were in earnest, and that we did mean to enlist. Whereupon he began by putting the formal question, 'Are you free, able, and willing to serve his majesty, King William the Fourth?' But there was a hitch; two shillings were requisite to enlist two recruits, and there was only one shilling. We proposed that he should enlist one of us with it, and that this one should lend it to him to enlist the other. But his wife would not have the enlistment done in that way. She said, 'That would not be *law*; and a bonny thing it would be to do it without it being law. Na, na,' she continued, 'it maun be done as the law directs.' The corporal made a movement as if he would take us out with him to some place where he could get another shilling; but she thought it possible that another of the recruiting party might share the prize with him, take one of us, or both; so she detained him, shut the door on us, locked it, took the key with her, and went in search of the requisite king's coin. Meanwhile, as Niven was impatient, I allowed him to take precedence of me, and have the ceremony performed with the shilling then present. On the return of the corporal's wife, who, though younger than he in years, seemed to be an 'older soldier', I also became the king's man.

Next day we were taken before the garrison surgeon in Edinburgh Castle, the late Mr. Jemmett, who died from mortification by pricking his hand when dissecting a dead body. I was called in first and stripped naked, and examined carefully as to soundness of the internal system, the limbs, and the eye-sight. I was ordered to walk fast and slow, and to put my body into different positions of difficulty. The result of all was, a certificate declaring me fit for service.

William Niven followed, and was similarly examined; but he came out declared not fit for service. He was greatly chagrined, and did not recover his spirits so long as I saw him. In the course of a few days he went to Glasgow, and enlisted into one of the regiments of foot guards. There the medical inspector passed him without difficulty. He joined his regiment in London, was drilled, was promoted to be corporal, and soon after discovered that, through one of those remarkable incidents which make 'truth strange—stranger than fiction', his nearest, if not *dearest* relative, whom he had never known, and whose real condition in life he had never been correctly told of, commanded that regiment of guards! He was at once discharged from it, and provided with a good outfit to Canada, and the promise of patronage if he remained there and did not return home. But the ship he sailed in never reached Canada. It was wrecked on the western coast of Ireland, and he, with some of the crew and passengers, reached Cork, the others being lost. Money was sent to Cork to fit him out again; he took the money, but declined the Atlantic voyage, and returned to Scotland. I saw him several years ago, and heard all these and other particulars from him; but know little of his subsequent history; nor is it within my present design to digress far into the memoirs of second parties.

[11] Originally meaning a slipper, '*chopine*' still means a half-bottle in French café slang. A typical Scots gallicism.

CHAPTER XII

From Edinburgh to Brighton—From Brighton to Birmingham

WITHIN a few hours of being certified as fit for service by the medical inspector, I was attested before one of the city magistrates. Within two days of that time the gentlemen in whose employment I had been, offered to re-engage me. I found that the keen sense of errors committed had at first caused me to take too gloomy a view of my situation; but it was now too late—I was sworn, and must go. The regiment was quartered at Brighton, the course of journey to which from Edinburgh, was by Leith Walk, two miles to Leith Harbour; from that, five hundred miles by sea to London, and from London fifty miles, through Surrey and Sussex, to Brighton. Several recruits were proceeding to their respective regiments by way of London, but only another and myself to the Greys. This other was Andrew Ireland, a cabinet-maker, from Edinburgh. A youth, from the labour of the plough and the spade, in the parish of Garvald Kirk, in my county, named William Tait, brother of John, the sawyer, enlisted with the Greys a few days after me, but was rejected for being half an inch under the standard of that time, five feet ten inches. He was young, and promised to grow an inch or two more, still they would not have him; a succession of years of low wages and little employment had given them as many men as they required. He enlisted into the Royal Artillery, joined the 4th battalion, became one of the best soldiers in that select branch of the service; was an excellent accountant, a particularly steady man, one of the smartest and ablest non-commissioned officers that ever drilled and exercised other soldiers on Woolwich Common; was married; became a widower with a motherless child; sent the child to his relatives in Scotland, while he proceeded to the West Indies; was there promoted to be sergeant and quartermaster sergeant; and, in 1846, the hardest periods of his service over, and a provision to the end of life, after he might cease to serve, before him, almost like a certainty, he left Barbadoes for England. But the devouring climate, enemy of the men of Europe, would not spare him, though it did not destroy him there. It came after the ship, as if it had been so busy with his comrades that it overlooked him; or, as if, after attacking him, it had found the constitution of a Lothian ploughman not soon overcome, and had not had time to finish him before he got away, it came after him in pursuit, wormed itself into him afresh, gnawed at him, overcame his strength, took the last breath from him and, as if resolved that he should never get home alive or dead, got his body over the ship's side into its ocean grave, when almost within sight of the British shores.

A staff-sergeant from Edinburgh went in charge of all the recruits of the party to London. We embarked in a sailing smack called the *Eagle*. During the first two days and nights, the sea being moderate, I stood in the forecastle and had waking dreams, or lay among the storm sails stowed in the gelly and had other dreams, some of them sleeping, some of them waking, there being but little difference between them. Several songs or farewells were begun, and two or three reached a kind of finish. One that took the lead of the rest towards a finish began—

> *Oh! speed thee, speed thee,* Eagle *ship,*
> *And bear me fast away!*
> *For,* &c. &c. &c.

But the *Eagle* carried us into fogs, and next into contrary winds, and began to heave and roll, until she heaved all the poetry out of my head, and rolled soul and body of me into the bottom of the gelly, with the cook's kettles, the sailors' lockers, and the other 'raw recruits'; they sometimes above me, and I sometimes above them; occasionally the sea pouring down the hatchway over us all, and all of us at once floundering in the waters of the interior, which drowned out the fires, and left us no dry spot to lie upon, perch upon, or cling to. One of the sailors, Geordy Punton, afterwards captain of a Leith trader, and subsequently drowned in the Thames at London, had been familiar with me in the early part of the passage, as he was a Dunbar man, and I was almost one. He spoke lightly of the storm at first, and joked at it; but he ultimately altered his tone, and told us we had got among breakers on the dangerous sands near Yarmouth. Both he and the carpenter came to the gelly, and took their money and watches out of their lockers; and the carpenter, and other sailors who had Bibles, fastened the Bibles around their waists with handkerchiefs, and seemed to prepare for the worst. Nothing happened that was very dangerous. Nothing to me looked half so alarming as their conduct on the day after the storm, when proceeding to the mouth of the Thames; they threw off the Bibles and the handkerchiefs that tied them, drank more whisky, and swore more oaths than they had done during the previous ten days which the passage had lasted.

At night, on the eleventh day of the passage, we came to anchor at Gravesend, and were overhauled by custom-house officers. Next day, with the wind contrary, we got to Greenwich with difficulty, about two in the afternoon. The sergeant landed us there, and marched us to Westminster, distant eight miles, most of the way through streets, by way of Deptford and the Borough, across Westminster-bridge. The rendezvous for all recruits proceeding to their regiments by way of London, is in Duke-street, Westminster. When we had been there two hours, standing before the door of the office in the street, we got billets on public-houses; and then we had to go in search of the public-houses. I and my comrade, Ireland, had billets upon the Gray's Inn Coffee-house. On presenting them, the clerk scrutinized us, and said, perhaps the billets were right, yet he had been often imposed upon, as it was known that they paid the men billeted on them to go and sleep elsewhere. We replied that we did not want to go elsewhere; we were excessively wearied, having landed after a tedious passage from Scotland only that afternoon. He rejoined that they had no accommodation for the like of us, but he would give us 1s. 6d. each to go elsewhere. We had been solicited by persons belonging to the Ship, the Robin Hood, and other public-houses in Charles-street, Westminster, which lodged unfledged soldiers like us in mean beds at 4d. each, to return there if we should have the good fortune to be paid not to sleep where we were billeted. We returned to the sign of the Ship, where soldiers recruiting, men seeking to be, or sought after to be made, soldiers assemble to perform business and join in riot. We soon discovered that no 'Johnny Raws' like us were permitted to retain the pay of 1s. 3d. per day, nor the 1s. 6d. each received for lodgings, which last we had been silly enough to mention. Nor could we spend it as we chose. The reckless and abandoned of the recruits, who had sold almost every rag of covering from their bodies, fastened upon us to pay for their drink, and to sell our clothes or exchange them for rags, as they had done. Old clothes' dealers, one after another, came to us; but as I had left Edinburgh in my best dress, with the design of having a respectable appearance on joining the regiment, I was resolute, and no persuasion, cajolery, nor threats, would induce me to a change of garments. Nor would I drink with them. The mischief that had befallen me on the night of the fair of Dunbar, was as yet too fresh in my memory. The determination also to be a meritorious soldier, and, by good conduct, rise above the ranks, was too strong in me to be overcome by the persuasion of associates so brutish and intellectually blank as most of them were. We were detained two weeks in London, for the want of an escort to take us to the regiment at Brighton. I offered, one day, at the office in Duke-street, to go with my comrade to Brighton, and assured the authorities there that I would take *command* of myself and him, and deliver ourselves safely over; but they ordered me to hold my tongue. I thought, innocently enough, that by so doing I would save his Majesty's service the expense and trouble, and ourselves the delay, of an escort. *They* only saw in this an attempt to get a fair opportunity to desert. Such a thought was converse to all thoughts passing within me. At that time, having fairly left home and gone so far, I would not have accepted my freedom had it been offered. And we were anxious beyond expression to reach the regiment. Of all that reckless gang of recruits, numbering from fifty to a hundred, assembled there, Ireland and I were the only two who were to be in the Cavalry service. We had 1s. 3d. per day, while they had 1s.; the full pay of cavalry and infantry is 1s. 4d. and 1s. 1d. respectively; there being a penny added to each, called beer-money, which, as recruits, we did not receive. We were troubled more by having 3d. per day above the others than it was worth to us; and all the more annoyed because we sought, amongst that disorderly set, to regulate our own conduct, and spend our own money. We had to go out among them every afternoon, at the heels of a staff-sergeant, to get fresh billets, most commonly in the suburban parishes; to Chelsea one day, Camberwell the next day, Poplar the next day, Hampstead the next, and so on. To go through the streets with such a disorderly and ragged gang, was inexpressibly annoying to both of us.

At last, one morning, a private of the 7th Dragoon Guards, who was on recruiting duty in London, got orders and a 'rout' to march us to Brighton. It was a morning of hard frost, early in January, 1832, with the sun shining brightly on the Surrey Downs; and as we walked smartly along, I felt a lightness of spirits which I had not enjoyed for several weeks before. That day, and the next, I built upon fancy, and castellated the buildings of my hopes in visions of what I would have attained to when I was leaving the regiment as fast as I was then approaching it. I thought I might be a captain, possibly a colonel, but certainly not less than regimental sergeant-major.

On the afternoon of the second day from London, we approached the barracks at Brighton, which are reached by a branch road to the left, between two hills, without obtaining a sight of the town. It being a town of fashionable celebrity, I regretted that we did not see it; yet hoped to parade its streets before long. I was disappointed; I did not see Brighton until twelve years afterward; and then I entered it under very different circumstances from those under which I entered its barracks in 1832.

On approaching the barracks, more than one dealer in cast-off clothes offered to buy ours before we entered the gates; for, they said, we would have to give them up to be burned, and submit to be fumigated in the hospital ourselves, and be shut up in quarantine, to save the regiment from the infection of cholera. Symptoms of cholera had appeared in the north of England, in Scotland, and in London, though we knew nothing of the fact. The alarm about it was excessive in Brighton. Nobody except soldiers was allowed to enter the barracks, and all foot travellers from London who could be prevented, were prohibited from entering the town. I would not sell my clothes, being resolved now, more than ever, to go into the regiment with a respectable appearance. We accordingly, by consent of our escort, washed and brushed ourselves before approaching quite near, both of us expecting to meet men whom we knew.

At the gate, the sentry asked us, hurriedly in a whisper, if we were the recruits they had heard of, who had a set of bagpipes with them; 'for if you be,' he said, 'don't bring them in; everything you bring in will be burned.' And then, in a tone of duty, as if he had been questioning us also in discharge of duty, he said—'Oh! recruits are you? Pass on.' It had been rumoured that recruits were coming with bagpipes, and pipes not being regimentally allowed, the men on guard had secretly agreed to warn the recruits before they came within the gates, to save their bagpipes; some of the wives of the soldiers were hovering about for the purpose of smuggling the pipes. But we were not the pipers.

Instead of the men rushing out of the rooms as they usually do when fresh recruits enter the barrack-yard, to look at them, inquire

124

who they are, and where they come from, no one came near us; they were ordered not to speak to us. They looked over the windows, and one or two called 'Where do ye come from?' and 'What do they ca' ye?' but nothing more: nor were we permitted to answer them.

The report of the appearance of the Asiatic cholera in Britain was new to us; for we did not know what the newspapers had published concerning it. And besides the reports in newspapers, a case of sudden illness, pronounced to be one of cholera in its worst form, had occurred in the barracks that day, in the person of private James Miller, the servant of Cornet Macquarrie. This was the first case in the regiment, and I believe the first in Brighton. The alarm it excited was great; and the alarm was aggravated by our arrival from Scotland, where the epidemic was reported to have appeared. A large room in the hospital, as far apart from other rooms as one could be found, was disposed as the cholera ward. In this the patient Miller had been placed, and in the same ward with him, he writhing in agony with cramps all over his body and raving in delirium, we were placed, the door bolted upon us, and orders given through a window, that we were to employ ourselves in heating flannels, and rubbing liquids with the hot flannels on the cholera-stricken patient.

In less than ten minutes after this, one of the hospital orderlies came to us with hospital dresses of light blue woollen, and ordered us to strip off our clothes and put them on. When we had done so, he got a pitchfork and took our clothes away, as if afraid to touch them with his hands. He was ordered to burn them in a back-yard, apart from any person that might be contaminated. I felt some curiosity to watch the process from a window which overlooked him. He laid several things together and set fire to them, an old coal sack, a door mat, an hospital blanket, with the board of ordnance mark on it, and some portions of our clothes. But neither my Sunday's dress coat of good broad cloth, nor my trousers nor waistcoat, nor Ireland's coat were burned. He threw straw over the other things, and got up a blaze with a thick smoke, which being supposed to be cholera smoke, prevented the hospital sergeant or doctor or any one else from going near him, to see that the work of purification by fire was effectually done.

Next day, on coming into the ward with medicine for the cholera patient, who now seemed in a condition less alarming than he was in the day before, the orderly went to the window, and possibly recollecting for the first time that we might have watched him yesterday, said, as if to settle the matter, 'There lie the ashes of your clothes; it was a pity to burn good clothes; I could have got a pound for *your* coat,' addressing me; 'but there was no help for it; cholera is a dangerous thing, and military orders must be obeyed; I'm sure it gaed to my very heart, so it did, to burn sitch good claes.'

I turned somewhat sharply on him, and told him that he did not burn them. Whereat, in a hurricane of oaths and asserations, he swore that he did; and, still in a passion, and with the tone of a wrongly-accused man, he went away, and once more locked the door upon us. He soon returned with a small bottle containing brandy, and without a word of apology or explanation as to his previous asseverations, told us that brandy was recommended as a preventive for the cholera, gave us each the bottle to drink from, and added, 'Noo, was it not better to sell your claes to get brandy to keep away the cholera than to burn them? But mind ye, never moot it; if ye hope to be good sodgers, and respected by your comrades, never tell on another comrade if he *should manage a bit scheme o' this sort*. If it were kenn'd that I did it, I would have a court martial and be flogged as sure as I am a leeving sinner and a sodger. As ye hope never to be flogged yersels, dinna speak o't.'

Thus appealed to, we kept silence. We employed ourselves day and night during the first week, as nurses to our cholera patient. The doctor came once a day to see him, but no one else entered the room save the orderly, and he as seldom as possible. During the second week Miller was able to get up. We found him an agreeable companion. He was exceedingly grateful to us for nursing him as we had done. His master, who was a rich youth, son of the late General Macquarrie, of New South Wales, allowed him the use of much money, more possibly than did him good. He did not fail to remember us when we were all out of hospital. I occasionally assisted him when I had a spare hour in his stable, and received from him each time a sixpence, which, to a hungry recruit with heavy stoppages on his pay for his new outfit, were sixpences not to be despised.

Cornet Macquarrie was a very young officer, being then in his eighteenth year only. His friends had suggested that an old and experienced soldier should be appointed as his servant, and the choice fell on private James Miller. This poor fellow, a native of Airdrie, died, I was grieved to hear, some years ago in a lunatic asylum.

There were no more cholera cases in the regiment; and we, at the end of fourteen days, having no sign of cholera upon us, were visited by the regimental tailor, who measured us for over-alls, stable jackets, and regimental dress coats. The master bootmaker, who had soldiers under him as journeymen, but was himself a civilian, came next, and measured us for stable shoes and regimental dress boots. The regimental hairdresser came next, and trimmed our locks to the prescribed length. Then the tailor came with the jackets and over-alls. Next the bootmaker came with the boots; and though he was a civilian and not a soldier, he deemed it to be his duty to seem lofty and severe, almost terrible, in his manner of commanding us how to put a foot into a new boot—how to draw the boot on; and telling us, heroically, how we required to be drilled fourteen hours a day, to break our stubborn knee joints into pliability; and how he could tell us, that before we required another pair of boots, we would have learned how to draw them on.

The troop sergeant-major, to whom I was allotted, brought me a forage cap, a leather stock, four linen shirts, two flannel waistcoats, two pair of flannel drawers, four pairs of worsted socks, two pairs of gloves, a pair of gauntlets (gloves reaching to the elbows), a curry comb and brushes, a horse's mane comb, sponges, soap, bath brick, save-all, with knife, fork, spoon, razor, comb, shaving tackle, two towels, turn-screw, picker (for horses' feet), button stick, button brush, rot-stone to clean buttons, boot brushes, blacking, clothes brush, brush bag, horse's nose bag, corn sack, horse cloth (the cover for the stable); account book with printed regulations, saddle bags, military cloak, and two pair of straps for overalls (trousers), which he proceeded to show me how to affix to the buttons. His manner was quite different from the civilian bootmaker. 'Now, my man,' he proceeded to say, 'one of the first things a young soldier must learn is the proper way of dressing himself, and he must do it very quickly. You will occasionally find that every article of your clothing and accoutrements must be put on in a minute of time, and your horse accoutred, turned out, and mounted in another minute; I am serious with you; such a thing will require to be done, though not always. But to be able to do it at any time, you must practise yourself to put everything on and off in the proper way, in the briefest space of time. For instance, your straps; there is a right way and a wrong way of fastening them, and you are proceeding in the wrong way. Here, turn the outside of your foot upward; button the strap to that side first; turn the inside of your foot up next, and now bring it under your sole and fasten it to the inside. Now you do it right; the other one do in the same way—*that's* right; you will be a soldier in no time. Now the stock about your neck; why you have buckled it behind already. Ah! I see you'll get on. Button up your coatee; hook the collar; draw down the skirts; throw out your chest; no, not your stomach, draw *that* in; throw back your shoulders; up your head—up yet; don't throw your head back; stretch it upright; don't bend your knees—stretch your knees; put the forage cap a little to the right side; bring it a little over the right eyebrow—not quite so much; now the strap down upon your chin, not under the chin; let it come just under your lip. Now, look at yourself in the glass. Don't be afraid to look at yourself in a glass; I like a soldier who looks at himself in a glass; he is never a dirty soldier. Don't laugh at yourself. What do you see in the glass to laugh at? you only see yourself; and you will get used to yourself. But I was like you; I laughed too when I saw myself in regimentals first.' And to this effect he continued to explain my duty, in a manner exceedingly kind and encouraging.

This was Sergeant-Major Simpson of B troop. There were six troops, extending to the letter F. Ireland had been allotted to A troop, and I was destined as a present to E troop; but as it was not at head-quarters I was attached at first to the B's, subsequently to the D's, with troop Sergeant-Major Gardener. He was equally kind and encouraging in his manner towards recruits, at least to me, as Simpson was. Gardener was one of the very few Waterloo men remaining in the regiment. I felt much interest in listening to him, when I could induce him to tell about Waterloo, what he did, and what he thought when in battle. He soon became familiar with me, and used to invite me to his room—an unusual thing for a sergeant-major to do with a private, particularly a recruit. He was originally a lad driving a jobbing cart in the streets of Perth, had received almost no education, learned to write and keep accounts after he joined the regiment, was promoted to be corporal when coming out of Waterloo, and had gradually risen to be troop sergeant-major.

I received nominally a bounty of £2. 12s. 6d.; but only 10s. of it in cash; the remainder went to help to furnish my outfit. A cavalry soldier requires two pairs of cloth overalls in a year—and he is only allowed by government one pair. He is allowed 6s. a year for boots. All his shoes, and repairs, and an extra pair of boots, probably every third year; every article which I have named, including the saddle bags and corn sack, must be paid for out of stoppages from his pay, with the following exceptions: one pair of cloth overalls, one stable jacket, and one dress coat annually; six shillings a year for boots, and three shillings for gloves, and a new cloak every six years.

Besides the sum of £2. 2s. 6d., which was appropriated from the bounty, I was indebted to the regiment about £3. 10s. for this outfit. All other recruits were the same. The rations, costing from 6d. to 8d. per day, according to the contracts for provisions, and 1d. per day for vegetables, were first paid for by stoppages. We got 2d. as daily pay, and all remaining went to pay off the debt. These stoppages, during the first year of a recruit's service, together with the endless drilling on foot and on horseback, and the hard stable work, generally give young men an unfavourable opinion of soldiering. But the beginning is not so disheartening now, since the period of enlistment is shortened. The recruit keeps up his spirits when he sees a limited time before him, at the end of which he will still be a young man, and may leave the service if he dislikes it, or remain if he does not choose to leave.

Having received the route for Birmingham, the precise date I do not now remember, we were all astir by the sound of early trumpets one morning, and marched out of the barrack gates; the band playing, horses prancing, crowds accompanying, with baggage piled upon waggons, followed by the hospital sergeant, orderlies, convalescents, tailors, shoemakers, saddlers, women and children, dismounted invalids, and unmounted recruits. I was an unmounted recruit, and with the others on foot formed the baggage guard.

Our march from Brighton to Birmingham occupied either nine or ten days. I had seen but little of rural England before that time; and though that was but a glimpse compared with what I have seen since, it was fresh, vivid, and impressive. I retain it to this day distinctly: and can at will, sitting by the hearth, looking dreamily into the fire, or vacantly upon a book, draw out the whole line of country before me: the villages, roadside inns, half-way houses where we halted to rest, swinging sign-boards, village greens, broad commons, cross roads, finger-posts, travellers journeying with us, and telling where a gibbet once was, or villagers shrinking out of sight with the recollection of the swing riots of 1830 and 1831 still fresh—with the dread still upon them of the special commission accompanied by soldiers, which had consigned a few to the gallows, many to the hulks, and had probably missed the chiefs who fired the rick yards or led the multitudes to break the thrashing mills—some of these chiefs now looking upon us from a distance, without any desire to come nearer. Other villagers, where no riots nor Swing[12] fires had been, and no fears for troops of cavalry were felt, came out to be critical on the horses, and to approve of the long swords, the carbines, the bright scarlet, the black bear skin on the men's heads, and the white feathers on the bear skin. They stood, and I can see them standing now, on the play-worn ground beside the parish stocks, in front of the churchyard walls. Behind them the churches, venerable and grey, not always with lofty spires, conspicuously upraised to heaven, but oftener lowly and half-concealed among the trees, as if retreating there for humble worship; the trees with the dead of many generations under their roots, bearing on their branches, one might suppose as fruit, a young generation of miniature men in round white hats, smock frocks, leather leggings, and laced-up boots; the fathers and elder brothers of these miniature men thus clustered on the trees, standing on the ground in their round white hats, smock frocks, leather leggings, and laced-up boots, as if they had dropped from the trees when they grew large and heavy; all were out to look at the soldiers—who taking cross country roads went through villages where soldiers are seldom seen, and where a regiment mounted on grey horses was never before seen.

Women also and babies were out. And laughing little maids, the future brides and mothers of rural England, climbed on the gates and stiles to see; and hearing the boys in the trees call, 'Soldier, give I that long sword, wilt thee, soldier?' cried, 'Soldier, take I on that horse with the long white tail, wilt thee, soldier?'

And gentlemen and ladies from the mansions, that stood within the wooded parks, walked out to look upon the unusual sight. So did grave vicars, and rectors, and their servants from vicarage and rectory, look out when the trumpets or the band played. And when the rear came up, they inquired where we were going, was there swing rioters abroad again?

The village live-stock upon the commons—dogs, hogs, and asses; and old horses, which had once been in military service, now capered when they heard the trumpets, as if young again; all were set astir by the marching of a regiment among them. The cows hobbled to the farthest side of the common, having no sympathy for bright scarlet, or kettle drums. And the geese, which had survived the killing and the roasting at Christmas sheered off, and faced round at a distance to hiss us, as if they were disloyal geese, hissing a regiment of royal dragoons, or as if they knew that we, being Scotch dragoons, were ignorant of roast goose.

The dinners provided for us each day at the inns or public houses on which we were billeted, so different in quality and style of cooking from the dinners to which I had been accustomed, were also matters to be remembered. I had tasted roast mutton at the winter suppers at Branxton, the annual festivals after harvest, but never at home. At Horsham, which was our first day's destination, we had roast beef and apple puddings for dinner at the house where I was quartered; the first roast beef which I had tasted during my life, and the first apple puddings which I had any recollection of. At Guildford, Chertsey, and Windsor, the fare was English, but I do not remember if it was entirely new to me. At Thame, in Oxfordshire, where we staid on the Saturday night, the Sunday, and the Sunday night, I was billetted on a house where we had roast goose for dinner on the Sunday—that was my first introduction to roast goose. Bicester, Banbury, and Warwick, were our next quarters. At Warwick I was made acquainted, for the first time, with Yorkshire pudding.

Soldiers on the line of march are freed from stoppages on their pay; they receive their daily pay entire. They are also allowed tenpence per day for dinner, which is paid to the landlord of the house by the sergeant-major; and the landlords are bound to furnish a hot dinner for tenpence. Their usual custom is to provide a dinner for which that is not sufficient payment. It is characteristic of the innkeepers of England to give soldiers a good dinner, irrespective of the price at which they are bound by law to furnish it.

Soldiers on the line of march in Scotland receive no marching money nor dinner, as in England. They must there live on their bare pay, and take billets on farmers, where they usually sleep in barns or hay lofts. They can claim a bed, the second best of the house, but the farmer usually gives them a sixpence or a shilling, or some whisky, or bread and cheese, so that they may the more willingly go to the barn to sleep. If you listen to soldiers who have frequently marched in England, Scotland, and Ireland, you will hear the Englishman calling Scotland anything but a respectable portion of Her Majesty's dominons. Scotchmen are not satisfied to hear their country miscalled, but they are obliged to shake their heads and admit that there is no dinner for them, when marching there, as in England. They rally for Scotland, however, and remind the Englishman of the whisky, how plentiful that was. The Englishman reminds them that there was as much of it in Ireland; and that the 'mess' was cheaper in Ireland. They all agree that Ireland is the place for cheap messing; it costs sometimes but five pence per day for each man (when its cost is eightpence in England) except, perhaps, in Dublin. Very few soldiers like Dublin. The ever-lasting parades, the furnishing of guards of honour to the castle, and the continual field days in the Phœnix Park, all to please the person-ages who for brief periods of time play at royalty as the lord lieutenants, render the soldier's life in Dublin like the treadmill.

From Warwick we marched to Birmingham, and as is the custom, on going into barracks, got no allowance of marching money for that day. Every soldier in the service has at some time complained of this. Going into the cold, empty barracks, where no one has preceded them to prepare fire or food, they do not receive the extra allowance, where, of all places and of all times, it is most requisite.

During the first three days of the march, I continued with the hospital corps, and the other fragments of the regiment which formed the rear. We found the time pass pleasantly. The armourer-sergeant was an intelligent man, and so were two or three of the privates. There was one Laidlaw, six feet four and a half inches high, who, when King George the Fourth was in Scotland, was selected by Sir Walter Scott, so he said, to attend the king at Dalkeith Palace, as orderly. He could have found recollections of that distinguished office to rehearse to us through months of marching; and there was a young schoolmaster, aged only nineteen, who over-topped Laidlaw by an inch, and who was alleged to have grown so tall that he could not get into the school room, and so came to be a soldier, to get room to grow. Laidlaw, who was jealous of any one overtopping him, accused this exalted school-master of having grown so tall that no human creature could see his learning, it was so high. Even Laidlaw himself could not see into him. We had also the regimental tailor—a grave, religious sergeant—who reproved us for joking at the tall young man, whose learning was so high that we could not see it, and at Laidlaw, who had so much to tell of the time when he was orderly to the king. He said that they having been made one of them six feet and a half inches high, and the other six feet five and a half inches, there was a purpose for them to fulfil. He had no doubt that a purpose proportionate to their size was made for them, even as he (the tailor) had made for each of them a coat to fit their size. This sergeant of the tailor's shop was an agreeable and instructive companion to walk with. The only man of the party who was not, was the hospital sergeant; he was an ill-tempered gentleman, whose chief study seemed to be to make the lives of those who were so unfortunate as to be in the hospital as miserable as possible. The surgeon was quite different; he was kind and soothing in his manners to the patients; the sergeant pretended to be kind also, in presence of the surgeon; but as soon as he was away the good nature disappeared, and the ill-nature returned as before. Some patients complained; but the sergeant had the gift of persuading all the officers, the surgeon included, that he was one of the best of sergeants, and that the soldiers who complained of him were the most unreasonable of privates. Those who knew him best (for myself I had never any cause to complain of him) alleged that there were only two other men in the regiment as disagreeable as he, one of them a Highlandman from Lochaber. I was one of nine men in the same barrack room with him. He was a genius for the invention of misery. The regimental tailor, after much theological and philosophical study, could only arrive at the opinion that this Highlandman had come out of Lochaber to trouble other men for their sins.

Recruits are not mounted on the line of march until they have had practice in the riding school. It is assumed that none of them can ride until they have been taught regimentally. At Thame, in Oxfordshire, I was billeted with one of the rough-riders of the school. He had charge of a vicious horse. It was one of two cream-coloured Arabians, presented by Queen Adelaide to the band of the regiment. No training nor breaking would make this animal tractable. And no man in the regiment who had yet attempted to groom him had succeeded in doing so unhurt, except this rough-rider. Men possessing more courage among horses than I were afraid of him, and I should not have been easily induced to go and handle him, had I known his propensities. But every recruit must submit to tricks, and nothing is more common with the soldiers than to get a recruit, if they think he is a person unacquainted with horses, to go into a stall beside a vicious one. I heard them talk of this beautiful Arabian, how gentle he was, and affectionate to any one who would groom him well. The rough-rider was not present, else he would have prevented me from falling into the trap. I had heard of Arabian horses being gentle and affectionate, and from my stable experience when a lad, I did not hesitate for a moment to strip off my new scarlet jacket, put on my flannel waistcoat,

133

and go to work to comb and brush this beautiful stranger of the east—gift of a queen. He allowed me to get up to his head; but the moment I was there, he sprung upon me with his teeth, like a furious dog. I perceived the trick in a second of time or less: an old soldier had warned me against such tricks, and his warning rushed to my recollection. Prompted to an action of self-defence, as also with the resolution that the onlookers should not have their expected laugh at me, I gave the ferocious brute such a blow with my clenched hand in the jaw, as to leave him a toothache as long as he was in the regiment. The veterinary surgeon puzzled himself many a time in his endeavours to ascertain what had fractured that horse's jaw and deranged his teeth, but the men who knew had the good sense, for their own sakes, to say nothing about it. I groomed the horse without a moment's farther hesitation, and was still rubbing him down when the rough-rider came in. He said it was wrong, and professed to be angry with me; but when we were alone, he said I had served the savage right. To fracture his jaw was more, however, than, under the impending consequences, he dared to have done. He got me next day to take charge of a spare horse; and by the sergeant-major's permission, I mounted and rode the remaining days of the march, leaving behind me the staff and the invalids, who were on foot, for ever.

This incident was fortunate. I was more favourably treated in the riding school by this rough-rider, and also by the riding master[13], than most of the other recruits attending the school at the same time. And except once, I had no more tricks played upon me by the older soldiers, an unusual degree of good fortune for a recruit. Persons who have no experience of what it is to be in the chrysalis, or Johnny Raw, state of a soldier, think that the tyranny he suffers is from his officers, the truth being that a soldier comes very little in contact with his officers. The drill sergeant, rough-riders, riding master, regimental sergeant-major, and possibly the adjutant, may be severe upon him if he be a dull soldier; but for unqualified, unprovoked, deliberate tyranny, the recruit, if he be not a spirited young man, and discreet as well as spirited, suffers it without measure and without mercy from his equals in military rank—the privates who are in the stable or barrack-room with him. Many more of the young soldiers who desert or become dispirited, desperate, and abandoned, are shattered in their morals and driven into misconduct, by equals rather than by superiors in rank. If a recruit seems to have lively affections, and a sweet memory of friends and home, that most amiable part of his moral nature becomes the sport of the older soldiers, and they proceed systematically to break him into reckless hardihood and vice. Every full-fledged soldier does not join in this persecution of the Johnny Raw, nor is every Johnny Raw subdued and corrupted; some have strength of mind to resist all assailants, others have tact to yield in some things gracefully and resist in others, and so establish their independence. But too many are otherwise. That they may be looked upon as spirited young men, they seek the society of the most vicious of the older ones; are not particular as to where, or how, they get drink; dare to sell some of their *kit* to get liquor, and so run the risk of punishment, and incur the certainty of debt in the troop books, as the articles sold will be replaced at the next weekly inspection by the troop sergeant-major and the captain. Lies are told, and the things are alleged to have been stolen. Innocent men are thus liable to be suspected, or by some bold rogue accused of theft. And thefts are committed. Fortunate is the young soldier who passes through his Johnny Raw state, and does not get his 'eye opened'. Eye-opening means to steal something from him. It is a crime resented by all soldiers who are beyond the condition of recruits, to steal from one another; but to 'open a recruit's eye' is hardly an offence: it is accounted a greater offence for one soldier to divulge that he knows another to have done it.

Still I believe that a recruit of ordinary ability and good nerve, may take a position among his comrades, and let them feel that he cannot be seduced or subdued. Such a man will be respected by the very worst of them, though for a time they profess to despise him. As for the officers, if a soldier keeps out of the guard-house, by returning to barracks in time when he has leave to go out, by being always ready for duty when required, and always clean, he may be a soldier for years without an officer speaking to him personally. The danger that awaits him from his officers shows itself when he does something to make them mark him, or to go before a court martial. For myself, I have confidence that I could have proceeded up to this day as a soldier, without committing any moral offence or breach of military discipline that would have brought me under the censure of the officers; also, that I could have continued to be on friendly terms with all the non-commissioned officers; and further, that I should long before this time have been a non-commissioned officer myself, had not an extraordinary series of events arisen close upon one another, which could not have happened at any period of time before or since; which may never again be possible to occur to any soldier. I have not yet arrived at the point of my narrative where they begin.

An old cavalry soldier in Edinburgh gave me some words of counsel, to be observed in the stable and the barrack room. I refer to them now because I have found them, or similar rules, useful elsewhere than in a stable or barrack room. One was, to observe when the soldier's wife, who might be in the same room with me, was about to go for water to the pump, or was in want of water, I was to take her pail and say, 'Nay, mistress, let me go to the pump for you,' and go instantly. Another rule of conduct was to anticipate a comrade who might require his clothes brushed, and rise and do it for him before he had time to ask the favour. And so in the stable, if I had charge of a comrade's horse in his absence, he on guard perhaps, to be as kind to his horse as to my own; and at any time, if I had nothing to do myself, to put forward my hand and help some one who had something to do. The same readiness to oblige may be practised in a workshop, in a literary office, or any other office, and is as necessary to be observed there as in a stable. But I fear that if there be not a natural inclination to be obliging, the desire of acquiring the good-will of associates will fail to make one always agreeable. Almost all men, probably all, who have risen above the social level upon which they were born, or who have created new branches of trade, or have been inventors, or have made discoveries, have been men who were ever ready to put forth their hands to help a companion in his work, or to try to do something more than what was allotted for them to do by their employers. The apprentice, or journeyman, or other person who will not do more than is allotted to him because he is not bound to do it, and who is continually drawing a line to define what he calls his rights, with his fellow-workmen, or with his employer; or, if in the army, with his comrades, and the non-commissioned officers immediately over him, is sure to remain where he is, or sink to a lower level. He is not destined to be a successful master tradesman; to be a discoverer in science, an inventor in mechanics, a propounder of new philosophy, nor a promoter of the world's advancement, and certainly not of his own.

It may, to some, appear like vanity in me to write what I now do, but I should not give my life truly if I omitted it. When filling a cart with manure at the farm dung-hill, I never stopped work because my side of the cart might be heaped up before the other side, at which was another man; I pushed over what I had heaped up to help him, as doubtless he did to help me when I was last and he first. When I have filled my column, or columns of a newspaper, or sheet of a magazine, with the literature for which I was to be paid, I have never stopped if the subject required more elucidation, or the paper or magazine more matter, because there was no contract for more payment, or no likelihood of there being more. When I have lived in a barrack-room, I have stopped my own work, and have taken the baby from a soldier's wife, when she had work to do, and nursed it; or have gone for water for her, or have cleaned another man's accoutrements, though it was no part of my duty to do so. When I have been engaged in political literature and travelling for a newspaper, I have not hesitated to travel many miles out of my road to ascertain a local fact, or to pursue a subject into its minutest particulars, if it appeared that the public were unacquainted with the facts of the subject; and this at times when I had work to do which was much more pleasant and profitable. When I have needed employment, I have accepted it at whatever wages I could obtain, at a plough, in farm drain, in stone quarry, at breaking stones for roads, at wood cutting, in a sawpit, as a civilian, or as a soldier. I have in London cleaned out a stable and groomed a cabman's horse for a sixpence, and been thankful to the cabman for the sixpence. I have subsequently tried literature, have done as much writing for ten shillings as I have readily obtained—been sought after and offered— ten guineas for. But had I not been content to begin at the beginning and accept shillings, I would not have risen to guineas.

I have lost nothing by working. Whether at labouring or literary work, with a spade or a pen, I have been my own helper. But the moment I have tried commercial enterprise or speculation, all good fortune has seemed to forsake me; yet the fault was not that of fortune. My faculties were not made to allow me to live by speculation.

---

[12] Peasant riots, usually involving rick-burning, and preceded by an anonymous letter signed 'SWING'. See Disraeli's *Sybil*. 'Parliamentary Reform in a full and fair representation of the People, or Death. Mark this thou contemptible Cad. SWING TO ROBERT PEEL'—is a fair specimen of 'Swing's' style.

[13] An appointment held by a ranker officer, in this case Lieutenant Gillies, who had been R.S.M. More will be heard of him.

CHAPTER XIII

Daily Duties of the Dragoon while yet a 'Johnny Raw'

I SHALL now introduce you to the daily life of a young dragoon. At a quarter to five or six o'clock in the morning, according to the season of the year, the warning trumpet sounds. All soldiers must get out of bed then, but the recruits must spring out, as they have more to do, and less time in which to do it, than the others. They must dress, roll their bedding on the iron bedstead, fold the blanket, the two sheets, and the rug, so as the colours of the rug shall appear throughout the folds of the sheets and blankets like streaks of marble. They must take the point of a knife, and lay the edges of the folds straight, until they look artistical to the eye. This must be finished by the time the 'warning' is over, which is a quarter of an hour after. At that time the stable trumpet sounds, and all must hasten down to stables. The litter must be shaken out, all that which is dry is tied up, the other is cleared away, and the stable swept by two men who take the sweeping for one morning, while two others take it another morning; there being twelve or fourteen men in each stable. The dry litter is tied up thus: four neatly plaited bands are laid out on the stones behind the horses; a few handfuls of clean straw, combed and carefully preserved by each man for his own use, is spread upon the four bands. The litter is laid on this straw, and the bands brought round and fastened. The bundle is then set on end against the post, at the horse's hind quarter. One of the bands is carried round the post to keep it steady. The top of the bundle is neatly plaited, and the comb used for the horse's mane and tail is taken, and the outside straw is combed. If the recruit has not been active in getting downstairs, to have his turn on the limited space to do this, others will be before him. Yet if he be in good favour with the other men, they allow him to get his straw put up sooner, knowing that he is going in an early class to the riding school. If he be not in good favour, or not yet beyond the period of having tricks played upon him, he may be seen laying out his plaited bands and handfuls of fancy straw on the stones, horses on each side of him, kicking with their hind feet within a yard of his head—able at any moment to kick across the whole space on which he is doing his work. A man tickles one of them, to make him prance and strike the stones, or toss back his litter upon the recruit. As if in a rage, the man professes to be earnest and loud in commanding his horse to stand still; and asks it if it means to kick until it knocks Johnny Raw's brains out? does it not know that Johnny Raw is behind it? Immediately opposite, another man causes his horse to plunge, and also demands if it means to kick until Mr. John Raw is killed? and if it is determined that Mr. John Raw is not to go to the riding school that day? If John discovers the trick, and complains to the corporal or sergeant, woe unto him. The only chance he has of getting over persecution of that kind, is to take no notice of it.

If it is not to be a field day, the men and horses not going to the riding school go out in watering order, into the country, a mile or two, for exercise. The youngest recruits go to the school first about seven o'clock, on trained horses; the youngest untrained horses go to the school in the same class, with rough-riders on them. The recruit prepares for the school at seven o'clock, after having combed and brushed his horse until it is spotless; by running upstairs to the barrack-room, putting on a pair of clean boots, brushing every horse hair and spot from his trousers, strapping them down, putting on his stock, buttoning his jacket, getting his cap, his white gloves, and a cane in his hand. Thus equipped, he goes to the stable, and finds his horse where he left him bridled, and standing fastened, with his head outward, his tail stallward. Johnny leads him out, walking backward, a hand at each side of the horse's mouth, and he must take care that no spot from the animal's mouth gets upon his gloves; and also that the horse does not rear up in play or mischief, and put his fore feet over his scarlet jacket, or knock one of his teeth out. We had a horse which put up his fore feet, and knocked a recruit's brains out, when being led through the stable-door.

I shall not now follow the recruit to the riding school. He returns in an hour, and others of an advanced class succeed; they return at nine, and another class takes their place, which returning at ten, are succeeded by the highest class. All save the youngest ones, who went at seven, are riding in saddles; they had only a cloth beneath them, in watering order. Those going at nine and ten o'clock get their breakfasts before leaving the stable; and they go with carbines and swords, and practise the sword exercise, galloping and wheeling round and across the school. Those who went at eight o'clock had pistols with them, and one or more of their pistols would be fired. If the riding master or rough-riders have a dislike to a man, or wish to annoy him, they will probably take his pistol day after day, and fire it. They require a pistol to fire suddenly behind the ears of the young horses, and occasionally behind the ears of the young men, to use them to the report. He whose pistol has been used, must clean its barrel and lock, on his return to the barrack-room.

On returning to the stable, he must rush upstairs, put off his gloves, jacket, cap, stock, and boots, and put on his stable shoes. He may see his breakfast of coffee and bread ready—but not yet, no, not yet, Johnny; you can have no breakfast yet. He must return to the stable, use a straw wisp, a brush, and cloth to his horse for at least half an hour. He must pick its feet, sponge its hoofs and its nostrils, dress it neatly, and feed it; then he may go to the room to look after his coffee. He is a fortunate youth if he is not sometimes, or often, a party to such a dialogue as this:

Soldier A: 'What is the matter with that recruit? What is he talking about?'

Soldier B: 'He says they have taken all the *thick* of the coffee, and left him the *thin*; he says he likes *thick* best. Isn't that what you like, Johnny?'

Johnny Raw: 'No, it is not, and you know it; you have left me no coffee to drink; nothing but the thick grounds. I shan't have it.'

Soldier B: 'Why, have you not told us that you prefer the thick? Nothing seems to satisfy you, Johnny.'

And Johnny must submit to eat his dry bread. If a non-commissioned officer come in and ask, 'What is the matter with that recruit?' the men answer before he can, 'The matter with him! he is only grumbling as usual.' The non-commissioned officer most probably replies, 'You must not grumble, young man; we must have no grumbling.' If he holds his tongue and suffers all gently, or if he imitates the other men, and bullies and swears at them, he may have easier trials; but if he reports them, tells his superiors what his comrades have done, woe be to the life of young John Raw!

He has not time to waste upon a dispute about his coffee. He must once more brush his boots and stable shoes, have everything spotless which is upon him, and which he leaves in the room behind him. If it be summer, he must put off his cloth overalls which he wore in the stable, and put on his white ones, and a pair of clean gloves, and be out at ten or eleven o'clock, as the case may be, to foot drill. He is drilled on foot until within a few minutes of twelve o'clock. When dismissed, he puts off his white trousers and gloves, resumes his cloth overalls, and runs to the twelve o'clock stable hour. He rubs down and feeds his horse. He comes up to the room with the rest to dinner; they all button up their jackets and stand at attention, while the orderly officer and sergeant come their rounds to inspect the dinners, which is done by a glance, and occasionally the question hastily asked, 'Have you any complaints?'

The dinners are then cut out, each man's allowance laid upon a plate. One turns his back towards the table, and another touches a plate with a knife, and calls, 'Who shall have this?' He whose back is to the table names some one; and so on they proceed until all the plates are touched, and all the men in that room named. If Johnny Raw is to be once more vexed or victimized, a bone without meat, or almost without it, is laid upon a plate. He whose back is turned has been secretly told that this plate will be touched, we shall say, the sixth in turn. Accordingly, when the man who touches the plates with his knife says for the sixth time, 'Who shall have this?' the reply is, 'Johnny', or 'Cruity', or whatever they may call him.

The recruit proceeds to pick his bone, or to turn it over and over to examine its nakedness; upon which some one says, 'Johnny, what is the matter, lad? You do not get on with your dinner—what is the matter, lad?' If he says they have given him a bone, and no meat on it, they reply that he is always grumbling. If he complains to the officer who comes to inquire if there be complaints, he will not improve his circumstances. A corporal may then be ordered to see that the men deal fairly with the recruit; but the men will vex him quite as grievously in some other way. If he can swear horribly, and introduce an oath never heard before in the regiment, or if he finds means of getting drink to some of them, he may escape farther persecution. If not, some of his brushes, or his scissors, or soap, or bathbrick, or blacking, disappears. He hears a soldier say, 'Who has lost a brush?' And he replies, 'I have.' The soldier goes on, 'What is it like?' Poor Johnny proceeds to describe it. The soldier asks, 'Would you know it if you saw it?' Johnny says, 'Yes.' 'Well, then,' says the other, 'go and look at it, and tell us if you know it.' 'But where is it?' asks Johnny. 'Where is it!'

rejoins the other, 'what do I know? go and find it.' The probability is, that Johnny never sees his brush again. It has been sold for threepence for a pint of beer, and he is supplied with a new one at a shilling, which adds to his debt with the troop sergeant-major.

Dinner over, the recruit prepares for afternoon foot drill and the sword exercise. This lasts two hours; and when it is done, and he is dismissed, if he be not too tired, he may walk outside the barracks and see the town until six o'clock. There is then the stable roll call, at which every man must be present, if not on duty or absent with leave. The regimental orders are read for next day, stating if it be 'watering order first thing', or a field day. The horses are rubbed down, fed, littered, and the bands with the handfuls of fancy straw are put carefully away until the morning. The recruit may now go to his room and fold down his bed, and stretch himself upon it to rest; or he may go into the town until eight o'clock or nine. If he be a wise lad, he will stay in and brighten his sword, scabbard, and his buckles, and whiten his belts and gloves for the school in the morning. There is no help for him but to persevere. Once or twice I almost despaired; but seeing there was no alternative, I resolved to do my best. I was fortunate in having few tricks played upon me, and no persecution in any shape in the barrack-room.

With a few other recruits, I fell first for foot drill into the hands of Sergeant Stephenson, of whom I have little to say, except that he was a smart-looking and well-conducted soldier. From him, after learning our 'facings', we joined an advance squad of recruits, under Drill-sergeant Keith. This was a remarkable man. While he gave the words of command with a tone of authority, his voice was as mild and kind to every recruit as the voice of an affectionate brother. He never on any occasion swore oaths, never showed himself out of temper, though more than once I have known him turn away his face for half a minute, to hide the vexation which some of the very awkward men, who would not or could not understand what he had explained to them, impelled him to feel. To drill fresh recruits year after year might be allotted as a punishment to bad men. But it requires the best of men to be good drill-sergeants. Keith was one of them. He was a philosopher. At the sword exercise he was one of the most dexterous and perfect. The wrist of his right hand seemed to have a universal joint, and with my more stubborn wrist I have often envied him. Keith succeeded some years ago as regimental sergeant-major.

The regimental sergeant-major of that time, Michael Nelson, had been a Paisley weaver. He was a Waterloo man; one of the cleverest soldiers that ever mounted a horse, but of a different temperament, with a harsher manner than the philosophic Keith. Nelson is now a commissioned officer in the regiment. In the month of February, 1847, I met him in Clonmel, with several other officers, some of whom I knew; but though we were frequently in the same hotel together, and held conversations on different topics, none of them knew me. While engaged in their arduous duties of escorting flour and provisions through the counties of Waterford and Tipperary, during the famine season, I frequently hired a car or a horse, and accompanied them. I rode the greater part of one day with a sergeant who had been drilled as a recruit with me; but I did not introduce myself, farther than that I had come from England, as the representative of the *Manchester Examiner* newspaper, to examine and report upon the state of the country.

In the riding school I was under the tuition of Sergeant Glen and Riding Master Gillies. With the exception of once from the latter, I never had an unkind word from either of them; but that exception is to me a memorable one.

The first horse which I got for riding-school exercise was an animal of good appearance, respectable behaviour, and deep sagacity—Farrier Simpson's horse. The farriers are not often on horseback, except when marching; accordingly their horses are allotted to recruits. Farrier Simpson had a strong regard for the stately trooper upon which I was to learn how to 'mount', 'dismount', 'mount' (for those mountings and dismountings are repeated many a time, until the recruit is perfect in his style), 'march', 'trot', 'canter', 'gallop', 'draw swords', 'leap the bar', cut at 'heads and posts', 'turn', 'circle', 'front', 'halt', 'make much of your horses', 'dismount', 'front your horses', 'stand to your horses'. 'mount', 'march', 'trot', 'canter', 'gallop', 'load', 'fire', 'draw swords', 'charge', and a hundred other things which would not be intelligible if here repeated. And having that regard for his favourite horse, Simpson impressed upon me the duty of taking kindly care of him. He needed not to have done so. I had as much natural regard for a horse as he could possibly have had, in addition to which there soon sprung up an intimacy between me and this one, which was more than is usually seen between a recruit and his school horse. In some cases these animals, when well trained themselves, evince a contempt for recruits, which a close observer of equine nature cannot mistake the causes of—the causes being the ignorance of the rider, compared with

143

the learning and conscious superiority of the horse under him. Others understand the recruits upon their backs, and sympathize with them. Mine was one of these. If a word of command were suddenly given when trotting or galloping, he would not only evince that he had been listening for it, by instantly obeying the order, halting if it were 'halt', turning if it were 'turn', wheeling if it were 'wheel', or anything else; but he would detect at the same instant if I made a mistake, or had not heard distinctly what the command was, and he would yield as far as he could consistently with his notions of duty, to bring me to the true knowledge of my duty. He would not, like some horses, take a pleasure in halting from a gallop with a jerk backward, to throw the rider over his head, should that rider not be keeping his ears open for the word of command. He would sometimes feel by his mouth that I had not heard the word of command, or if hearing it, had not communicated to him the intimation by the bridle reins or pressure of the knee to obey it; upon which, if it were 'halt', he would halt, but would bear his shoulders forward, to save me gently from the shock. The same too in turning; if it were a sharp, indistinct command, given when we were at the canter or the gallop, he would throw his body round with a sweep, though keeping his feet to the proper turning distance, to bring me round with him, if he felt that I was not on the alert.

Soon learning the kindly nature and excellent educational abilities of this horse, it was natural for me to have a high regard for him. If he had been a biped with the gift of speech, and not a dumb quadruped, he would have been a philosopher of the best order—teaching the world the truths of nature in language of benevolence and love—subduing the enemies of truth, and displacing ignorance, by gentleness and the power of goodness. Farrier Simpson and I became acquainted and respectful of each other, through our mutual respect for this noble animal. As a recruit, I had little time to be in the farrier's personal company; yet we met occasionally. The forge was from two to three hundred yards from my stable. I would sometimes tell the horse that he might go to the forge. If he seemed to doubt what I said, I lifted one of his feet, shook the shoe to intimate that it was loose, undid the chain of his collar, fastened the end of it up, and let him go. He went direct to Simpson, and selected him from among the other farriers; of whom there are one for each of the six troops, besides the farrier-major. The farriers are privates; the farrier-major wears four stripes on his arm, and ranks with the troop sergeant-majors. The only non-commissioned officer above them is the regimental sergeant-major; to whom the soldier says 'sir', when addressing him. No one else, beneath the rank of a commissioned officer, is addressed as 'sir'.

I would sometimes send the horse to see Simpson at the forge when he needed no shoeing, if I had a spare hour. At such a time I followed after him, and gave the generous creature the opportunity of being with both his favourite masters at once. I do not know if Farrier Simpson was a man possessing much intellectuality of a philosophical bent; but he was a man of average good sense; and speaking of the horse, he used to say to me, 'It is kindness does it all; I like you because you are kind to my horse; that horse likes us both, because we are both kind to him; you may do anything with man or beast by kindness.'

Nothing occurred to interrupt the good feeling which thus began between the farrier and myself. It became his duty as farrier of D troop, to which I was then attached, together with the trumpeter of the same troop, to give me, each of them fifty lashes with a nine-tailed whip on the bare back, each tail of the nine with six knots upon it. Simpson gave the first five-and-twenty lashes; then rested while the trumpeter gave the second five-and-twenty; proceeded with the third instalment of five-and-twenty; again rested while the trumpeter completed the hundred; and was about to proceed with the remainder of two hundred, which was the amount of the sentence of a regimental court-martial, when the commanding officer said, 'Stop!' This unpleasant affair did not interrupt the friendship between the farrier, whose duty it was to give me the first and third instalment of five-and-twenty, nor with the trumpeter; but with the trumpeter I was nothing more than an acquaintance, not a friend. Simpson began as if mindful of being a friend rather than a farrier, but the loud command of 'Do your duty, Farrier Simpson!' reminded him that he must 'cut in'.

My trial and punishment occurred on the 29th of May, 1832. It was ordered, proceeded with, and completed, all within a few hours; a circumstance altogether irregular by military rule, and which, coupled with other irregular matters, led a general Court of Inquiry to report against the commanding officer, and draw upon him an official reprimand.

———

In consequence of this Autobiography not having been written to be published in my life-time, nor so soon as the year 1848, had I died before, I find in it several names of persons which for the present must be omitted. Yet in respect of every event or incident which occurred to myself during the evenful summer of 1832, this is a faithful and for the first time a fully published report. Besides what my own vivid recollection serves me with, I have referred to the official documents presented to the War Office and to parliament, from the sitting of the court martial on the 29th of May, to the termination of the business on the 25th of August following. If I linger somewhat tediously on the details, the reader's time may not be all wasted. A narrative of the most exciting scenes of the reform agitation in Birmingham; the rejection of the bill by the lords in parliament; the resignation of the Grey cabinet; the Duke of Wellington alone in power, and alone relying on the army; the king bewildered; the nation with one voice crying, 'Stop the supplies'; all the county representatives of England except six, a majority of the borough members, a large minority of the lords, and the entire nation save the fractional parts called anti-reformers, already declared for the bill; the newspapers of the highest class, in London and the provinces, daring the duke to prevent the passing of the bill, by the army; the political union of Birmingham drawing upon it the eager observance of all Britain, and Britain of all Europe; the anti-reformers daring the political union of Birmingham to move, and pointing to and naming the Scots Greys in their town ready to prevent them; the Greys booted and saddled night and day; their swords taken to the barrack grindstone and sharpened for work; their pouches replenished with ball-cartridges; and *they*—shall I say *thinking* on what was to be done, and what it was to be done for—that they were armed against their country, against the House of Commons, and against their king? Yes, they did *think*; but they did something more; and it was the unmistakeable rumour of that something more, from the stables of the barracks of Birmingham, through the streets of that town, flying fast to the War Office in London, and the palace, that drew forth the letter of the 17th May, from Sir Herbert Taylor, by command of the king, to Earl Grey, announcing that his majesty had succeeded, for the safety of the nation, in inducing as many anti-reform peers to withdraw their opposition, as would allow the bill to pass. This narrative shall be as brief as it can be intelligibly rendered; but if it should seem tedious, it ought, nevertheless, to receive a patient perusal. Readers of more classes in society than the one in which I have most of my life moved: readers of various politics, religious believers in various creeds, may all find something to reflect upon.

146

CHAPTER XIV

The Political Crisis of 1832

IN chapter ten I spoke of the introduction of the first Reform Bill to the House of Commons, by Lord John Russell, on the 1st of March, 1831, and of the divisions of the house on it in its earliest stages. These were, on the 22nd of March, for the second reading of the bill, 302; *against* the second reading, 301; on the 18th of April, on the motion of General Gascoyne against reform, 'that the number of members be not reduced,' *for* that motion, 299; *against* it, 291; majority against the reform ministry, 8. Three days after, the ministers were again defeated on a division of 164 to 142 upon a question of adjournment, whereby the voting of supplies was postponed by the anti-reformers.

This last division recalled to the public mind a power which is invested in the House of Commons, and which is the sole defence of the popular branch of the legislature against the lords and the crown— the power to refuse to vote the supplies. The effect of this division was, in the first instance, a threat to the reform government that the anti-reformers could and would stop the supplies. Its effect, in the second instance, was, to make the nation cry aloud for a dissolution of parliament, so that a new election, even with the unreformed constituencies, might decide which party in the house should have the power of withholding the supplies. A third effect was, that the nation, not losing sight of this constitutional power vested in its representatives, urged the application of it upon the House of Commons in the following year, when the great military commander of the age unconstitutionally held the government in his own hands, and attempted to overcome the national will by the power of the army. His Grace's declaration, in 1830, that there was no need for reform, that the old system of representation worked well, and that there should be no reform while he had the power to resist it, had given an impetus to the public determination never before known on a strictly constitutional question. Every act of the anti-reformers added strength to that national determination. Their acts of opposition, though constitutional, were often violent, sometimes undignified, and at last they ceased to be constitutional.

On the 22nd of April, parliament assembled in both houses, under an impression that a prorogation and dissolution would immediately take place. The anti-reformers deprecated dissolution. Animated debates arose; and tumults, such as have seldom been witnessed within the walls of parliament, ensued. In the midst of the most undignified and angry discussion known to Hansard, his majesty, William IV, arrived at the House of Lords, and summoned the angry commons to meet him among the angry peers. Few of the anti-reformers were loyal or composed enough to answer the summons. Those who did appear, heard from his majesty's mouth, that parliament was prorogued and would be dissolved, in order that the sense of the country might be taken on the question of a change in the representation.

London and almost every town and village in the kingdom were illuminated. To the disgrace of the street mobs, the windows of the Duke of Wellington, Lord Londonderry, Sir Robert Peel, Sir Robert Wilson, and other leading anti-reformers, were attacked with stones, and broken. The mobs were led by the ignorant guides to mischief, who neither knew the real power of a multitude, which is its moral power, nor how to take up and occupy a position of dignity, nor what the quality of dignity is. Such persons have always been foremost to lead mobs. They lead mobs still, when they can find them; and until the population which is spoken of as the 'masses', or the 'millions', is elevated by an intellectual system of instruction, universal in application, mobs will continued to be what they have been. Their leaders, too, will continue to be what they still are, violent when there is no immediate danger, dangerous in their cowardice when leading the multitude beyond safety; abounding in words; incapable by nature of philosophic reflection; uninfluenced by the higher moral sentiments; and powerless to convey moral influence to others. The leaders of mobs have been, and are, and will continue to be, of this kind. Not that there are no intelligent and reflective men in the multitudes: there are many; but the men of philosophic reflection, acting under the influence of the moral sentiments, though believing in a political principle which with the multitude is popular, and though powerful by the higher order of their intellectual nature to accomplish the attainment of the popular principle, are restrained from occupying the same position with the unintellectual competitor for leadership. They cannot compete with him. The absence of the moral sentiments in him renders his opposition to them unscrupulous, and they shrink from him. He obtains the leadership and keeps it. The more intelligent and reflective among the multitude retire into privacy, with the intellectual men who are beaten out of the positions of leadership. Or, if young men of good intellectual power grow up within the multitude, after the men of moral power have been driven away, they learn to say that those who were once political believers in, and supporters of, popular representation, or any other popular question, have retired to privacy, because they do not longer believe as they once believed.

The street mobs of London and many other towns, misled by such persons, powerful in their violent conduct to lead to violence, powerless by their want of moral influence to restrain, committed outrages on property, at the general election in April, 1831. The reform cause was dishonoured by their outrage, and would have been weakened, had not the virtuous and the intellectual of all classes been in the position of leaders. The national opinion was formed. Had it been less than national, with one party striving to form it by convincing other parties not yet believing with them, the violence to persons, to window glass, and the threats of outrage which occurred, would have retarded the reform progress indefinitely. Those who did not yet believe in the justice or expediency of reform, would have been confirmed in unbelief. But happily for ultimate success, the national movement had the highest order of intelligence, morality, and political philosophy at its head.

At the general election of April, 1831, few changes were made in the boroughs; but the counties, which up to the passing of the Reform Bill, were the repositories of most of the popular power which then existed, returned seventy-six members out of eighty-two pledged to vote for the bill.

The new parliament met on the 14th of June; and on the 24th Lord John Russell introduced the Reform Bill to the House of Commons a *second* time. As on the first occasion, his lordship made a luminous statement, strengthening himself by references to the opinions of Chatham, Fox, and Pitt, in favour of an extended system of representation. The second reading was adjourned to the 4th of July, to afford time for bringing in the Scotch and Irish Reform Bills. On that day a debate ensued, memorable for the oratory displayed on both sides. Sir James Mackintosh (now dead), Mr. Henry Bulwer (now our ambassador at Madrid), his brother, Sir Edward Bulwer Lytton, Sir Robert Peel (against the bill), Mr. Macaulay, Mr. William Brougham (brother of the then Lord Chancellor), and Lord Althorp (the late lamented Earl Spencer), were eloquent and effective. The debate ended on the third night by a division. There were 367 for the second reading, and 231 against it; majority for the bill, 136. The bill was then committed, and underwent a rigid scrutiny, which occupied the house until the 19th of September. On that day it was moved that the bill be read a third time. Another eloquent debate ensued, which lasted three nights. Sir James Scarlett (the late Lord Abinger), Mr. Macaulay, Mr. Wilson Croker (editor of the *Quarterly Review*), were conspicuous. At the division there were—for the bill, 345; against it, 236; majority for the third reading, 109. The bill then passed the commons, loudly cheered, the plaudits oft repeated, and caught up without the house and carried through the streets of London, and repeated during the whole night; and again throughout the kingdom, to the great joy of the inhabitants of every town and village, and almost of every hamlet. On the day following the passing of the bill in the House of Commons, it was carried up to the house of peers by Lord John Russell and Lord Althorp, attended by upwards of one hundred members.

On the 3rd of October, the Prime Minister, Earl Grey, moved the second reading of the bill in the House of Lords. In opening his address he was deeply affected by the weight of responsibility which it imposed upon him. He said the great object of his political life had been parliamentary reform. If the present measure had the revolutionary tendency which some attributed to it, he would not defend it, far less propose it. He traced the growth of the spirit of reform, sketched its '*present irresistible power*', pledged himself to the support of the institutions of the country, his object being to improve not to injure them, and concluded a great speech by the announcement that he and the government would stand or fall by that bill. Loud cheers, such as are seldom heard in the House of Lords, gave acclaim to the noble and venerable orator when he sat down.

Lord Wharncliffe immediately rose, and after a lengthened speech against the bill, in which, however, he did not defend the rotten boroughs which were to be swept away by schedule A, moved, as an amendment, that 'this bill be rejected'. This was considered unnecessarily offensive, and was altered to the usual form of negatives, 'that this bill be read a second time this day six months'. The debate began on Monday, and lasted five nights, ending at five o'clock on Saturday morning. Parliamentary history affords no records of eloquence, learned research, and dignified argument superior to that debate. The House of Lords probably never equalled it. Besides Earl Grey, the chief speakers for the bill were Lords Lansdowne, Melbourne, Holland, Mulgrave (now Normanby), Plunkett, Rosebery, Radnor, Goderich, his Royal Highness the Duke of Sussex, the Duke of Richmond, and the Lord Chancellor Brougham; the latter pleading for the bill in the greatest oration of his life. Besides Lord Wharncliffe, who led the opposition, the chief speakers against reform were, the Archbishop of Canterbury, the Dukes of Gloucester, Wellington, and Buckingham; Lords Harrowby, Dudley, Carnarvon, Eldon, Mansfield, Bute, Winchelsea, Haddington, Londonderry, Lyndhurst, Wynford, and Harewood.

The question of '*What will the Lords do?*' had been eagerly asked and speculated upon among all classes—among reformers and anti-reformers—during several months; and as the time of division drew nigh, no other question was asked when friend met friend; even strangers in the street would stop strangers, and ask, 'What will the Lords do?' The question was now solved. After this great debate of five nights, at 5 o'clock on the morning of the 8th of October, 1831, the Lords *rejected* the bill. There were *content* for the second reading, 158; *non-content*, 199; majority against the bill, 41.

Expressions of disappointment and indignation arose loudly, and ran swiftly through every street of London, and with every mail coach out of it; along every turnpike road; into every bye-path in the kingdom, and almost to every hearth, save in the houses of the fractional minority of the population, the anti-reformers. The church received a blow in the loss of popularity from which it did not recover for years, if, indeed, it has recovered from it yet; of the majority of forty-one against the bill, the bench of bishops gave twenty-one. Riots once more prevailed. At Derby the prison was broken open, and the property of the anti-reformers destroyed. At Nottingham, the populace, blind to respectable, moral, and intellectual leadership (as in 1848 they seem still resolved to be), rioted, destroyed property, fired the castle belonging to the Duke of Newcastle. His grace was unpopular, and had given a great impulse to reform, though intending the reverse, by his declaration relative to the voters in Newark, who depended on him, 'May I not do as I like with my own?' Some of the London newspapers were published with black edges, to indicate mourning. But a feeling of confidence in the ultimate success of the bill soon gained strength, by the influence of the political unions, which, following their great original of Birmingham, were now established throughout the kingdom.

On the 20th, the king prorogued parliament, and announced from the throne, the necessity of resuming, in the ensuing session, the consideration of reforming the House of Commons.

On the 29th, Sir Charles Wetherell, recorder of Bristol, and one of the most resolute opponents of the Reform Bill, proceeded to that city, and made a public entry as recorder. Riots ensued, beginning on Saturday, continuing through the whole of Sunday, and suppressed only on Monday. The Mansion House, Excise Office, and Bishop's Palace, were plundered and set on fire; the toll-gates pulled down; the prisons burst open with sledge-hammers, and the prisoners set at liberty among the mad populace. The mob increased in madness as it increased in magnitude, and as the fuel upon which its fury fed increased in quantity—plunder in shops and houses, and liquor in vaults and cellars. One hundred and ten persons were injured less or more in life or limb, sixteen fatally, before the riot was suppressed. Of the sixteen who were found dead, three died from the wounds inflicted by the military[14]—the remainder died of apoplexy, inflicted on themselves by excessive drinking in the bishop's palace, and other houses which they plundered.

On the 31st, the political union of London met in the Crown and Anchor, and by adjournment, in Lincoln's Inn Fields; Sir Francis Burdett in the chair. It was agreed to form a national union with branch societies, each having a delegate at the central board. At subsequent meetings resolutions for universal suffrage were proposed, and led to the breaking up of the union; all the members not being favourable to such a measure on principle, and many who were favourable to it on principle opposing it as impossible of attainment at that time. 'If the moderate reform of the bill, which had been twice rejected by the legislature, was so difficult to obtain,' they asked, 'what must universal suffrage be?' The working classes of London, however, led by persons not eminent for discretion, resolved, that so far as they could defeat the Reform Bill, they would do so. They formed a political union of their own, called a metropolitan meeting, at White Conduit House, the advertisement stating, amongst other things, 'that all hereditary distinctions of rank are unnatural, and opposed to the equal rights of man, and ought to be abolished'; and farther, 'that the political union of the working classes should not support any measure of reform,

152

but one including universal suffrage and the abolition of all hereditary power and ranks.' An intimation from the police magistrates and the Home Office that such a meeting might be treasonable, caused it to be postponed. This and similar conduct on the part of large bodies of the people, led by persons who could expound their wrongs but could not practically guide them to the acquisition of their rights, gave the anti-reformers new strength and zeal in their opposition to all reform. It alarmed the king, and the more timid of the aristocracy who had declared for the Reform Bill. And when the Reform Bill had become law, the recollection of that and similar declarations, and all the excesses of the turbulent and indiscreet committed at that time, led to a re-action in public feeling in favour of conservatism, which rendered the reform ministry almost powerless.

On the 6th of December, 1831, parliament was opened by the king. The royal speech recommended the settlement of the reform question.

On the 12th, Lord John Russell introduced the Reform Bill to the House of Commons a *third* time. He said, government was pledged not to propose a bill less efficient than the former. But he was prepared to accede to some alterations, the chief of which was that in boroughs the rent of £10 should qualify for a vote, and not, as proposed before, a valuation of £10 for poor rate. Sir Robert Peel deemed the alterations to be improvements. The bill was read a first time; and on the 10th a second time, after a debate of two days; the division taking place at one o'clock on Sunday morning. There were *for* the second reading, 324; *against* it, 162; majority, 162. The House then adjourned until after Christmas.

On the 17th of January, 1832, parliament again assembled, and resumed the business which has made that year memorable. The opposition to reform, though still coming from fractional numbers of the population, was more vehement in tone than formerly. The in-discreet discussion of other questions bordering upon treason and well charged with sedition, by those leaders of the uneducated multitudes who vied each to 'go further than the other,' as the favourite expression was, rendered the anti-reformers more determined not to yield any measure of reform. The largest number of signatures appended to an anti-reform petition was that of the Protestants of Ireland. On the 28th of February the king held a levee, at which the Earl of Roden presented a Protestant petition against the Irish Reform Bill, signed by 230,000 persons.

The Reform Bill again passed the House of Commons. On the 14th of April, after an arduous debate of four nights, the second reading of the bill was carried by a majority of *nine*, at seven o'clock in the morning, in the House of Lords. The numbers were—*for* the bill, 184; *against* it, 175. An accession of fifty votes had been obtained for the bill since October, when it was rejected. Several bishops had joined the ministers, and voted for the bill. A new party among the Lords, called 'waverers', had sprung up. They contributed to the majority on the second reading; but little dependence could be placed upon them for getting the bill, unmutilated, through committee.

On the 7th of May, on the motion of Lord Lyndhurst, that the disfranchising clauses of the bill be postponed, and the enfranchising clauses considered first, the ministry was defeated by a majority of 36, the numbers being 151 to 115. Upon this, Earl Grey moved the adjournment of the committee until the 10th. On the 9th, the reform ministry resigned; the reasons assigned being their inability to carry such a measure of reform as they held to be indispensable.

Up to this time, it was generally believed that Earl Grey had obtained the king's assent to the creation of new peers to carry the bill, if necessary. The fact was now published, that this extreme measure had neither been granted by the king, nor asked for by the minister.

The sovereign summoned and consulted Lord Lyndhurst, the Duke of Wellington, and Sir Robert Peel. The precise nature of the consultations never transpired, though explanations were subsequently made, which led to the belief that Sir Robert Peel declined to be pledged to the king to carry, or propose, any measure of reform, having so recently opposed the bills of Lord John Russell; and he did not see before him a possibility of carrying on an anti-reform government, with the majority of the House of Commons pledged to reform, as it then was.

The Duke of Wellington, it was reported, declared himself willing to be one of an anti-reform cabinet, though not holding any political office. During nine days his grace was in constant communication with the king; and all that time no government was formed.

The House of Commons met, and, on the motion of Lord Ebrington, passed, by a large majority, a resolution of undiminished confidence in the late cabinet. In London, public meetings were held every day, declaring, by unanimous resolutions, that no taxes should be paid until the bill passed into law. Meetings of the most formidable magnitude were held in all the provincial towns, at which petitions to the House of Commons, to withhold the supplies of money for the public service, were adopted. The constitutional power of the commons to control the peers and the crown, by refusing to vote supplies, and the unconstitutional power of the crown, or of any subject under favour of the crown, to overawe the commons and the country with the army, were the topics of eager discussion at every meeting, club, dinner table, and fireside. Nearly all mercantile transactions were suspended. Intimations of an encampment of all the political unions in the kingdom in the vicinity of London, was seriously made—to remain there until the bill was carried! The anti-reform newspapers dared them to make the attempt, and spoke of the army. The reform newspapers, including the leading daily journals of London, spoke of resistance to the army; constitutional lawyers, of the highest eminence, were reported to have spoken at public meetings, within four hundred yards of the palace, of kings having trusted in armies against their people, and the 'royal heads rolling in the dust before night!'

At Birmingham, two hundred thousand persons, under the guidance of Thomas Attwood, the eminent banker, the father and the hero of political unions, met on Newhall Hill (where now stands the Town Hall), petitioned against supplies, resolved to pay no king's taxes until the bill passed, and, if need were, to remove bodily the whole two hundred thousand of them, and encamp, with other political unions, on Hampstead or Penenden Heath, to be near parliament. Every day, for months previously, hundreds of people walked into the cavalry barrack yard of Birmingham, to see the Greys. On the Sunday before the meeting on Newhall Hill, there were upwards of five thousand people within the gates, most of them well-dressed artizans, all wearing ribbons of light blue knotted in their breasts, indicating that they were members of the political union. Next Sunday, the barrack gates were closed. No civilians were admitted. We were marched to the riding school, to prayers, in the forenoon, and during the remaining part of the day, or most of it, were employed in rough sharpening our swords on the grindstone.[15] I was one of the 'fatigue' men, who turned the stone to the armourer and his assistants.

It was rumoured that the Birmingham political union was to march for London that night; and that we were to stop it on the road. We had been daily and nightly booted and saddled, with ball cartridge in each man's possession, for three days, ready to mount and turn out at a moment's notice. But until this day we had rough-sharpened no swords. The purpose of so roughening their edges, was to make them inflict a ragged wound.[16] Not since before the battle of Waterloo had the swords of the Greys undergone the same process. Old soldiers spoke of it, and told the young ones. Few words were spoken. We had made more noise, and probably looked less solemn, at prayers in the morning, than we did now grinding our swords. It was the Lord's day, and we were *working*. The House of Commons had three times passed a bill declaring that fifty-six rotten boroughs should be disfranchised; that the new boroughs of Manchester, Birmingham, Leeds, Greenwich, Sheffield, Sunderland, Devonport, Wolverhampton, Tower Hamlets, Finsbury, Marylebone, Lambeth, Bolton, Bradford, Blackburn, Brighton, Halifax, Macclesfield, Oldham, Stockport, Stoke-upon-Trent, and Stroud, should have each two representatives. On this memorable Sunday, we sharpened our swords to prevent these new boroughs from obtaining any representatives.

Ashton-under-Lyne, Bury, Chatham, Cheltenham, Dudley, Frome, Gateshead, Huddersfield, Kidderminster, Kendal, Rochdale, Salford, South Shields, Tynemouth, Wakefield, Walsall, Warrington, Whitby, Whitehaven, and Merthyr Tydvil, were, by the bill, three times carried in the House of Commons, to have one member each. Our swords were rough-sharpened on Sunday, the 13th of May, that these towns might have *no members*, all other arguments against reform having failed. The Irish and Scotch reform bills were not in the same position; but the swords with ragged edges were for them as well as the English Reform Bill.

The negotiations then pending between the king and the anti-reformers, were unknown to the country, and in their details still are. Most of the transactions beyond the town of Birmingham were unknown to us, though, from general rumour, we knew, unfortunately for our profession, that the country was alarmingly unanimous. When closed within the barracks, booted and saddled, we had no communication with the townspeople night nor day, and knew nothing of their movements. We did not apprehend an immediate collision until the day of the sword-sharpening. The danger now seemed imminent. Those of us who had held private and confidential conversations on the subject, had agreed that the best means of preventing a collision with the reform movement and the national will, as expressed by the House of Commons, was to give circulation to the fact that we were not to be depended upon to put down public meetings, or prevent the people of Birmingham from journeying to London, to present their petitions, and support the House of Commons by their presence, if they chose to undertake the journey. We caused letters to be written and sent to various parties in Birmingham and London, to that effect. Some were addressed to the Duke of Wellington, some to the king, some to the War Office to Lord Hill, and some were dropped in the streets. Those letters were necessarily anonymous, but they contained no violent threats. They firmly and respectfully urged that, while the Greys would do their duty if riots and outrages upon property were committed, they would not draw swords or triggers upon a deliberative public meeting, or kill the people of Birmingham for attempting to leave their town with a petition to London. In the letters dropped in Birmingham streets, or sent to parties resident in that town, we implored the people, as they valued success to reform and political friendship with the army, *not* to allow rioting, window-breaking, or any outrage on property; else, if refusing to fire or draw swords on them, in the event of our being brought before a court martial for such disobedience, we would have no justification. We would be condemned and shot. 'If you do nothing but make speeches, sign petitions, and go peaceably to present them, though you go in tens of thousands, the Greys will not prevent you.' One of my letters contained that passage, and concluded thus: 'The king's name is a tower of strength, which they upon the adverse faction, want.'

The belief with the public, however, was that the king had turned anti-reformer; and, possibly, he wavered. There is too much reason to fear that the queen-consort was influenced by the anti-reform ladies of the aristocracy, and operated on her royal husband. But these are secrets of the royal household, not to be soon revealed; perhaps never. As to what we would have done in the event of an armed movement of the people, as discussed or suggested by many of the leading London newspapers, is not for me to speculate upon now. Such probabilities were speculated upon then.

Happily, the *nine* days of a nation without a government—all classes fervently excited and nearer unanimity than was ever known of the English nation—came to an end. The renewed vote of confidence in the late cabinet by the House of Commons; the petitions of the country to the commons to stop the supplies; the political unions guided by the greatest of them all—the union of Birmingham—resolving not to pay assessed taxes until the bill passed; the rumour industriously spread and conveyed to the highest quarters, and founded on a well-determined resolution of certain soldiers, that the army was not to be relied upon, if the constitutional voice of the country was attempted to be suppressed by the unconstitutional use of military power—especially at Birmingham, upon which town the eyes of Britain and of Europe were fixed; all those concurrent causes, of which the last was not the least effective, brought the attempt to establish a government by military power in defiance of the House of Commons to an end. May such attempts be at an end for ever!

The king's private secretary, Sir Herbert Taylor, was made the medium of concluding the interregnum—those fearful nine days, upon which a great kingdom had laid aside its usual avocations of industry, its citizens meeting in council daily, its working millions standing in the streets asking what they should do next—the cry of all being, 'Encamp at London!' and its dragoons sharpening their swords on the Sunday! Sir Herbert Taylor, then private secretary to the king, communicated the following letter to Earl Grey:

'St. James's Palace, May 17th, 1832.
'My dear Lord—I am honoured with His Majesty's commands to acquaint your lordship that all difficulties to the arrangements in progress will be obviated by a declaration in the House to-night from a sufficient number of peers, *that in consequence of the present state of affairs*, they have come to the resolution of dropping their further opposition to the Reform Bill, so that it may pass without delay, and as nearly as possible in its present shape. I have the honour to be, yours, sincerely,   'HERBERT TAYLOR.'

The bill went through the committee accordingly, and on the 4th of June finally passed the House of Lords, on the motion of Earl Grey; the numbers being 106 *for*, and 22 *against* it.

The troubles of our regiment about reform, and particularly my own, did not end with the circumstances in which they began. The fate of the bill was settled by that letter from the king, announcing that in '*consequence of the present state of affairs*' (which *affairs* some of us had assisted to place in that state). The newspapers continued to discuss the constitutional question, warmly. On the 21st or 22nd I was on guard. When off sentry I found myself, early in the morning, alone in the guard-house, all the other men, save those on sentry, being asleep. I had read during the night, in an anti-reform paper, a vehement denial of the Duke of Wellington having yielded to reform from a distrust in the army; also that the rumours of the Scots Greys at Birmingham, having expressed or held any political opinions, were fabrications of certain of the reform papers. I took the opportunity of being alone to write a letter to that paper[17] which affirmed that the soldiers had expressed political opinions, to corroborate what it had said. A passage from the letter was published. As it led to all the subsequent proceedings before a court martial and court of inquiry, which I am about to relate, I give it here.

'As a private in that regiment, I have the means of knowing fully the opinions which pervade the rank in which I serve. It was true that a few sent their names to the roll of the political union. But let no one think that those who refrained from doing so cared less for the interests of their country. I, for one, made no such public avowal of my opinons, for I knew it to be an infringement of military law; but I was one who watched with trembling anticipation the movements of the people of Birmingham. For while we ventured to hope that any collision between the civil and military forces would be prevented, by the moral energies of the former, we could not help having a fear that *the unprincipled and lawless*, who are everywhere more or less to be found, *might take the opportunity* of that turning in the national affairs, *to commit outrages on property; in which instance, we should certainly have considered ourselves, as soldiers, bound to put down such disorderly conduct.* This, I say, we should have certainly felt to have been our duty; but against the liberties of our country we would have never, never, never raised an arm. The Scots Greys have honourably secured a high character in the defence of their country, and they would be the last to degrade themselves below the dignity of British soldiers, in acting as the tools of a tyrant. The Duke of Wellington, if he sees or hears of this, may assure himself that military government shall never again be set up in this country.'[18]

This was published on the 27th of May, 1832. The words printed in *italics* show that the opinions relative to the duty of soldiers to protect property and suppress riots expressed then, were the opinions which I have since expressed. To write, or say, or think (a soldier has no business to think, they tell him) that in any case we were not to do what we were ordered was a grave offence, nothing short of mutiny. I was aware of that grave fact. I remonstrated with the soldiers who had joined the political union, and succeeded in persuading them to recall their adhesion to it. With the same regard for my own safety, I never went near the political union. Had the time and the circumstances come for us to act according to our design and judgment, and not according to orders, it would have been an occasion great enough to risk all that we were risking. It would have been a national necessity. We would have either been shot dead, or triumphant with a nation's thanks upon our heads. For either alternative we were prepared. I had no fear that my memory would suffer, even if shot dead in the first act of crying, 'For the king, the constitution, the commons, and the people!' In this chapter I have related the circumstances in which the country was then placed. They show how nearly the constitution was suppressed by military force. The only dread which distressed me was the fear that we might be called out to quell some contemptible window breakers, in which case we could have had no justification for refusing to cut them down. Our hope was that if we came into collison with the people at all, it would be to disperse some meeting met to petition the House of Commons, or one deliberating on the Reform Bill, or one conveying a petition to parliament, or a memorial to the king, as had been proposed to be done from Birmingham. There would *then* have been an occasion worthy of a bold adventure.

It ended, however, in the less dignified visitation of a flogging. But *that* I have not yet looked upon as a disgrace. I would have felt disgraced had I allowed it to fall upon other backs than my own.

[14] Dragoons commanded by an officer on leave. The garrison commander stood idly by, was court martialled and shot himself. This was, no doubt, very much in the minds of Somerville's officers, and helps to account for their rash initiative.

[15] The order came from London. When it reached the Royals, at Canterbury they put the sharpening out to contract with a local cutler who, being a radical, refused it.

[16] This sentence, and most of this and the next paragraph, were significantly suppressed in the second edition.

[17] *The Weekly Dispatch*, then a radical, later a patriotic, organ.

[18] A groomed version of the original, which included the here suppressed phrase— 'We well knew the position in which we might be placed should events require the physical action of the community'—which would not have squared with Somerville's later repudiation of physical force.

CHAPTER XV

The Military Crime

I MUST here direct attention to some of the usages of the cavalry service, that you may the more clearly understand the first occurrences which befel me, in consequence of the publication of that extract of a letter which you read in the last chapter.

Almost every man has two horses, with their accoutrements, to keep clean and to feed; some have three. The six troops of a regiment consist of fifty-five men each. The commissioned officers select each a servant from the ranks; some, two. Those servants leave their horses behind them in the troop stables, and attend only to the horses of their masters. The horses left are either given to recruits, to go to school upon, or are allotted as spare ones. The regimental sergeant-major, the six troop sergeant-majors, the farrier-major, the six farriers, the ten or twelve sergeants, the sixteen or twenty bandsmen, and the bandmaster, are all allowed a man to take care of their horses. The men so selected have their own horses to attend to also, which gives them each two. There are a number of young horses always in training, to replace old ones condemned at the previous yearly inspection, but which are still retained to do duty until the young ones, usually purchased when two years old, have reached the age of three years, or three and a half, and have been trained. Thus there are a number of spare horses; some of them old, some young. They are allotted among the men, so far as they go, each man having one of them in addition to his own. There are also some men in hospital, sick; their horses are, in like manner, allotted. There may be some men in confinement; their horses are allotted. Each day, eight, ten, or twelve men go on guard on foot; their horses are left during twenty-four hours to the other men of their respective stables. And as it occurs every day that some of those who have two horses go on guard, they each leave two to be taken care of in the stable. Thus it happens that one man may have three horses.

The corporals are not exempted from taking care of their own; but they do not take spare ones; consequently, as they, the sergeants, farriers, troop sergeant-majors, and bandsmen, are all included in the numerical strength of fifty-five to each troop; the number of men daily in a condition to take spare horses, is much below the strength of fifty-five. Those who are appointed to the care of the horses of the officers, non-commissioned officers, and bandsmen, are paid for so doing. The bandsmen pay about two shillings a week; the sergeants and sergeant-majors two shillings and sixpence to three or four shillings. The men who act as grooms to the latter, clean their boots, belts, and clothes also. The men who are grooms to the bandsmen, clean nothing but the horses. It is an object of favour with a private to get a second horse which is paid for; because, while he has it, he is not required to take his turn of the spare horses which are not paid for, those of men on guard, sick men, prisoners, or the condemned, or untrained young ones.

On the line of march there are fewer spare horses than in quarters, as the farriers and others are then mounted; yet there are always some. They are led by men appointed to the duty; which, on the march, is frequently imposed as a punishment. The men who turn out latest in the morning, who are imperfectly polished or brushed, or who evince signs of having been tipsy during the night, have the spare horses given to them. And as all horses and accoutrements must be thoroughly cleaned at the end of each day's march, before the man can attend to himself, he who has two, feels the duty to be punishment in reality.

Another way of punishing men when marching, is to make the offender dismount from a favourite horse (if he be so mounted), and ride on some odious trotter, which may be the dislike of all the regiment. It is sometimes a grievous punishment awarded to men who give offence, to be separated from favourite horses, and have ill-tempered, ill-going animals allotted to them instead.

Men are occasionally punished for gross misconduct by saddle-bag drill. In such a case, the offender is accoutred in full marching order, carrying his sword, carbine, and saddle-bags, with every article of his kit packed into them—the bags strapped upon his back, and the horse's saddle above the bags; and thus loaded, he is turned out on foot, to march on a space of ground marked out for him, from six o'clock in the morning until six at night. In warm weather this is a terrible punishment, if it lasts a week or a fortnight.

For lesser faults offenders are turned out in full marching order once an hour, or, it may be, three or four times a day, without any warning as to the precise time when they will be ordered out. If not down stairs, spotlessly clean, in full dress, on the instant of being called, they get additional punishment; to avoid which they must be ready and on the watch all day. Those punishments are usually awarded for drunken offences of a minor character. If a man be found four times intoxicated within twelve months, he may be tried by a court martial, and have one penny per day stopped from his pay, besides such other punishment as the court may award. And this may be repeated three times, until threepence is stopped. But I believe the law does not stand the same in this respect as it did. There is now some attention about to be paid, though not much, to a system of rewards and other inducements·to good conduct.

The most vexatious punishments to which soldiers are liable, short of those which have positive cruelty or torture in them, are the petty persecutions of some of the non-commissioned officers, or perhaps the riding master, when they take a dislike to some particular man; they may weary his life almost out of him, and he be still unable to point to any act of theirs as contrary to order, or illegal. If a recruit attending the riding school for lessons, he may be ordered to load and fire every day, while no one else loads and fires; so that he may have his lock, stock, and barrel, to clean and burnish up every day. If a soldier beyond the condition of taking lessons, he may be one of eight, ten, or twelve men, selected to make up the number requisite to form the different 'rides' in the school. And if the riding master be 'down upon him', as the soldiers name the persecution which has no definite form, but which takes advantage of every circumstance that can be pressed into the service of the persecutor, he may have the same man there every day, and on each occasion give him unnecessary work to do. He may have a horse, outcast of the regiment, hopelessly unmanageable, and mount the man he is 'down upon', on that horse, and require him to do all manner of exercise upon it, with the same precision as upon the best trained horse.

On Sunday, the 27th of May, 1832, the passage from my letter, as printed in the preceding chapter, was read in Birmingham Barracks. Viewed in connection with previous rumours of what the Greys would do or would not do, in the event of the army being called out to obstruct the progress of the Reform Bill, it excited much attention, more than came to my knowledge at the time. But I ascertained that inquiries were made to discover the writer. One of the men, who had a confidential knowledge of certain transactions done, and of designs which *were* to have been transacted, had circumstances required us to act, came to me, and said that he already knew that a number of men were suspected; that the sergeant-major, adjutant, riding master, and commanding officer would be 'down upon' all of them, until they were driven into some fault, and caught in it; that he himself was suspected more than any other man, in consequence of having joined the political union, and being known to have some talent and practice in letter-writing. He proceeded to assure me that he did not write that letter, nor did he know who had written it; but that he knew they would be 'down upon' him. He said he wished he was as safe as I; and was sorry that he had not been as careful to keep away from the political union. To which I replied, that he and others who went there were blameable for indiscretion; but I was not so free of blame in respect of indiscretion as I had been. I then confided to him the secret that the letter was my production, and that he need have no fear for himself, as I would avow it rather than let him or any one suffer on account of it.

I never ascertained who all of the suspected men were; but before the Court of Inquiry, at Weedon, the commanding officer stated that I was not one of those at first suspected; that during the Sunday evening, in a conversation with the riding master and another officer, it was suggested that I might have been the writer, or that I knew something about it, as I had been seen reading newspapers; but that he himself was not inclined to believe that it was me, and only believed the act to be mine when I acknowledged it, on the following Tuesday.

Had the commanding officer been careful to say as little before the Court of Inquiry as the riding master said, it might never have transpired that I was one of the subjects of their conversation on the Sunday evening. But he told the court that, though suspecting others, he yielded to the suggestion that I might be the writer; and observing in the paper a notice that to prove to the public that the original was a genuine soldier's letter, it could be inspected at the newspaper office, he endeavoured to obtain a specimen of my hand-writing that evening, to send to London to be compared with the original letter.

What was said to the riding master I know not, but on the Monday morning I was ordered by a sergeant not to take Farrier Simpson's horse, D 36, but another horse, B 30. This latter had no connection with the troop to which I was attached; the troop to which it belonged was stationed at Kidderminster, and it was at headquarters at Birmingham, unfit for regular troop-duty, though it was a young horse, and had been three years in training. It was not then trained, and never was. It was given first to one man, then to another, and again to a third, and so on to others, as punishment. For mere riding it was not unmanageable, but it had been used in the riding school so often by men who had committed some fault, and were riding for punishment, that its temper, naturally bad, instead of being sweetened or subdued by them, was soured and aggravated.

I had once or twice, after returning from the riding school with my own horse, been sent thither with this one, for a civilian and some of the rough-riders in the school to ride upon. This only happened when no one else was at hand, to accoutre and take it from the stable to the school.

On the morning of Monday, the 28th, on being ordered to accoutre this horse and take it there, I did so, under the impression that I was so ordered, because no other person was at hand to take it but me. I therefore went in ordinary stable dress, not in boots and spurs, but in shoes, and without a cane or switch, having no expectation that I was to ride. Up to this day the riding master had never been otherwise than kind to me. From the time of joining the regiment I had not committed a single fault of the most trivial nature. I had not received so much as one reproof or severe word from any officer or non-commissioned officer. In showing the 'tackle' once a week, which was done by taking every part of the horse's accoutrements to pieces, arranging it artistically, each man on his bed in the barrack-room; every buckle and chain burnished and shining; the locks of pistol and carbine, taken to pieces to show the interior works, all brightened; the barrels out of their stocks, the stocks varnished and the brasses burnished; the gleaming sword unsheathed by the side of its shining scabbard; each man standing at attention at the head of his iron bedstead, upon which his 'tackle' was spread, while the captain and other officers of his troop, the sergeant-major and the sergeants came and inspected it—at this weekly show it was the misfortune of some men to have their buckles minutely inspected, they having got a name for indifferent cleanliness, while others had the fair fortune of being passed by with a glance; it had become a weekly occurrence for the captain to glance his eye to my accoutrements, upon which the troop sergeant-major said, 'that man's things are always clean'; and without further inspection they passed to some one else.

Until this memorable Monday morning no fault had been found with me. Having been practised as a rider in my boyhood, I had little difficulty in the school, except to unlearn some unmilitary positions. Every direction given I studiously obeyed. When I was in the first class, and 'back sticks' were used to make the recruits sit upright, I was always called out of the ride and left to look on; the riding master saying that I did not require that department of teaching. Indeed, from the official documentary evidence laid before parliament and the War Office, I find him bearing testimony to the fact that I had been always obedient and active for duty. I had advanced into a superior class, leaving recruits whom I found before me when I joined the regiment, behind. I had been sooner sent to mount guard and go out to field days than most other recruits. Without being again at the riding school after this day, I went regularly to field days three times a week on joining my own troop, letter E, which lay at Coventry. And I doubt if there be a rougher piece of ground for cavalry exercise anywhere, than that upon which we had our field days, a common lying about two miles west of that city. We used to charge at the gallop with swords drawn, and carried above the forehead as the position of St. George, taking a leap of a quick-thorn fence of moderate elevation, with a ditch behind it. I was fortunate in getting a horse of rare ability for a leap at Coventry, though an animal of a different temperament from that which I previously described as Farrier Simpson's horse. He had little of the equine philosophy of the latter; but while at every charge over this fence and ditch, some unfortunate man, ill-mounted, found himself and horse left behind, this fine young animal, which was allotted to me, used to go over like a bird. The only difficulty I had with him was to preserve the line, not to bound out ahead of the squadron, his inclination being to make a race of the charge, instead of a mere military manœuvre.

These matters I mention now, to show what my position really was at the 28th of May. On taking the horse to the school, I was surprised that instead of some rough-rider taking him from me as before, to allow my return to the stable to attend to my own horse, the riding master ordered me to 'fall in', and join the 'ride', which was about to be formed. I did so, and was the second file of the 'ride'; Sergeant Glen, the head rough-rider, being the leading file. Mr. Gillies, the riding master, seeing me without spurs, demanded why I had come to the school without boots and spurs. I was about to reply that I had been sent with the horse, and had no intimation that I was to ride. 'Hold your tongue! . . . Don't answer me,' he exclaimed,—'dismount!' I dismounted. 'Mount!' I mounted. 'Dismount!' I dismounted. 'Mount!' I mounted. 'Dismount!' I dismounted. All this was only the work of a minute; but his manner was so different from anything that I had seen in him, and he cracked his whip with such vehemence, that I did not know what to think. The horse nervous, ill-tempered, and alarmed, reared, plunged, and chafed. I attributed the riding master's ill-humour to the fact that I had come without my spurs. And, on being ordered to go to the barrack room and dress, I darted out of the school, to run as if life and all that life is worth depended upon the speed of getting booted and spurred.

He seeing me run before I was out of the school, recalled me in a thundering voice, and demanded if I did not know how to go out of the school otherwise than I had done. He told me to get a switch, instead of spurs. I then walked out, instead of running. As soon as I was clear of the door I ran; and though the distance was three or four hundred yards to the room in which I had quarters, I returned in a very few minutes.

Arrived with my cane, I took the horse from the hands of the orderly, who attended the classes to fire pistols behind the ears of young horses and young men, and standing for orders, got the word 'mount', and mounted; 'dismount', and dismounted; 'mount', and mounted; 'dismount', and dismounted; 'mount', and mounted. Once more the commanding voice, the loud whip, and the maddened animal kicking the boards, mingled together. I could not, and no dragoon that ever bestrode a trooper could, have calmed a horse thus irritated, and brought him into line with the seven or eight others all at once. I could not do so; but I did my best. To make the matter worse, because I did not do so, the riding master, as I thought, whipped the horse. There was afterwards some doubt about this; and probably he only 'cracked' the whip. The effect, however, was to make the animal plunge, dash backward on the boards, and be unmanageable in circling, turning, and wheeling. At first we were to move slowly; but my horse was in that state of irritation that it would not go slowly. We then trotted and cantered, circled, wheeled, turned, and many other things; the horse sometimes halting and rearing up, when it should have been trotting, until it disordered the whole ride.

The riding master vociferated that it was my own fault; and, as if

167

to make me manage the horse better, ordered me to ride without stirrups. The stirrups were thrown across in front of the saddle. I now saw that he was determined, for some purpose or other, what I could not even suspect, to give me a tumble. This I was determined should not happen. It may do in the amphitheatre to ride fantastically; but it is more than play in a military riding-school to ride without stirrups, on a saddle, with a horse foaming and enraged as mine then was, the riding master now worse tempered than the horse, and the rider now thinking that he had most cause of the three, to be out of good humour.

I rode on without stirrups, and kept my seat; though more than once, with sudden rearing and swerving, I felt myself unsteady. We got the word 'halt', and formed in line up the centre. Upon which, I being the file No. 2, the riding master spoke thus: 'Number two by himself, the remainder stand steady, a horse's length to the front; march!' This I obeyed as well as I could make the horse do it, by taking three yards (a 'horse's length') to the front. Then by myself I was dismounted and mounted some half dozen times at least; which being done without stirrups, I had to breast the saddle each time. It exhausted my breath, and almost my patience.

The ride went on again; my horse seemingly more resolute in rearing and swerving out of the ride than ever. It made a spring from the side of the school towards the centre; and in the vexation of the moment I dismounted. The riding master rushed forward, and gave the word 'mount'; I did not move. Turning to the orderly, he called, 'Go for a file of the guard.' A corporal and file of the guard came. 'Now,' said he, looking on me sternly, 'will you do your duty? Mount!' I said, 'I cannot manage this horse.' He then said, 'Guard, take this man to the guard-house; he is a prisoner!'

They came: one of the file on each side of me, and the corporal behind. The latter gave the word 'March!' and we marched away. The men on guard were much surprised to see me a prisoner; and were all eager to know what I had done. The day passed over. At mid-day, dinner was brought to me, and supper; and next morning my breakfast. Soldiers are more careful of one another, and kind, when one happens to be a prisoner, no matter what the crime may be, than at any other time.

Between nine and ten o'clock, on the 29th, the regimental sergeant-major came to the guard-house, and called me out. He said, 'Well, what do you think of yourself now?' I replied, that I thought I had been a fool yesterday in the riding school, and was very sorry for having disobeyed orders, but it was my first fault in the regiment. He rejoined, 'Ah! I see you are getting afraid of us.' 'No,' I replied, 'there is a difference between being afraid, and being sorry for committing a fault.' 'Come along,' said he; and went away. I followed.

He led me to the orderly room, where the adjutant and the commanding officer, Major Wyndham, were. Lord Arthur Hill was our lieutenant-colonel, but was absent on long leave in London, and the major commanded. Major Wyndham was a very tall, dark-whiskered, pleasant-looking, middle-aged gentleman. His character with the men was that of a mild, amiable officer, more likely to be ruled or imposed upon by others than to do wrong to any one. And, notwithstanding all that occurred to me at that time, all that was said in the newspapers against him, and all the errors he fell into in point of military law and official discretion, I still believe him to have been at fault only in being led or advised, by harsher natures than his own, to proceed as he did.

First he said, 'Well, my man, you are getting sulky on our hands.' I replied, 'No, I am not sulky; I unfortunately disobeyed orders yesterday, in the riding school, but am now very sorry for it.' 'Ah, but,' said he, taking up a newspaper which lay ready at hand, 'you are fond of newspapers, I understand,' (or of writing to newspapers).

I saw what was coming; and having heard from the men on guard, and another who came to the guard-house with my breakfast, that there was a great commotion in the regiment about the letter, and that several men were accused, and were likely to be made prisoners and brought to trial, I resolved to confess myself the writer. The major, exhibiting a slip of paper, said, 'You are fond of writing to newspapers, I believe?' This paper contained some verses as I believed at the time, with my name attached. They were but silly as poetry, yet having something sentimental about them, they had been printed in the poet's corner of a Birmingham newspaper. A gentleman belonging to the Staffordshire Yeomanry, who with other gentlemen came to the military riding-school to take lessons, and for whom I had several times accoutred one of the troop horses, inquired, one day, if I had written the love verses which had been in the newspapers. I said, 'Yes.' He proceeded to inform me that his sister and other young ladies had admired them, and had desired him to get some copies of them in the soldier's own handwriting, for their albums or scrap-books. I did not think so much of their literary merit myself, as to deem them worth the honour of being placed in the albums or scrap-books of ladies who rode in carriages with liveried servants, but as he was urgent I consented, and on another day I gave him one copy. (The subject was the nameless ONE for whom I had crossed the Lammermoors, but had never spoken to, written of in previous chapters.) I shall not, I cannot, do any lady the injustice of believing that a copy of sentimental verses, sought by herself and placed in her scrap-book, were taken out again for the purpose of assisting in getting the author flogged. But having been told that the copy was placed in a lady's scrap-book, and that the other ladies requested each a copy, while I had made no copies but the one; it was evident, seeing that the major had one, that some person had taken it from the lady's scrap-book, to be used for the discovery of evidence, in this case.

From what the major subsequently said, it appeared that he had then sent it to London, for the hand-writing to be compared. He said, again, 'You are fond of writing to newspapers, I believe?' I replied that I had written very little to newspapers. He then, taking hold of the newspaper which contained the extract from the political letter, said, 'I have something else to say to you; do you know anything of this libel which has been published about the regiment?' I replied that I did not know if it was a libel; but I had written a letter, and I believed part of it was published. He then asked, sternly and formally, if I had written that letter, and I answered 'Yes.' He proceeded—'You do not think that letter a libel, but I think it worse; it is treason.' Some further remarks were made, which I did not state before the Court of Inquiry to be more precise than 'to the best of my recollection.' As the major gave a somewhat different version of this examination, I shall, in the next paragraph but one, quote his version. He asked if I did not know that I was sworn to the king, paid by the king, and bound to support him. I replied that I was sworn to the king, as the head of the nation and the constitution; that I did not know who would have paid me had the House of Commons refused to vote the supplies, as it seemed likely to do a fortnight ago; that as to the oath of allegiance, circumstances might have arisen in which it might have been a question to whom—the king individually, or the constitution and government— the oath was taken. (In relating this to the Court of Inquiry, I was stopped by the judge advocate and the president; they said it was their duty to inform me that I need not state anything which would criminate myself. I replied, that I was advised not to withhold any part of the conversation which had passed between the major and myself.)

After coming to that part of the published extract from my letter, which mentions some of the Scots Greys having joined the political union, the major asked how I knew that any of them had done so. My reply was that I had had very good information. The major asked who they were, what were their names? I replied that I would not give their names. He asked again if I was determined not to give their names. I said that I would not say that I would never, under any circumstances, give their names; but I would not do so at that time, nor under present circumstances. Again he asked if I refused to name them, and I said, 'Yes, I do refuse.' On his reading the passage which stated that, in 'the event of rioting or outrage being committed on property, we, as soldiers, would have considered it our duty to put down all such disorderly conduct'; he said, 'That is very right; I perfectly agree with you.' Coming to a remark which the editor of the newspaper had made about this 'brave and patriotic soldier,' the major said, 'I dare say you are intelligent enough, but God knows we know little of your bravery!' He made some other remarks about the political unions being 'illegal and treasonable,' and said that, looking at my disobedience of orders yesterday in the riding school, and the confession that I had now made of writing that letter, he thought I had committed a crime—a very great crime indeed. I again pleaded guilty to the disobedience of orders in the riding school, said I was very sorry for it, but the writing of the letter was a different and distinct affair. He rejoined, emphatically, 'My lad, you will repent of that'; and ordered the sergeant-major to take me back to the guard-house.

I now give that portion of the major's statement before the Court of Inquiry, on the 27th July, which refers to my examination before him, on the 29th May, which I have just related.

Question: 'When he was brought to you, will you state what passed between you and him?'

Answer: 'I found him in the passage, and I had been in the room probably a minute when I sent for him. Lieutenant Ricketts was in the room, and the sergeant-major brought him in by my order. I presented the *crime* to him and said, "This is your crime, I am sorry it should have appeared." That was the commencement of the conversation. I said I did not expect it of so young a soldier; he looked at me, and I think the words he said were, "*I am sorry for it.*" I do not think he said anything more, except that he mentioned something about his horse being unruly; I think *he said he "could not manage the horse"*; those were his words. I said, "It is highly improper conduct, a high disobedience of orders, and I regret it very much"; *I was sorry to see he did not express some contrition. I thought* a soldier would have said more. *My object in seeing him was, if he had spoken well for himself, to have released him*; he did not say that which I expected. I said it was an act of insubordination, and as near as I can recollect, I said, "it cannot be overlooked"; he said nothing more.

'The newspaper was lying on the table; I took it up and said, "I am afraid, my lad," I think that was the expression, "you are fond of writing in the newspapers." He seemed surprised. I then said, "Is this letter from you?" He then stopped a short time and said it was, that he had written the letter. I then read the letter, or extracts from it, and I think I commented on the letter, saying, I was sorry to see a young soldier writing in a newspaper, and particularly on political subjects, which I considered was not a soldier's duty. He then said, he did not know; he thought he had a right to write in the newspapers. I said, "You have no right to comment upon the conduct of your regiment, and say what is not the fact; you have written a libel on your regiment"; I said, "that is not the business of a soldier."

'I read some more lines, and came to a passage about what the Scots Greys would do, in case they were called out to act. It is a long time since; I cannot recollect the words, but they were to this effect, *that to quell a mob they would so, but would not lift up arms against the people.* I said, "this is strong conversation"; and asked him, what he meant by it? I said, "You ought to know your duty better than to express any such libel on the regiment," and I asked him, what he meant by it? Then I said, "Do you recollect, my good fellow, that you have sworn allegiance to the king, and you are paid by the king?" Then that began a conversation, the words of which I do not recollect, except having seen them in the paper, something about his being paid by the king, and that only so long as he was paid for the people, or words to that effect.'

Question, by the president: 'Is that your own recollection, being refreshed in any manner, that he did use those words in particular?'

Answer: 'Yes; he said he was bound to the king as long as he went with the people, or words to that effect. I then told him that I was sorry to see so young a soldier commence in that manner. Again I said it was not the business of any soldier to meddle with politics, and I regretted very much that he had libelled the whole regiment. That, I think, ended the conversation. I then desired the sergeant-major to take him back to the guard-house, which was instantly done.'

This is the direct statement of Major Wyndham. On cross-examination he said farther, that (speaking of himself in the first person) 'I was surprised; I had been twenty years in the regiment, and never heard of a soldier using such language, making use of all our names in that kind of way. It had been a conversation throughout the whole of the barrack-yard ever since Sunday; no one could make out who it was. Various people were suggested; one man in particular, and everybody believed it was him but myself.   *   *   We were still in doubt as to the writer, until the man confessed he was the writer in my room. My idea was, that it was too well written for a soldier; one part, I thought, might have been written by a soldier; the rest, I said, could not have been written by a soldier; that was the first remark I made.'

'Did you, in commenting on the letter, apply to it the epithets, "seditious" and "treasonable", or either of them?'

'No, I used the word "libel", and, I think, afterwards in the school, when I spoke to the men.'

'For anything you could say, you might have used the words seditious and treasonable, or either of them?'

'No, I think I said "libel upon the whole regiment'. It had been commented on throughout the yard, and a great deal of vexation caused by the letter. The town was in a state of confusion; the barrack yard kept constantly shut; *we were spoken of as unionists*; one report was that I was dismissed; that the commander was coming down; and that, at one place, they had nearly pulled him out of his carriage. Altogether I was excited; and, I believe, every man in the regiment was excited. Banners were flying, drums beating (outside); the gates of the barracks were locked; and what with the gates being locked and the other circumstances that occurred, one cannot be surprised at there being angry feeling about the letter being written.'

At a subsequent part of the major's statement, wherein he relates what took place in the riding school, in the afternoon after the sentence of the court martial had been carried into effect, he adds to his description of the state of Birmingham and the regiment, as given by himself in the last paragraph; that he had been written to from London to know if the Greys could be depended upon, for that reports had reached the highest quarters that they could not. This is corroborative of the statement made by me, in the preceding chapter, as to the part which 'we' had acted in producing that 'state of affairs', which caused the king to write, by his secretary, to Earl Grey that the farther opposition of the peers would be withdrawn, and the Reform Bill allowed to pass.

As that statement of the commanding officer refers to what occurred after the court martial, on the 29th of May, I do not now quote it. His statements, already quoted in this chapter, refer to the proceedings before the court martial was ordered, or even thought of. The major says, honestly (it would have been well if every other witness had told all which they knew as honestly), 'My object in seeing him was, *if he should have spoken well for himself*, *to have released him*, but he did not say that which I expected.'

I could not, with punishment impending over other men, do otherwise than tell him that I was the writer of the letter, for which they were suspected. For this confession, if his words have any meaning at all, I was sent back to the guard-house with the sergeant-major. In about ten minutes after leaving me there, the sergeant-major returned, with a slip of paper, upon which was written my 'crime', or indictment, and said, 'You will prepare for a court martial immediately; that is your crime.'

He went out, and again returned in a few minutes, and told me if I had any witnesses to call, to name them, and he would order their attendance. My thoughts instantly turned to the persons who had been in the riding school the day before, and had witnessed the extraordinary conduct of the riding master; but I could not recall all the circumstances in a moment, and the probable evidence of the different men—some of whom saw one thing, some another, according to the part of the ride they were in. I therefore said I would require a few minutes to consider who might be of use to me; to which the sergeant-major replied, angrily, 'We have no time to lose in that way,' and left me abruptly. He did not return. I was taken before the court martial at eleven o'clock, and had no witnesses.

CHAPTER XVI

The Court Martial—Sentence, Two Hundred Lashes

THE following is a copy of the orders upon which the court martial was formed:

'MORNING REGIMENTAL ORDERS BY MAJOR WYNDHAM[19], BIR-MINGHAM BARRACKS, 29th MAY, 1832.—A regimental court martial will assemble in the mess-room, for the trial of such prisoners as may be brought before it. President: Captain Fawcett. Members: Captain Clarke, Lieutenant Somerville, Cornet Ferlong, Cornet Macquarrie. The troops to parade in stable dress, with side arms, at half-past four o'clock. A true copy from the regimental order book of the 2nd Dragoons.

(Signed) ST. VINCENT WILLIAM RICKETTS,
Lieutenant and Adjutant, 2nd Dragoons.'[20]

It was stated by Major Wyndham, in his examination by the Court of Inquiry, to be customary in the Scots Greys to order a parade of the men in side arms, to hear the proceedings of every court martial at the same time that the court was ordered to assemble; and that consequently by doing so on this occasion, it was not to be inferred that he anticipated the finding and sentence of the court. I would have proved by the oldest soldiers in the regiment, whom I had summoned to the inquiry, that the custom was otherwise, and that in no case within their recollection had a regimental court martial been assembled immediately, by orders issued during the day; the custom being to issue the orders on the previous evening. My purpose in summoning witnesses to prove these customs was to show that, though I had been in confinement for the crime in the riding-school from Monday morning until Tuesday forenoon, no court martial was ordered nor intended to be ordered for me, until after I had confessed myself the writer of the newspaper extract. And it will appear soon, that Adjutant St. Vincent Ricketts admitted the irregularity to be greater than this. I had also witnesses to prove, that though nominally tried and punished for the riding-school offence, the major, by his address to the regiment after I was punished, showed, that it was for the letter-writing, and not for the other offence, that I had been punished. But it became unnecessary to call those witnesses when the major made his statement. He made the case against himself, as clear a one as I could have proved it.

Much time was wasted in the Court of Inquiry, upon the question of the hour at which the regimental court martial assembled. It had been reported in the newspapers that it assembled at eleven o'clock, or at half-past eleven. This was a point of little importance, but Major-General Sir Thomas Bradford, and the other field officers forming the Court of Inquiry, made it one of my charges against my commanding officer which was 'not proved'. They took a variety of newspaper reports, without questioning me as to their correctness, or whether I had authorized them to be published, and forming these into a series of charges, *after the Court of Inquiry closed*, reported upon them to the commander of the forces, Lord Hill, and to parliament, that they were 'not proved'. The only charges which I in reality made, were two; first, that I had been entrapped and almost compelled into an act of disobedience in the riding school, in order to get me into trouble about another offence of which I was only suspected; and second, that I was tried and sentenced for the disobedience of orders which I could hardly have avoided, while I was punished for the other offence of writing in a newspaper. I did not then, and assuredly do not now, allege that I and others were to act politically as we did, and not to be called to account. We knew the penalty for our contemplated actions to be *death*; but we were prepared to risk that, for the constitutional privileges of the House of Commons and the great cause of reform, for which the nation, with a decision never before equalled in unanimity and earnestness, had pronounced.

The petty crime for which I was tried, was thus worded:

'For highly unsoldier-like conduct on the morning of the 28th instant, in dismounting without leave, when taking his lessons in the riding school, and absolutely refusing to remount his horse when ordered to do so.'

When the officers had assembled, I was sent for. The corporal of the guard placed me between two of the privates of the guard. We marched in that position to the officers' mess-room. A table stood in the centre of the room. The president sat at one end, the four officers sat two on each side, dressed in regimentals and swords; and I was placed and stood at the other end. The corporal and one of the guard withdrew. The other man stood with his carbine (a short gun) at the position of 'carry' by my side, as sentry over me. His name was Thomas Scott. I summoned him to the Court of Inquiry, to prove that the official minutes of the court did not report all the proceedings. He was an unwilling witness. It was dangerous for him, or any of my witnesses, to give evidence in my favour; but he established most of my allegations of unfairness, on the part of the officers who interfered with my questions to the witnesses for the prosecution, the questions to Sergeant Glen, the rough-rider, in particular. Thomas Scott's evidence also proved that the official minutes of the court were only a partial report of the proceedings before it. The Court of Inquiry, in its report to parliament, overlooked this important fact. It censured the conduct of Major Wyndham, and he was reprimanded accordingly; but it should have censured the officers composing the court martial. Here is their official report. The order upon which it was formed, the names of the officers, and the crime, are already quoted:

'The prisoner having been asked by the president whether he objects to any member of the court? answers—

'That he objects to Cornet Macquarrie, as being a *minor*.' (The word *minor* not correctly reported; see the remarks.)

'The objection of the prisoner is overruled by the members of the court.

'The prisoner pleads guilty to the charge.'

'First evidence

'Lieutenant and Riding Master Gillies being duly sworn, states to the court—

'That the prisoner, on the morning of the 28th inst., when taking his lesson in the riding school, turned in out of the ride and threw himself from his horse. Evidence asked him his reason for so doing. He, prisoner, told evidence, "because he could not ride the horse."

He, evidence, told him it was his duty to teach him to ride his horse, and he, evidence, ordered him to mount the horse again, which the prisoner refused to do. Evidence then sent for the corporal and a file of the guard to take the prisoner to confinement, and on their arrival evidence again ordered the prisoner to remount his horse, which he again refused.'

'Second evidence

'Sergeant John Glen, being duly sworn, states to the court—

'That on the morning of the 28th inst. he was in the riding school, in the same ride with the prisoner. Evidence saw the prisoner turn out of the ride and dismount his horse, without receiving any order from the riding master to do so. The riding master went up and asked him "Why he did so?" But evidence did not hear the reply. The riding master then ordered him to mount again, which he did not do.'

'*Question by the prisoner:* Did you or did you not hear my answer?

'*Answer:* I did not hear it.

'Was your impression, when you saw me dismount, that of thinking me disobeying orders, or because I could not ride the horse?

'*Answer:* I did not form an opinion, being in front of the ride.

(See Scott's evidence.)

'*Question by the court:* Upon hearing the riding master order the prisoner to remount, what then was your impression as to the prisoner's conduct?

'*Answer:* I think he was disobeying orders.

'*Question by the court:* Did you ever before see a soldier refuse to remount when ordered?

'*Answer:* Yes, I have; but the man was punished for it.'

'Third evidence

'Corporal Adam M'Clure being duly sworn, states to the court—

'That on the 28th instant he was corporal of the barrack guard, when one of the men came to the guard-room and desired evidence to take a file of the guard to the riding school, which he did. Evidence, upon going into the riding school, saw the prisoner standing near his horse. The riding master said, in presence of evidence, that he would give him (the prisoner) another chance, and asked him to

178

mount the horse. The prisoner said, "No"; evidence then took him to the guard-house.

'*Question by the court:* Did the man appear to have been drinking?

'*Answer:* No.'

'*Defence*

'The prosecution being here closed, the prisoner is put upon his defence, who states to the court that the horse which he was riding was one upon which he never was before, and being unqualified to sit steady upon the horse, the prisoner found it to give way to the reins frequently, which he could not keep easy.'

'*Opinion*

'The court, having duly considered the evidence against the prisoner, are of opinion that he is guilty of the crime laid to his charge.'

'*Character*

'The prisoner calls upon Lieutenant Gillies, who, being duly sworn, states in answer to the prisoner's question as to his general character in the riding school, that until the present time he has considered the prisoner attentive to his drills.

'The prisoner further calls upon Sergeant Glen to speak to his general character, who, being duly sworn, states that he never before saw him refuse to obey any orders.

'*Question by the prisoner:* Do you consider that I was as attentive in the riding school as the other recruits?

'*Answer:* I consider you to have been so.'

'*Sentence*

'The court, having found the prisoner "guilty" of the crime laid to his charge, the same being in breach of the Articles of War, do by virtue thereof sentence him, the prisoner, Alexander Somerville, to receive two hundred lashes in the usual manner of the regiment, at such time and place as the commanding officer may think fit.— M. J. FAWCETT, President. Approved, C. WYNDHAM, Major, commanding Second Dragoons.'

These are the official minutes. They do not set forth all the proceedings of the court. I shall here make a few remarks upon what they omit.

My objection to Cornet Macquarrie was not that he was a 'minor'; but that he was 'too young', being under eighteen years of age, as I and most of the men in the regiment at that time believed; and because he was only learning to ride in the school himself; also, that this was the first court martial he had been upon, and that he could have no experience. Much sensation and unhappy feeling had prevailed in the regiment before I entered it, and still prevailed, arising from an order issued by the Duke of Wellington, which cut off all the years and months from the service of those who had entered the regiment at any age below eighteen. In the time of the war, many youths of sixteen entered the service; some of whom were now old soldiers, and found, by the duke's order, that two years were to be subtracted from that period of service which entitled them to pensions. The order had declared it illegal for any man to be a soldier under the age of eighteen. The duke had more disrespectful words spoken of him in the regiment, for this capricious regulation, than I had heard spoken against him in civil life, for his declaration against reform in all its shapes. The men used to point to Cornet Macquarrie and say, 'There is a boy gets into the regiment because he is the son of a general, and exercises all the privileges of an officer, though under the age declared to be illegal.' And several of them had said in my hearing, in the guard-house, on the day the court was held, that if they were in my place, and about to go before a court martial, they would object to him sitting upon it.

But I regretted having made the objection, almost as soon as it was made. He was not likely to be friendly to me, or even fair in the court, after I had objected to him. Nor was it of any importance to me whether he was under or above eighteen years of age; that question was not involved in my case, as it might have been in the case of an older soldier, who had lost some years of service by having entered the regiment too young.

The question to Sergeant Glen, 'Did you, or *did you not* hear my answer?' is reported as the first question put by me to him. If it had been the first, the form of it would indicate a presumptuous style of examination on my part, which not even the officers accused me of. It was a question several times repeated. I knew that Sergeant Glen did hear my answer, which was, 'I cannot manage the horse.' He made no reply before the court martial, until I repeated the question several times, seemingly, because he did not know whether any reply should be made to a question of mine; or, if any, what reply would be acceptable to the court.

Again, when I put this question, 'Was your impression, when you saw me dismount, that of thinking me disobeying orders, or because I could not ride the horse?' the sergeant stood silent for a considerable time. He knew well that I had been used, and the horse also, to drive it mad, as no recruit or soldier of any age had been. Conscientiously, he could not answer that question against me; but he had twenty-six years of service and was about to be discharged upon a pension, and could not afford to give an answer in my favour. I put several other questions to him, to elicit evidence upon the extraordinary conduct of the riding master, but he did not answer them. The president, Captain Fawcett, interfered, and addressing me angrily, said he could not sit there to hear such questions asked by a prisoner. Captain Clarke said he thought the prisoner had a right to put any questions to the witness, which he might think useful to his defence. Lieutenant Somerville, perhaps because he thought I was a discredit to the name, sneered, and mocking my broad Scotch dialect, repeated the questions after me, and without giving the sergeant time to answer them, said, in the same sneering tone, 'What a mighty great lawyer you are!' (he was an Irishman); and then resuming his natural voice, with a severe tone of military dignity in it, said, 'But you will find it is of no use to be a lawyer here.' The youthful cornet, Macquarrie, laughed, and had his sneer also. The only dignified officers, who behaved as such, and as gentlemen, were Captain Clarke and Cornet Ferlong.

Sergeant Glen at last answered my question in these words: 'I did not form an opinon, being in front of the ride.' Whereupon Captain Fawcett said, pettishly, 'You have made a great deal by that question!' None of these remarks appeared in the minutes of the proceedings of the court martial. Here is an extract from the minutes of the Court of Inquiry referring to this:

'Weedon Barracks, July 26th, 1832.—Private Thomas Scott examined.

* * * * * * * * *

'*By Private Somerville:* Were you present at the court martial held on me, on the 29th of May last, in the barracks at Birmingham? I was.

'Do you remember that Captain Fawcett was president of that court martial? Yes, he was.

'*By the Judge Advocate:* How came it that you were present at that court martial? I was on guard: I went in with the prisoner.

'*By Private Somerville:* Do you remember Captain Fawcett having made any observation on any question put by me to the witness? Yes.

'State what it was. (This was repeated by the court, to whom Scott answered); "When Somerville asked Sergeant Glen, what impression it made upon him, when he turned out of the ride? I cannot tell what Sergeant Glen said; he was some time before he answered it. The question was answered. Captain Fawcett said, 'You have made a great deal by that question!' " '

This answer occasioned looks of surprise in the Court of Inquiry. Those *looks* seemed to interfere with Thomas Scott's memory; not that I believe them to have been so intended. His answer caused a sensation on one side of the table, where it was not expected; and he seemed afterwards to be afraid of renewing the sensation, for he took a long while to answer the subsequent questions. He answered some of them, however, and I quote a few more. The answers printed in *italics* are worth notice.

'What else passed? I cannot exactly recollect; it is a long time since; I cannot say whether it was, "You have made, or, you have not made"; I cannot say which was the expression.

'Do you remember Captain Fawcett saying that he did not sit there to hear such questions put? No; *I cannot say that I do.*

'Do you remember Captain Clarke making any observation on the questions put by me to any witness? Yes; he told the prisoner he was allowed to put any questions he thought proper, through the court.

'What occasioned Captain Clarke to tell me I had a right to put any questions I thought proper? *That is a question I cannot answer.*

'Was it an observation of Captain Fawcett that occasioned the remark of Captain Clarke? *Yes, it was at the time that Captain Fawcett told you that you had made a great deal by that question, that Captain Clarke spoke to you.*

'Did Lieutenant Somerville make any observation on any question I put to the witness? I cannot say; *if he did, I do not remember it.*

'*Cross-examined by Major Wyndham:* Had Sergeant Glen completed his evidence previous to Private Somerville putting the question, which produced the observation of Captain Fawcett? He had answered the question.

'*By the Court:* Had Sergeant Glen said all he had to say before this question was put? I cannot exactly say whether he had or not.

'Was he done speaking? *He was done speaking.*'

The object of these questions put to Thomas Scott, was to make it appear that I had interrupted Sergeant Glen in his evidence before the court martial, and that therefore the president interfered with me. This was not the case. I put no question to Sergeant Glen until I was told by the president, that if I had a question to put to the witness I might now do so. Thomas Scott excused himself from recollecting some of the answers which he should have given on the inquiry, by saying that so many things were said at the court martial, he could not remember them all; that 'Somerville was talking to them almost all the time he was in.' Whereupon there came the following questions:

'*By Major Wyndham:* How did he conduct himself during the trial? I cannot answer that question. I do not understand it.

'*By the Court:* How did he behave in the room; was he proper and respectful, as a soldier should be under the circumstances of being before a court martial? I never was in any court martial before this.

'*By Private Somerville:* Did Captain Clarke say that I had a right to put what questions I thought proper, immediately after the observation of Captain Fawcett? He did.

'*By the Court:* You have said that Somerville spoke nearly the whole time of his trial; to whom did he speak? and was it in a loud tone, or otherwise? He spoke to the members of the court.

'Was it in a loud tone, or what manner, or respectful? *Yes, I think respectful.*

'Do you remember any of the remarks he made to the court? I do not remember them now.'

The manner was respectful. It might be earnest and firm. It was the same then as Major Wyndham stated it to be, when I was ordered to strip and take my punishment. 'He quietly placed himself in the situation to be punished, and received a hundred lashes.' The major might have said that he took them quietly, too. The custom with soldiers is, when accused of a crime, and brought before the commanding officer, to humble themselves and make piteous pleas for forgiveness. 'Please, sir; do, sir; God bless you, sir; do forgive me; it was wrong; I shall always be a good soldier; forgive me this once;' and so forth. If a soldier of manly dignity omits to perform this dog-like cringing, and does not whine and beg to be forgiven, he is looked upon without favour, it may be with enmity. From the evidence of Major Wyndham, quoted in last chapter, it appears that he would have released me from confinement, had I cringed and begged to be forgiven. 'I think the words he said were,' says the major, '*I am sorry for it*; he mentioned something about his horse being unruly; I think he said he could not manage the horse. Those were his words.' And then the commanding officer says, 'I was sorry to see he did not express some contrition; I thought a *soldier* would have said more.' He expected me to beg, implore, and whine, and be unlike a man. So it is with punishment. If the soldier howls like a dog, and cries out, 'Stop, and I'll never do it again! Forgive me; oh! pray do forgive me; as you hope for salvation, by forgiveness of your sins, colonel, have mercy! oh! have pity! I am a bad man, I confess it—mercy! have mercy, good colonel! Every man will call you a good colonel, if you have mercy!' These are a sample of what is usually expected from the *soldier*, according to the major's ideas of him when under punishment. Men who cry out, suffer less than those who do not. The vociferation eases the internal organs which are overcharged with blood, almost to bursting, and are wrung with pain; and it usually procures a remission of part of the sentence. I took the punishment as I conducted my defence before the court martial, with firmness, and, I believe, dignity. Before the court I used no disrespectful word, nor tone, nor gesture; but I endeavoured to prove, by the witnesses for the prosecution (not having been allowed time to call witnesses for the defence), that I was driven into an act of disobedience. It was not an open court, with an applauding auditory present, nor with reporters writing for the world to read. I was a close prisoner, with a sentry over me with a loaded carbine, not a friend on earth knowing my situation, except those comrades in the regiment who trembled for themselves. I knew that punishment was before me, but of what kind I could not assure myself. Indeed I did not think of the punishment when before the commanding officer or the court, so much as I thought of the meanness of the treatment which had brought me to be a prisoner.

The sentence of the court martial was not known until the afternoon parade, at which time the minutes were read. This is customary with all courts martial. The corporal of the guard and a file of men were sent for, when the court was done with me. I was placed between them, and marched back to the guard-house. I had now time to think about the sentence, which was unknown to me; and, forming what I believed to be the worst anticipations of it, looked forward to two months of solitary imprisonment in the black hole, or possibly something less. But, that I might not be disappointed, I placed before myself what seemed to be the worst punishment they were likely to inflict; judging, as I did, from what I had heard of the punishment of other offenders, who had committed worse acts of disobedience than I had done, without any provocation or excuse.

The first intimation which I received of the kind of punishment which I was to suffer, was by overhearing the corporal of the guard say to a trumpeter, named Charles Hunter, who seemed to be asking leave to speak with me in the black hole, that he could not give him leave, but he would go out of sight, and would not *see* that Hunter got access to me, to do what he was going to do. The other men on guard got an intimation that, though it was contrary to orders, they were not to *see* what Charley Hunter did. Accordingly, Charley got the key of the black hole, opened the door, entered, and took a bottle which was hidden about his clothes, and told me that it contained half a pint of rum, to drink it all—I should probably have need of it at the parade, in the riding-school. I asked what he meant? He said some of the men in my room had put pence together, to buy the rum for me. 'But what do you mean by offering me rum? You have not seen me drink liquor of any kind; what do you want me to drink all that rum for?' 'I do not know that you may require it,' he replied; 'but I advise you to drink it. I saw old Owen (the sergeant of the band) go across the barrack-yard a short while since, to the riding-school, with *the green bag* in his hand; perhaps they only want to frighten you: I dare say they won't do more than tie you up; but you know *the green bag* means something.' 'What does it mean?' I asked; 'do you infer from seeing it, that the cats were in it, and that I am to be flogged?' 'Not flogged, perhaps,' he replied; 'but they will try to frighten you. Drink this, and be *plucky*.' 'Not a drop,' said I. 'If they flog me for that charge of disobedience in the riding school, I need no rum to sustain me; I shall have strength enough to bear it.' 'But do; come, drink; it is a common thing. All soldiers try to do this for one another; I have known men drink a pint of rum, and go and take their punishment *like* men.' 'Not one drop for me,' said I, firmly. 'But you will require it when you can't get it.' 'I shall not require it.' 'But I have known men *sing out* dreadfully when punished; if they had got enough of rum, it would have supported them, and they would not have *sung out*.' 'Not one drop for me, Charley Hunter; I shall not *sing out*, I promise you, if they cut me to pieces; but if they do lay a lash on my back, they will hear of it again. Take away that rum; I shall not drink it; no, nor the half of it; nor a drop of it: I shall not touch it.'

Charley replied to this, 'Well, there's no use losing it; if you won't drink it, I know who will.' He took some of it himself, and gave the remainder to one of the men on guard standing close by, and who had promised not to *see* what was done.

I heard the warning trumpet sound; and soon after the trumpet for parade sounded the 'turn out'. A few streaks of light entered by the chinks in the door of the black hole. I could see nothing more of the outward world. I heard the band play, and knew by the sound that the troops were marching. By the music of the march I knew when they had reached the riding school. When the music ceased, I waited anxiously for the door of the black hole to open. The key rattled in the lock; it opened; two of the guard entered, laid hold of me, one on each side, and led me out. I told them they need not lay hold of me; I would go quietly. All the men of the guard, save those on sentry, were formed at the black hole door. I was placed in the centre of them. The regimental sergeant-major gave the command 'quick march', and we stepped off. The large folding doors of the riding school were thrown open; and when we entered were closed behind us. The regiment was formed four deep round the walls, facing inwards. We proceeded to one end of the school. The commanding officer then gave the command to the regiment, 'attention!' and immediately after, 'draw swords!' upon which the regiment drew swords, bringing them to the position of the 'carry', each man's sword upright a few inches in front of his shoulder. The officers stood in an oblong space within the lines of men. The regimental surgeon was also there, the hospital sergeant, and two hospital orderlies. The sergeant of the band stood with the *green bag*, and Farrier Simpson and a trumpeter each stood

186

with a nine-tailed whip, vulgarly called a 'cat' in his hand. The sergeant had two more in the bag, to be ready in case these should give way. The handles were of wood or whalebone, about two feet long, the 'tails' about the same length, each tail two or perhaps three times the thickness of ordinary whip cord, with six hard knots upon it. A form and chair stood close by, and on the form a pailful of water, with some towels in the water to apply to my back, and a basin containing water on the table to give me to drink, should I become faint. These were in charge of the hospital sergeant and his orderlies. A ladder was placed upright against the wall, and several strong-looking ropes, half an inch thick, or thereabouts, with nooses to them, hung about the ladder, and lay on the ground. All these things I saw while advancing to their vicinity, at the upper end of the school. When arrived there, we got 'right about turn', and then the word 'halt'.

The guard withdrew a few paces, so that I should be fully within view of the regiment. The adjutant then handed the written minutes of the court martial to the commanding officer, which the latter held in his hand while giving the commands 'attention', and 'draw swords'. When the men had brought their swords to the 'carry', he gave 'slope swords', then 'steady', and, lastly, 'pay attention to the proceedings of a regimental court martial'. This done, he read the minutes as I have quoted them in the last chapter, his back to me, his face to the regiment. On conclusion he turned to me and said, 'You will take your punishment; strip, sir.'

I proceeded at once to unbutton, and take off my regimental jacket. The sergeant of the band, with great alacrity, came to assist. I said, in an under-tone, that I would take my things off myself. One of the orderlies took my jacket and cap, another my stock, and laid them on the form; I handed my shirt to the sergeant, who fastened it round my middle. One of the orderlies took a rope with a noose on it, and running the noose upon the wrist of my right arm, put the other end through a ring, which was fastened in the wall, at the distance of several yards from the upright ladder. Another orderly took another rope with a noose, and fastening it in like manner upon my left wrist, drew the other end of it through a ring, at the distance of several yards on the opposite side of the ladder. They then drew, each his rope, until my arms were stretched outward, and my breast and face were brought closely and tightly against the ladder. Two other soldiers came with two other ropes with nooses. They lifted my right foot, and put one of the nooses over my foot, and ran it up tightly upon my ankle; and then lifted my left foot, and ran the noose of the other rope tightly upon my left ankle. They each put his rope through a ring in the wall, near the ground, and brought the ends round the upright ladder, and each of my legs, several times, until I was bound so fast that I could not move.

The regimental sergeant-major, who stood behind, with a book and pencil to count each lash, and write its number, gave the command, 'Farrier Simpson, you will do your duty.' The manner of doing that duty is to swing the 'cat' twice round the head, give a stroke, draw the tails of the 'cat' through the fingers of the left hand, to rid them of skin, or flesh, or blood; again swing the instrument twice round the head slowly, and come on, and so forth.

Simpson took the 'cat' as ordered; at least I believe so; I did not see him, but I felt an astounding sensation between the shoulders, under my neck, which went to my toe nails in one direction, my finger nails in another, and stung me to the heart, as if a knife had gone through my body. The sergeant-major called in a loud voice, 'One.' I felt as if it would be kind of Simpson not to strike me on the same place again. He came on a second time a few inches lower, and then I thought the former stroke was sweet and agreeable compared with that one. The sergeant-major counted 'two'. The 'cat' was swung twice round the farrier's head again, and he came on somewhere about the right shoulder blade, and the loud voice of the reckoner said 'three'. The shoulder blade was as sensitive as any other part of the body, and when he came again on the left shoulder, and the voice cried 'four', I felt my flesh quiver in every nerve, from the scalp of my head to my toe nails. The time between each stroke seemed so long as to be agonizing, and yet the next came too soon. It was lower down, and felt to be the severest. The word 'five' made me betake myself to mental arithmetic; this, thought I, is only the fortieth part of what I am to get. 'Six' followed, so on, up to 'twenty-five'. The sergeant-major then said 'Halt!'

Simpson stood back, and a young trumpeter who had not flogged before, took his cat and began. He had practised often at a stable post, or a sack of sawdust, and could handle the instrument as scientifically as any one. He gave me some dreadful cuts about the ribs, first on one side and then on the other. Some one bade him hit higher up, I do not know whom. He then gave them upon the blistered and swollen places, where Simpson had been practising. The pain in my lungs was now more severe, I thought, than on my back. I felt as if I would burst, in the internal parts of my body. I could have cried out; and, I doubt not, would have taken less harm from the punishment had that *firmness*, which phrenologists say is strongly developed in my cranium, permitted me to break my resolution. I had resolved that I would die, before I would utter a complaint or a groan. I detected myself once giving something like a groan, and to prevent its utterance again, I put my tongue between my teeth, held it there, and bit it almost in two pieces. What with the blood from my tongue, and my lips, which I had also bitten, and the blood from my lungs, or some other internal part ruptured by the writhing agony, I was almost choked, and became black in the face.

The hospital sergeant, seeing this, brought the basin of water, and put it to my lips; I indignantly withdrew my head from it, and the revulsion, or change of feeling, somewhat relieved me.

It now became Simpson's second turn to give twenty-five. Only fifty had been inflicted, and the time since they began was like a long period of life: I felt as if I had lived all the time of my real life in pain and torture, and that the time when existence had pleasure in it was a dream, long, long gone by. Simpson got up among the old sores; the strokes were not so sharp as at first; they were like blows of heavy weights, but more painful than the fresh ones. It was now that he— probably more inclined to remember that he was my friend than a farrier—was commanded in a loud voice, in these words, formerly quoted, 'Farrier Simpson, do your duty.' He travelled downwards, and came on heavier than before, but, as I thought, slower. It seemed a weary slowness for the sergeant-major, to be only counting the fifteenth and sixteenth of the third twenty-five. I then uttered the only words which I spoke during the whole time, namely, 'Come quicker on, Simpson, and let it be done; you are very slow.' The poor fellow was slow, from aversion to the task; I do not know if he gave the strokes more quickly; they all seemed to last too long.

When the other youngster had reached, or nearly, his second twenty, I felt as if I could yield, and beg forgiveness; but the next moment the coward thought was rebuked within me, and banished. 'Not from them,' said I, mentally, 'shall I beg forgiveness,' but I prayed to God to put it into their minds to stop, and pardon me the remainder. When this five-and-twenty was completed, which made a hundred, the

commanding officer said, 'Stop, take him down, he is a young soldier.'
I was then unbound. One of the wet towels was spread upon my back, my jacket laid loosely over the towel, and I was led to the hospital between two men. There, a cloth dipped in a lotion of some kind, was put over my skin, and I was laid down on my back. It soon became so stiff, that to rise seemed as impossible as to rise with the weight of a ton fastened to me. I felt as if dragged down by tons of heaviness. When fresh lotions were put to my back, two orderlies came, one on each side, and lifted me by the arms.

The only remark I made about the punishment, was on entering the ward where I was to lie. Some of the patients expressed sympathy for me; and I said, 'This shall be heard of, yet; I shall make it as public over England as newspapers can make it.' I said no more; but the patients were carried to the Court of Inquiry, fifty miles, to prove that I had 'used threats' on entering the hospital.

You will remember the crime for which I was tried, which referred to the riding-school, and that only. Here is Major Wyndham's own statement of what he said to the regiment, as soon as I was removed:

'As far as I can recollect, I said—"Men, you are here assembled; I have a circumstance to mention to you, relating to us all." I think I said—"I have discovered, at last, the man who wrote the letter." I think I said—"I am happy for it, because the odium cannot fall on any other person." I think I went on to say—"I regretted it very much, and I am sorry to see anybody write in the newspapers, or publish a libel on the regiment, and particularly so young a soldier as the man just punished." '

*   *   *   *   *   *   *

'I then went on to say, that I had been written to on the subject of the state of the regiment, as much had been said about the political unions, and our having joined them; and I wrote back in return, that you would ever find the Greys steady and firm like rocks; and I remember bringing back to their recollections, two winters ago, when I had them in London, when we were up three nights in the riding school; I brought back to their recollection a circumstance that was asked me there, and I said, the Greys would be ever firm and would do their duty,' and so forth.

The report of soldiers who took special notice of what the major said, some of whom I summoned to the inquiry, was, that the major began with the words, 'Men, I am happy to inform you that I have found out the writer of the letter, and you have just seen him punished.' After the major's own statement, it was not deemed desirable to subject these witnesses to the hazard of giving evidence in my behalf. He had admitted nearly all which I sought to prove.

I may here add the testimony which Major Wyndham bore, both to my general character and riding qualities, before the Court of Inquiry:

'He had not been complained of before this circumstance. He had been well spoken of before this.'

And again: 'I always heard from the riding master that he was doing very well.'

And again, to the court: 'Had you seen him ride before the 28th?' 'Several times.'

'What did you think of his riding?' 'I think he rides very well for a man of his figure, for the short time he had been learning.'

[19] Major Wyndham had charged at Waterloo, and in spite of the censure passed on him as a result of the Somerville case, duly succeeded to the command of the regiment. He retired in 1837, but was given dignified employment as Lieutenant-Governor of the Tower, and survived beyond his eightieth year, to die in 1872.

[20] Wyndham being the only major, there was no officer of field rank to preside. Captain Fawcett seems to have been a ranker; Clarke ultimately commanded the regiment; Lieutenant Somerville had till recently been adjutant.

CHAPTER XVII

Discharge from Hospital—The Public first Hear of
My Punishment—The Sensation

FROM the evidence of the hospital sergeant before the Court of
Inquiry, which I shall here quote, it will be seen that I was only six
days in the hospital; that I went out as cured, and fit for duty; and that
he endeavoured to make it appear that I had been but very slightly
punished. I had a purpose to serve by escaping from the hospital as
soon as possible. While there, I could not communicate with the public
or any friend, being closely watched; and I had resolved that my
punishment should be made known, as soon as I could publish it. At
the same time it was desirable, on the part of those who had caused its
infliction, that I should be as short a time in the hospital as possible,
that it might seem to be a light punishment; for already, though unknown to me, there were disagreeable rumours about it circulating in
Birmingham. But I was neither cured nor sent to duty. I was not
ordered or permitted to mount a horse. The evidence of the sergeant
was given on the 26th of July, when the punishment, inflicted on me
on the 29th of May, had become the subject of parliamentary discussion
on more than one occasion, and of newspaper discussion every day, in
all parts of the kingdom. It now assumed a serious aspect for the credit
of the regimental commanding officer, and the court martial. This may
account for the hospital sergeant endeavouring to make it appear to
have been a light punishment. I was not so much cut and mangled as
some soldiers have been by the same number of lashes. But six knots
on each tail, nine tails to the 'cat', give fifty-four wounds at each stroke,
which, again multiplied by one hundred strokes, give five thousand
four hundred wounds, produced by the sharp blows of hard knots.
The persons who wield the instrument of punishment are taught by
long practice, at inanimate substances, to wield it so as each knot shall
'tell'. I believe it is quite correct to say, that those who bleed freely
suffer least pain, and run the least danger of losing their lives. Here is

the witness from the hospital, produced by Major Wyndham and cross-examined by me:

'26th July, 1832. Sergeant William Sykes, hospital sergeant of the Scots Greys, was called in; and after the usual caution from the judge advocate, was examined as follows.' (The caution was, not to divulge anything which occurred in the court):

'*By the Court:* How long have you been in the service? About twenty-six years.

'*By Major Wyndham:* Did you receive Private Somerville into the hospital, on the 29th May, after he had received his punishment? Yes.

'Describe the appearance of his back. I considered that he was very slightly punished.

'Was there much laceration, and did he bleed? He bled a little in one place; but there was very little laceration to what I have seen.

'Did you dress his back; and with what? I dressed it with goulard water; that was the first cloth put on his back when he came into the hospital.

'Was there, or not, any blood to be seen, except from the first cloth? None, that I saw.

'When was he discharged from the hospital as fit for his duty? On the 4th of June, about two o'clock in the day.

'How many days was that after he came in? He was six days in the hospital; because he came in on the 29th, between four and five o'clock, and was discharged on the 4th of June.

'Has he since been in the hospital at Birmingham? Not at Birmingham; at Coventry he was, as I have heard.

'*Cross-examined by Private Somerville:* Have you been medically educated? and have you had opportunities of frequently witnessing the consequence of military flogging? No; I have not been medically educated; I have seen several instances of military flogging.

'Is it not generally expected that the parties who are appointed to administer the lash, in such cases, will do their duty? Yes, certainly.

'Do you believe that the parties appointed to that duty, in my case, failed at all in the execution of the duty they had to perform? I could not answer that.

'Was there any indication, from the appearance of the back, that one hundred lashes had been inflicted? By the appearance of the back, I would suppose it had not been so.

'Then can you undertake to say, from the appearance of the back, that one hundred lashes were not inflicted? No, I could not say that.

'From your experience in such cases, how many ordinary military lashes would have produced the effects you saw? I have seen fifty produce such effects.

'If you have seen fifty produce such an effect, do you, as a military man, believe that the persons appointed to punish me did their duty? I could not say.

'If you have seen fifty lashes produce the effects which, in my case, were produced by one hundred, do you believe that the persons administering the fifty lashes, which produced the same effect, exceeded their duty? I could not say.

'Do you know or believe that the persons who punished me have been accused of neglecting their duty? No.

'Describe the width and depth of the effects of the punishment which I received. I could not exactly describe that; it was on both of the shoulders. I could not exactly describe the width.

'Describe it as near as you can. Ten or twelve inches, from one side to the other. It was on the shoulders, chiefly.

'How often did you remove the cloth from my back, yourself? Once or twice myself. I could not exactly say the number of times. When the doctor came round in the morning, I generally moved it off, and put another one on.

'Then why did you say there was blood only on the first cloth? Because the first lotion which was made, I emptied it from the vessel it was in, and there was no stain of blood in the vessel.

'*By the Judge Advocate:* Can you tell whether the same quantity of punishment produces different effects upon different subjects? I have seen one man get the same quantity as another, and not appear to be so much hurt; some men's skins are more tender than others; to the best of my judgment, that is the cause.

'Do you mean to say, that if a given number of lashes be inflicted in different instances, with the same severity, yet in some cases the effect may be more perceptible than in others? That is what I mean.

'Is it possible, from the appearance of the back, to judge with any degree of precision how many lashes may have been inflicted? I could not judge myself.

'Have you seen many cases, in which the infliction of one hundred lashes has produced more visible effects than in this instance? I do not remember any case in which one hundred were given.

'How long have you been hospital sergeant? Six years hospital sergeant; five years corporal in the hospital, before that.

'(The witness was directed to withdraw.)

'It was here stated, on the part of Private Somerville, that it was his wish that it should be recorded on the minutes of this inquiry, that he did not go into the hospital at Coventry, in consequence of the effects of his military punishment at Birmingham; *neither had he ever said to any person, that his going into the hospital at Coventry was in consequence of such punishment.*'

My object in stating this to the court, was to free myself from the imputation of being the author of all the reports which appeared in the newspapers about me. The assistant surgeon, attended by some of the principal medical gentlemen of Coventry, came and looked at me, and asked some questions while I was in the hospital there, for the purpose of disproving the newspaper reports.

As several days of the sittings of the court had been taken up in receiving evidence, to rebut newspaper rumours which I had not authorized nor originated, but for which I was held liable, and which were continually renewed and repeated, though I begged and implored the conductors of those papers to refrain from making such statements; I was desirous of freeing myself from the responsibility of them, as far as I could. Moreover, at that time, I did not believe that my ailments in the Coventry hospital were a consequence of the punishment. But I have since had good reasons for changing that opinion. I find the following evidence, on this point of the case, in the minutes of the Court of Inquiry:

'26th July, 1832. Alexander Stewart, assistant surgeon to the Scots Greys, was then called in, and, having received a similar caution to the other witnesses by the judge advocate, was examined, as follows, by Major Wyndham:

'How long have you been assistant surgeon to the Scots Greys? About eleven years.

'Are you now in the hospital at Coventry? Yes, I am stationed at Coventry.

'Have you been so during the last two months? Yes.

'Was Private Somerville admitted into the hospital, at Coventry, at any time since the 4th of June? Yes, he was; on the 28th of June.

'Was he admitted into the hospital at Coventry, with any complaint connected with any corporal punishment he had received? No.

'When was he discharged from the hospital? He was discharged the 8th of July; and he was seen on the 10th, and was excused from a certain duty; riding duty, for instance.

'You are quite sure it was not at all connected with his punishment? Certainly not.

'What was the matter with Private Somerville? Boils.'

I did not then believe that my illness, an eruption of very extraordinary boils, on my back, beneath the place punished, arose from the punishment; and Mr. Stewart, I doubt not, gave his opinion conscientiously. But, since the year 1832, I have had opportunities of studying the question, particularly in Spain, and I am now certain that, in almost every case of corporal punishment, there are secondary symptoms; that the violence to the muscular or nervous systems, or to both, or to some quality of the body, which is a mystery to an unprofessional person like me, and probably so to the profession, causes a diseased state of the fluids of the body, which disease takes an inward direction, in some cases settling on the lungs, or other internal organ, enfeebling, and, ultimately, destroying the life of the patient; or it takes an outward direction, as in my case, breaking through the skin in boils, thereby saving the life of the patient; or it remains, festers, inflames, and causes a speedy death by mortification, as in the case of Frederick White, of the 7th Hussars, whom a coroner's jury declared to have died, at Hounslow barracks, from the effect of corporal punishment, in 1846. Mr. Warren, the surgeon of the Hussars, was as certain, at the coroner's inquest on the body of Frederick White, that death was not the result of the flogging, as Mr. Stewart was, before the Court of Inquiry, that my secondary symptoms were not the result of my flogging. Mr. Wakley, the coroner, and the jury did not, however, follow Mr. Warren's opinion. On the medical evidence of other witnesses, they gave a verdict that Frederick White's death was caused by corporal punishment. I read the reports of the coroner's inquest in the newspapers, from day to day, with intense interest. Mr. Wakley was charged, by certain parties, with having a political object to serve, in prosecuting that inquiry as he did. I was residing at the distance of 200 miles from Hounslow at that time, and, from the business I was then engaged upon, could not, without extreme inconvenience, offer myself at that inquest as a witness. Yet I had resolved to incur the inconvenience, and to present myself as a witness, to state what the secondary symptoms were in my own case; what they had been in the cases of men who had suffered corporal punishment in the British army, and with whom, through a fellow-feeling, I had held conversation; and what they had been in the cases of men whom I saw punished, during two years of military service in Spain. But it was suggested that my evidence might be objected to, as prejudiced. The allegation against the coroner seemed likely to be more strongly urged against me; wherefore I proceeded no farther in my purpose of presenting myself at Hounslow. But I make this public statement now, that those who gave the verdict that Frederick White died from the effect of corporal punishment, may have such consolation, the justice of their verdict, and their impartiality, having been questioned, as they think fit to derive from one who has had some experience in these matters; but, more especially, I make this statement now, to direct the attention of the students of surgery, and medicine more pointedly, to this class of diseases. The profession has long admitted that lock-jaw may follow wounds which give a violent shock to the nervous system; cases are known in which death by lock-jaw has followed the cutting of a toe nail too near the quick. Is it unreasonable then to suppose that such a shock to the corporal system, nervous, muscular, or whatever it may be, should produce such effects as mortification at the lower extremity of the spine, as in the case of Frederick White, or boils at the lower extremity of the spine, as in the case of A. S.? I have little doubt now that, had those boils not appeared externally, I should have died of mortification, as Frederick White did.

I was discharged from hospital at Birmingham, on the 4th of June, at two o'clock. I felt excessively weak in body, and somewhat agitated in mind. I proceeded to the troop sergeant-major, and obtained the arrears of pay which had accumulated while I was a prisoner and a patient; and from him I went to the regimental sergeant-major, and obtained leave to go out of barracks. I walked up Coleshill-street, towards the Bull Ring. In a narrow passage opposite the end of New-street, there was a quiet-looking tavern, into which I went, and, sitting down, asked the landlord to be allowed to write a letter. There were several people sitting over their pipes, ale, and politics; and they, observing that I did not call for any liquor to drink, offered their pots to me, with that frankness which is so peculiarly a characteristic of the inhabitants of Birmingham. 'Come, soldier, drink!' said one; 'Drink with me,' said another. I declined; told them I had been ill, was not entirely recovered, and must not partake of strong liquors.

They allowed me to finish my letter without farther remark. While I was folding it, that landlord said, 'What about that soldier that was flogged a week ago?' I replied that I could hardly tell what about him. 'That is a strange thing,' said he, addressing the people who sat beside him; 'I have inquired of several of the dragoons about this case of flogging, and not one will give an answer. There is something about it they don't wish to be known. I cannot even learn what the crime was that the man committed' (addressing me); 'cannot you tell what the man was flogged for?' I replied, 'No; I believe there will be some difficulty in knowing what he was flogged for.' I rose to get a light to seal my letter, from a candle which stood on the mantel-shelf, for lighting pipes. While about to apply the wax to the candle, I observed a small piece of printed paper placed in a glazed frame. It was the passage of my letter, cut from the newspaper in which it had been inserted. 'Aye!' exclaimed one of the persons present, 'read that. There is a soldier for you! that man would not be afraid to tell us about his comrade, that has been flogged: the half of you soldiers are such mean-spirited tools of your officers, you are afraid to speak.' 'Perhaps you would not speak so fast,' said I, 'were you a soldier, and subject to the consequences of speaking.' 'Would I not?' he returned: 'were I a soldier, no comrade of mine should be flogged; I would run my sword through the first man, no matter what his rank, who offered to lay a lash on any comrade of mine.' 'But what if they laid it on yourself?' 'The man is not born who would dare lay a lash on me,' he replied. And to the same effect the others joined with him.

I had not sealed the letter while this conversation proceeded, as I wished to see what turn it would take. The speakers were all too vehement and boisterous about their heroism for me to trust them with my secret, except the landlord, who seemed more reasonable and calm. I called him aside, went into another apartment with him, and, unfolding the letter, asked him to read it. He took it; started with astonishment, trembled as he read; took me by the hand, and said, 'I see it all; great heavens! is it possible? My dear fellow, sit down; pray sit down; you will have justice done to you in Birmingham. By the just God of heaven! I do not know the people of Birmingham, if you do not get speedy and ample redress. Sit down, my poor, unfortunate man; tell me the first thing that I can do for you— everything, anything is at your service!'

I was completely overpowered by this outgushing of kindness. The firmness with which I had taken the punishment, and the sense of wrong which had sustained that firmness, had not left me at any time, night or day, until now. I gave way, sat down, and was a child, without the power of speech. He sat down with me, and was like myself.

There is no tavern now at that place, nor do I now remember his name. I had no opportunity of calling there after that day, the 4th of June, until the month of October. Unfortunate in business, he had left the house before that time, and I have never been able to find him since.

He saw from the letter that it was to go to London, to the newspaper in which the extract had appeared which led to the punishment. He suggested that it should be shown to the editor of the *Birmingham Journal*. He carried it to Mr. Lewis, who 'stopped the press', and gave a brief notice of the case; and then forwarded the letter to London. The notice of it, from the *Birmingham Journal*, was reprinted in an Edinburgh paper, in which my brother James saw it first; and I believe his eyes were troubled when it came before them. The late Mr. Samuel Smith, of London, editor of the paper to which I addressed the letter, caused the matter to be brought before the House of Commons, by Mr. Joseph Hume. Through those channels, it soon led to an amount of excitement, exceedingly disagreeable and dangerous in its intensity, both to the officers of the regiment and to me. The populace hooted the officers whenever they appeared in public; and the newspapers, from their Birmingham correspondents, published reports, few of them authorized by me, most of them exaggerated, some of them unfounded, but all of them charged upon me. In the streets of Birmingham and adjacent towns, scores of persons hawked papers about, and cried them, 'with a full, true, and particular account,' most of which was the invention of some enterprising printer, or flying stationer. On the first Sunday after the affair became known, the streets in the neighbourhood of the barracks were crowded with people all the day, and up to a late hour at night. The people were not allowed to come in, nor the soldiers allowed to go out. But I was told that no restriction was placed upon me. I availed myself of this leave, though more than suspecting that it would be satisfactory if I went out and did something indiscreet. I determined not to associate with any of the civilians without the gates, nor to go to the house where I had received so much kindness from the landlord. Nobody in the crowds knew me; but many of them inquired eagerly for Somerville. 'What are they doing to him?' 'Why don't they allow him to come out?' They thought the gates were closed to keep him in, and that all the regiment were detained within with him: none of them knew that they were talking to him. Mr. Chilton, a button-maker, and Mr. Massey, now in the office of the clerk of the peace, ascertained who I was, by some means—the particulars of which I have forgotten—and I spent a part of the evening at the house of one of them.

In the course of a few days, it was deemed advisable to send me to my troop at Coventry. A young horse belonging to my troop, which, like me, had not yet joined, but which had been trained at headquarters, was allotted as mine. I was ordered to get ready, in full marching order; a private, named Merry, who occasionally rode between Birmingham and Coventry with orders, was sent with me. Thus, mounted on as stately and spirited a grey trooper as was in the regiment, and attended by Merry, on his excellent trotter, I was paraded and inspected one morning, and sent to Coventry.

We had eighteen miles to walk, trot, canter, or loiter over, the time at our own taking; no orders given. It was a morning in June, the sunny June of England. The corn-fields, and the hedge-rows around them, were green; gardens were flowery; the windows and the cottage doors were bordered with blooming roses; the birds made music in the trees; the honey-bees made honey, and hummed in the chorus with the birds; the busy haymakers made hay; the eye, the ear, and every sense, confessed that June was one of the books of a great—a universal poem; the leaves opened, pictorial on every page, at every line, that the meanest creature might read; that the very breath of living Nature, the soft air perfumed in meadow hay, was poetry. Sunshine was brilliant everywhere, save on some spot where lay a shadow; but even the shadows had almost disappeared, the sun was so high. And so with me, the exhilarating influence of the summer scenery, enjoyed for the first time that year, and hope that rose and shone high over all troubles—not that I had any reason to bid hope ascend, but because it was natural that it should arise after a time of depression—it left upon me hardly the shadow of a trouble. I was only reminded of them occasionally by some mower in the fields, who, seeing two dragoons riding leisurely along the road from Birmingham, consulted seemingly with his fellow mowers, threw down his scythe, came to the wayside, and asked, 'Soldiers, how does Somerville get on?—what is he doing?—what are they doing with him?'—and so forth.

I was unwilling to answer those questions; but Merry, who had something of the nature indicated in his name, gave most of them an answer. At one place only, the halfway house, where we dismounted for half an hour, he told that this was the man himself present. I felt abashed that he had done so; for the news spread instantly, and people came running from every house, garden, and farm field. We could hardly get away from them; and when at last we mounted and trotted away, they set up shouts and waved hats after us, as long as we were in sight.

I was well received at Coventry by the soldiers, and most of the non-commissioned officers, and by all the officers of my troop. Two or three individuals made themselves as disagreeable as they could contrive the means of doing; one of them, the troop sergeant-major, who brought the letters from the post-office every day, used to bring my letters to me as if staggering under their weight; jeering me at the number and quality of my correspondents, which was the chief reason why I answered very few letters; but he, and those who joined with him, were exceptions. When he discovered that the officers did not treat me with derision, but with respect, he became respectful also.

People took it into their heads to pass resolutions at public meetings, and to send these formally written out; rhymsters sent rhymes, some of them lithographed or printed; others wrote letters avowedly to obtain my autograph in answer; and all of them were offended, most of them writing afterwards in newspapers, calling me 'an ungrateful man', 'unworthy of their sympathy', and so on, because I had not acknowledged their complimentary resolutions, rhymes, or letters. It did not occur to them, that I was still a soldier with daily duty to perform, and not possessed of an office and assistant clerk, to reply to twenty, forty, and sometimes fifty letters received in a day. I had comparatively few letters from Scotland, which probably led me to take the more notice of one or two which came from strangers there. One of these, from a person named Craig, in the vicinity of Airdrie, stated, that it was written on behalf of himself and a number of friends, who were desirous of knowing all the facts of my case; that I need not fear to give him every particular, as no improper use would be made of the communication. Being in the hospital when I got that letter, I had time to answer it in detail. I stated some matters, which though all true, I would not have written had I known the difficulty they were ultimately to place me in. I made it a special request that the letter should be considered private. Mr. Craig, it turned out, was the Airdrie correspondent of a Glasgow newspaper. He sent my letter at once to his paper, for publication, omitting only that part of it, in which I requested that the whole might be kept private. It was published in that paper; was copied into *The Times*, and other London daily papers, and was made part of the groundwork of the Court of Inquiry[21]; the statements in it being taken as the charges made by me against Major Wyndham. Most of these were a relation of private conversations with the major, and with soldiers who told me what the major had said, which I could not prove; and which I should not have dreamt of preferring as public charges for the Court of Inquiry. Yet this gentleman thought himself ill-used, like some others, when I complained of his putting me in that position. 'Oh,' said he and they, 'have we not caused the Court of Inquiry to be held, by publishing these statements?' 'Yes,' said I, 'but the court has declared the greater part of them to be not proved; private conversations, to which there were no witnesses, were not intended as public charges to be proved before the Court of Inquiry.'

I was not personally known in Coventry for a considerable time, save to a very few persons. It was amusing to hear the remarks that were made, and the questions asked of me about myself, by those to whom I was unknown. I usually made a joke of the subject. More than once this was like to have ended in mischief, by those who thought I treated a better man than myself with contempt, that better man being myself.

'Soldier, sup with me; come, take my glass,' one would say; 'Take my pot,' another would say, 'and tell us how Somerville gets on. How is it they don't let him out of barracks? eh? You don't know; you do know; you are one of those who are ashamed of him, I suppose. Drink his health; you won't drink his health? Here, Jim, hold my pipe, let me past you; I'll make this soldier drink Somerville's health. You won't drink it. By the pot in my hand you shall have this potful to his health, either in you or on you; will you drink long life and health to Somerville the soldier, and the freedom of opinion?' 'No!' 'Then you shall have it about you; will you drink his health?' 'No.' 'There it is then; now what do you say?'

This occurred one day in a public house, to which I had gone to read the news. A pot of beer was thrown on my clothes, and partly in my face, disfiguring white trousers and scarlet coat most foully. I started to my feet to shake it off; they thought I was going to fight them, and they cautioned me not to try that; for if I would not drink to the health of the best man in the regiment, they would not only throw the ale over me, but perhaps give me a thrashing as well; and that I had better be off with what I had got, lest I fared worse. I spoke to them to this effect. 'I shall go; but before I leave you, as we shall never meet again, if I can avoid the meeting, let me inform you, that you have spoiled the clothes of the man you profess to have a respect for; you have thrown beer in his face; you have committed a gross indignity upon him; you profess to admire what you call his assertion of the freedom of opinion; and because he has chosen to have his own opinions in your company, and to resist dictation as to whose health he should drink to, you commit a gross outrage upon him.'

'What!' they exclaimed together, and one after another, 'are you Somerville? If you be, let us shake hands; let us be friends; we did not know you.' 'Off hands!' I said; 'no shaking of hands with me. Your insult would have been equally unworthy of men who deserve to be called men, had you committed it upon another person. My notions about the freedom of opinion, which you profess to admire, differ from yours. If you would promote the freedom of opinion, do not begin by being social tyrants.' And so I left them.

One Sunday evening in July, about seven o'clock, I received an unexpected order to get myself and horse accoutred, and go to Birmingham. I was to take none of my kit with me, only to take my rolled cloak and sword. By this I knew that I was to return soon. I went off, and had a pleasant trot to Birmingham, alone, in the cool evening. I say alone, because nobody accompanied me; but the turnpike road was peopled, especially near Birmingham, the fine weather of the Sunday having invited the people to walk and loiter about. As I trotted past, the inquiry was renewed by every group—'Have you come from Coventry, soldier? how does Somerville get on?' But I did not halt to answer any question.

On entering the barracks things seemed changed. The regimental sergeant-major called to a man to come and take my horse, rub it down, feed it, and attend to it in the morning. And then he took me to his own room; invited me to take refreshment with him; told me that there was to be a Court of Inquiry held at Weedon; that I had been sent for, to choose and arrange my witnesses; that I was to give him (the sergeant-major) a list of them, to be taken to the orderly-room next day; but that he hoped I would not put him in the list; he was so nervous, if called upon to give evidence on the most trifling case, that he would esteem it a great favour if I would not summon him. I replied that I could not possibly do without him. He bade me not decide too soon, to take until tomorrow to consider. I considered until the morrow: but it was to tell him that he must go, I could not possibly excuse him. He said he could give no evidence that would do me any good. I said that, as to that, I should run the risk of it; his name must be on the list. I looked forward to the proof of the fact by him, that through him I had not been allowed to call witnesses on the court martial; and he knew that this was my purpose. He tried cajolery again, but I would not be cajoled: 'You shall be one of my witnesses,' said I.

Having given in the list of those whom I required on the Monday morning, my horse was prepared for me by the man to whom it was given on the previous evening; I mounted, and rode to Coventry. We were all to be at Weedon Barracks, in Northamptonshire, on the following day. Conveyances were provided for the men who were going as witnesses, none of them being mounted. I was at liberty to travel in any way I chose. I went by the London mail, with the late Mr. Richard Marriott, of Coventry. We left that city about 10 a.m. I got a number of letters just before we set out, which I read on the coach. One of them was of peculiar interest; its arrival at that time, and the arrival of the writer in England, after being long lost, was so remarkable, as to prove most truly, that 'Truth is strange, stranger than fiction'; as you will see in the next chapter.

[21] *The Times*, 17 July 1832; by that time the subject had already been debated in the Commons (June 19) and *The Times* had had a leader calling for an enquiry (5 July).

CHAPTER XVIII

At this Momentous Crisis, Singular Reappearance of a Long-lost Brother

IN some of the early chapters I mentioned my brother Peter, and alluded to his being apprenticed as a joiner. From the time of my herding the cows at Branxton, in my eleventh year, until now, I had not seen him; and, during nearly half of those intervening twelve years, none of our family knew in what part of the world he was, nor if living or dead. There was too much reason for our not knowing where he was, during the latter years of his absence, as I shall in this chapter relate.

He and I—he with a trade, and I only a labourer—were unlike our other two brothers; for that one of the other two who had learned no trade, raised himself from hedging and ditching as a labourer, by self instruction and sheer perseverance, to offices of trust and good emolument, which he still holds, and the other, with a trade, made a good use of it. Peter and I, circumstanced like them, did less than either. When he had served about two years and a half, as a joiner and cartwright, with Mr. Mason, of Spott, Haddingtonshire; he broke his apprenticeship, and went to the establishment of Mr. Weatherston, of Chirnside, Berwickshire, who was celebrated through the south-east of Scotland as a millwright and mechanical engineer. Though no cause whatever can or should justify a youth in leaving his apprenticeship until legally released, there were some extenuating circumstances in his case. In the first place, his mechanical ability was of an order, even when a youth, above the average of journeymen, and he was flattered by neighbours who could appreciate it, into the belief that he should aim at more than the life of a joiner or cartwright. His master gave him the best work to do, which, doubtless, was an advantage to the apprentice; but the latter receiving no wages, and having the certainty of receiving none until the four years for which he was bound were expired, the idea that he was giving the master more than an equivalent for board and lodging and instruction, was not unnatural, though it was improper. But there was a much stronger reason for his doing as he did. Our father was very poor during those years; his wages as a labourer, now that he was decaying in strength—literally worn down with hard work—did not average above eight shillings per week: in a year after, he was reduced to seven shillings, and in two years, to six shillings a week. Thus it was that, having seen the struggles in the family, to purchase joiners' tools for Peter when going to his apprenticeship, and find him in clothes, I gave up all thought of going to any trade as an apprentice; though my poor father said many a time, seeing that I had a natural bent for constructiveness (for I was continually making something, constructing and rigging ships, making water-wheels with machinery attached, making new gun-stocks for old gun barrels, and so forth)—my father used to say, that if I had set my heart upon any trade, he would pinch himself down a little lower in living (heaven knows he lived lowly enough!) to get me through my apprenticeship; that it would be unfair, because Peter had broken his indenture, to think that I would do so too. Then he would proceed thus: 'And may be, *Wull* (William) would help, though he has done a great deal for us already, and it would be hard to ask him to do more; yet, with the Lord's blessing, we might warsel (wrestle) through, and get you a trade; and, I dare say, you would na be unmindfu' of your auld mother and me, when we are worn out.' 'No,' I used to reply, 'I'll work at "my ain hand" at hedging, ditching, breaking stones, or be a ploughman, or whatever comes readiest: I have no desire to go to any trade.'

I hope that this reply to my father, which was not the truth, is not indelibly recorded against me. My personal desire was very different; but I saw that to carry it into operation was impossible; and he seemed so desirous of knowing if I inclined to go to a trade, was so incapable of maintaining me through an apprenticeship, yet was so willing and ready to 'pinch himself still lower' to do so, that I withheld my secret inclinations from him. Peter, as an apprentice, was similarly affected. He saw our father struggling to provide clothes for him, our mother to have them at all times in good order; and that, with those struggles, only the very humblest kind could be provided. Again, I say, that nothing of this natute can justify a young man in breaking his apprenticeship. But he did so, and caused more unhappiness to our parents, than all their struggles to provide tools and clothes for him had done. My father, with his keen sense of right and wrong, felt it a dishonour to have a son who had broken a contract. Peter, knowing the family sorrow which he had thus occasioned, refrained from visiting us as usual, though Chirnside was within an easy day's journey.

I did not see him again, as my herding kept me closely at home. Nor would I have known much, or anything of his mechanical talents, until years after, when I had an opportunity of seeing them, had it not been for an accidental meeting with Mr. Weatherston, some time in the year 1829. I was then engaged cutting timber with old David White-head, at Renton. David had no great pretensions to excellence as a joiner and cartwright. Most people who saw me working with him, thought I was a journeyman; and not knowing that I made sparred gates and doors, and mended carts and ploughs, sawed the trees into deals, and so forth, without having learned the trade, they thought that master and journeyman were much alike. And truth to tell, our handiwork was not greatly different; we put timber enough in it, and gave it strength; but for elegance and finish, it was somewhat behind the age we lived in. One wet day I was in Tammy Grant's, and found Mr. Weatherston sitting beside the half-mutchkin stoup. Somebody named me as I entered, pronouncing my name, as it is usually done in that part of Scotland, Simeral. 'What Simerel are ye?' said Weatherston. 'One of my faither's Simerals,' I replied. 'Onybody could tell that,' said he; 'but what are ye, what do ye do?' Some one present told him that I was David Whitehead's man—that I was a joiner. *'Dawvit's man!'* he exclaimed; 'ye are a queer joiner, I'se be bound, that works wi' *Dawvit.*' He mused a few minutes, as if searching in the lumber of a well-filled memory for a recollection that had not been in use for a long time; and, getting hold of the recollection, he said, 'Simerel! there *have* been men of that name that could work. I had one Pate Simerel some years syne with me' (Pate is a familiar substitute for Peter); 'Pate was a lad that could handle his tools. He was none of your *Dawvit's* joiners, not he; that Pate Simerel came to me when he had served little mair than half an apprenticeship; he offered to serve it out with me. I did not like taking him on, as he had run away; but he had a relation in our town, John Temple, a decent man; and he told me the lad had a decent faither and mother, and that the lad was decent too, and so I took him on; and when I found what was in him, I made him a journeyman in almost no time. That Pate Simerel (addressing some third parties) was one of the best millwrights that I ever had in my shop, and that is saying a great deal: he could put his hand to anything;

I could send him to mend an auld mill, or put up a new mill; and, though he was one of the youngest hands I had, he would make it go like clockwork, and get over all difficulties, though I was not there myself.' Then turning to me—'Aye, lad, Pate was a chiel that could work with his tools, and design work for others. He was none of Dawvit's sort of joiners. You! you are liker a ploughman than a tradesman; and yet, when I look at you, there is some likeness in the face; but he was a tall, thin, genteel lad, and didna look so like as if he suppit brose three times a day, as you do.'

'What became of that Pate Simerel?' I asked. 'Became of him! he gaed to be a sodger; that's what became of him. Him, and some mair young lads like him, got among the 'tillery sodgers at Chirsit fair, and listed; that's what became of him.'

'He was my brother,' said I. 'Your brother! Pate Simerel your brother?' 'Yes.' 'And you only a joiner, working with *Dawvit*?' 'I am not a joiner; I have only been a labourer, breaking stones on roads, or digging ditches; and I have been two or three months a sawyer; and now I am helping *Dawvit*; but that does not make me a joiner.' 'No, lad, it does not, and never will; come to me, and I'll make ye a mill-wright.' 'No,' said I, 'it will not do now; I am too old; I have grown past the right time.' With more conversation of a similar kind, we parted.

Peter, after being in the Royal Artillery somewhere about three years, part of which time was passed in the island of Barbadoes, signified his desire to leave the service, and return to the trade of a millwright. We got intimation of it at home through a letter from William, generous then as always, saying that he would provide the funds to purchase his discharge, and to defray the attendant expenses, amounting to something over £21; but stating that Peter would also require tools, and some stock of clothes to start with. Our father and mother, two sisters, and myself, all who were at home, set joyfully and anxiously to work, to do all that we could. We wrote to Peter for a list of the tools he would require; with which, when received, our father went to Dunbar, to Mr. Miller's ironmongery shop, with all the money he could get together, I engaging to go without some new articles of clothing which I was to have had, that there might be the more money. Both of my sisters, after out-field work in the day, went to work with our mother, and got out the linen web of shirting, which the latter annually provided by her own spinning, and, sitting late at night, made a stock of shirts to be sent to Peter; and also worsted stockings. My father sat by the fire, with his glasses on his venerable face, his eyes almost too old to see to knit stockings, yet persevering, taking several hours from rest at night; after his out-door work, betaking himself to them at every dinner hour, that he might hasten them to a finish; and, as he plied the wires, he would now and again make such observations as these: 'He will surely settle himself now. I will send him a volume of *Young's Sermons*, in the box with the things; and the *Marrow of Modern Divinity*; it should do him good. I'll send him that volume that has the sermons on the Prodigal Son. "He took his journey into a far country"—that is, he sinned, and wandered from righteousness. They sent him to feed swine: "and he fain would have filled his belly with the husks the swine did eat." He broke his apprenticeship, and ran away, and was a sodger, and lived among the sin in which they lived, and fain would have satisfied his soul with it; but sin will not always satisfy. "And when he came to himself, he said, I will arise, and will say unto him, Father, I have sinned against heaven and before thee. And he arose and came to his father, and when he was yet a great way off his father saw him, and had compassion, and ran, and fell upon his neck, and kissed him. And the father said, bring forth the best robe, and put it on him"; that is, clothe him in the Gospel; there is a great sermon of Young's on that text; and "put a ring on his hand"; that is, give him the sign and the outward mark of the kingdom of grace. And put "shoes on his feet", that he may be sustained in the faith, and fail not to journey to the end.

'These are all great texts in Young's hands; and if I send them to our poor prodigal Peter, they may take effect upon him. But even if not, it is our duty to do all that in us lies to bring back him that has gone astray. A parent will do more for one bairn that errs and goes astray, than for all the rest. What a high and all-glorious example have we poor mortals to do this! The faithless unbeliever looks abroad upon the universe, and sees worlds after worlds, greater than this globe of earth, and many in number; and he reasons, as he has grounds to do, that they are inhabited by other races of the Lord's creatures: and then he says in his unbelief—What reason have we to believe that God would give his only Son as the Saviour of this single world, almost the least of the worlds? But these worlds come from the one Almighty, the one Parent and Creator; and if one world has sinned, while all the rest have been sinless, might not the Father have given more to redeem that one lost world than to all the rest? Will not a mere mortal give more to bring back his bairn that goes astray, than to all his family? Would we not give all that we possess to bring back prodigal Peter? Yes; I'se send him *Young's Sermons*, and a volume of Jamieson's, of Edinburgh, and the *Marrow*. If he make a good use of them, they will bring him to the best robe, the robe of grace; and the ring for his hand, the mark of a Christian; and the shoes for his feet, the Gospel. But we shall also put the clothing of this world upon him, and give him tools to work with to get his bread; and if we dinna send shoon to his feet, we'll send stockings. Dinna make the feet ower short, for Peter has a long foot. The last shoon that Johnstone Steel made for him before he ran away from his 'prenticeship, silly dyted thing, were the longest pair of shoon that Johnstone had made for some years, he told me, except Geordy Ha's shoon.'

We who listened knew that, at such a point as this, the least touch would turn him into a channel where lay some pleasant anecdotes; and we gladly touched the chord to lead him from dwelling too long where his sensitive affections detained him. He would then tell us how there was once a ship in distress, within sight of the Cove farm, where he was barnman, and where Geordy Ha' was a workman. People cried to one another, why did they not go to the Cove shore, and get a boat, and man it, and go out? To which Mr. Hoy, the farmer, said, 'What need ye go so far to man boats? Man Geordy Ha's shoon!'

When the stockings and shirts were made, they were, with the tools, amounting to several pounds in value, and the books, put in a box, which I carried three miles, to a place where the Berwick carrier called, who took it to a Berwick smack, trading to London. It was addressed to Eltham, in Kent, at which place Peter was to find work, as a mill-wright, with an old shopmate. It reached its destination safely. But Peter's wanderings were not brought to an end by having obtained his discharge from the artillery, and tools to go to work with at his trade. Comparatively they were only beginning.

After working for a few months at Eltham, and in London, where he was a lodger in the house of our cousin, Mrs. Dunse, daughter of my venerable uncle and name-father, Alexander Orkney, of Square, near Berwick-upon-Tweed, Peter heard, as everybody else did at that time, that the gold mines of South America were to produce wealth for England, such as England never knew before, if Englishmen would only advance a little cash, to take shares in the different speculations.

Very much cash was adventured. Next bold and enterprising men were wanted to go out to work the mines, to explore the Andes for new ones, and work them. Fortunes were to be made easily by everybody; and, in any case, the mechanics—fortune or no fortune—were to have such wages and advantages as no millwright could have in England. Peter had an offer, giving him the chance of seeing the world, and of getting soon rich, to return home, and live all his life after in comfort. He accepted it, and wrote us a letter at Gravesend, on board the ship, which was already so far down the Thames on its voyage to Rio Janeiro.

This was a severe blow to my father and mother, who had been in the hope of soon seeing him in Scotland. They were so much afflicted, that it then seemed to me impossible that I should ever go away from them. But a tide in my affairs, as we have seen, carried me from home also. We heard nothing more from Peter himself. Inquiries, by letter, at the office of the company in London, brought no intelligence more favourable, than that he had quitted their service of his own accord, before the term of their agreement had expired; and that they had not sought to detain him, as his health was bad—bad health arising, as they hinted, with a feeling somewhat like malignity, from irregular conduct; the fact being, as I have subsequently ascertained from himself and corroborative witnesses, that the company having been generally unsuccessful in their gold mines, broke faith both with the shareholders in England, and their servants in South America.

He left them, and was readily employed at far greater advantage to himself, though in more arduous employment, by the Brazilian government. Twice he crossed the Andes, and traversed those vast mountains sectionally, exploring in their highest altitudes and deepest abysses for gold or silver ore. About two years, in the far interior, were thus occupied, during which he had no opportunity to write home, and say why he had left the company. And before setting out on the exploring expedition, he did not write, as he had no good news to send home. On returning to Rio, and being liberally and honourably remunerated by the Brazilian government, his wealth exceeded all that he had dared to dream about. Besides engineering and machinery, to which he now devoted himself for the government, he betook himself to ship carpentry. In this last capacity he was introduced to a new adventure, exceedingly dangerous, but highly lucrative. He saw the certainty of becoming speedily possessed of wealth in it, with *only* the chances against him of losing his life; and those he risked. A native of the United States, resident at Rio, had a vessel, half clipper, half cutter, half smuggler, half-fair trader, sailing sometimes under United States colours, and at other times under the colours of any nation which it might be useful to profess to belong to. She had a crew of the most daring and enterprising men: several Americans, French, a few Spaniards, Portuguese, and Italians, and a Yankee captain. Her trade was outwardly that of a merchant vessel; inwardly and secretly, it was that of a smuggler of specie and gold dust. Peter was first employed in putting secret fittings into her, in such places as no searcher should discover them. He got so far into the confidence of the American proprietor and the captain, while putting in those 'fixings', that they offered him high terms to join in the adventure. He joined them; went on board ostensibly as ship's carpenter; but, in reality, to have charge of the specie in the secret places.

They carried on a trade of this kind on the coasts of Brazil, about a year, carrying their treasure to ships which met them at certain places of rendezvous; and, so far as lucrative remuneration went, were highly successful. But I am unable to explain the nature of this smuggling. Peter was to have written it in an account of his voyages, when he was at home, which he did not do before going abroad again; and it will never be done now.

They had a black cook whom the captain flogged one day. During the night, being near Rio, the injured negro leaped overboard, swam ashore, and informed the authorities of the nature of the trade this Yankee brig was engaged in. They were taken in the river next day; some were executed, and others sent far into the interior of Brazil, to dungeons, under sentence of long imprisonment. All had their property confiscated. Peter was sent five hundred miles up the country, lost all that he possessed, and only saved his life by protesting that he was a British subject. It was doubtful if that would have saved him, had the Brazilians known that he had been more on board the smuggler than the ship's carpenter. He lay some months heavily ironed, in a dungeon beneath a convent, which served as one of the state prisons of Brazil. No human being visited him all the time but the gaoler, who brought him beans and oil, his only food, and a priest. Finding his prisoner to be no Christian, according to his definition of the character, the priest paid little attention to him for about five months, but left him to his beans and oil, his dark damp cell, his long beard and nails, which were never trimmed, his Scottish Presbyterian Protestantism, which was supposed to be too hopelessly bad for a priest to touch with argument, and to the companionship of all manner of noisome vermin. At last the priest became attentive to him, and brought books, and made considerable progress under Peter's tuition, in learning to read English. When he got so far as to understand some of the language, he became deeply interested in listening to accounts of England and Scotland. He then got his prisoner released from irons, and allowed him to go to work with such carpentering tools as they had. Peter made several pieces of cabinet work for the convent, which gave much satisfaction. They would have retained him to work for it as a cabinet maker, had he not continued to express a desire to escape. It was quite possible that an order might come any day for his execution.

The priest became his friend so far that he undertook to have a letter conveyed to Rio, to the commander of an English ship of war which was reported to be there. That ship turned out to be the *Undaunted* frigate, commanded by Lord Henry Thynne. His lordship on hearing that a British subject was imprisoned in the interior of the country, demanded him to be given up to British authority. An order was made accordingly. Peter and the priest parted; the latter telling him that he was a much bad Christian, but a much good cabinet maker.

As it was dangerous for him to remain in Rio Janeiro, and hopeless to attempt to recover any of his property, and as the *Undaunted* was in want of hands, he joined her, and was rated in the carpenter's crew.

The *Undaunted* being soon after ordered to England, he and other hands who had not served long, were transferred to the *Tyne* sloop of war, then commanded by Captain Hope, son of the Lord President of the Court of Session. In the *Tyne* he had charge of the ship's furniture; and had a cabinet workshop. While cruising on the South American coasts for about three years, he made many articles of fancy cabinet work for the officers and their friends. And also for those of the *Tyne* and other ships, he made large boxes of the richest kinds of wood, the planks of which were three inches thick, the purpose being to introduce the timber free of duty, under the semblance of boxes, to have it sawn into veneers in England, and worked into articles of elegance and fancy.

This has been an immemorial practice with officers on board of British ships of war, in returning from the South American stations; and, though it looks dimly like smuggling, it was not viewed in that light. But Sir Robert Peel's tariff has put an end to the chances of its being a smuggling transaction, by allowing those fancy woods to come in duty free.

The *Tyne* returned to England in the summer of 1832, called at Portsmouth for orders, and was sent round to Sheerness. Peter had not an opportunity of getting on shore until the second day. On setting his foot on British soil, for the first time after so long an absence, he turned with eager curiosity to the newspapers. The first paper he got hold of was the *Morning Herald*. He had not glanced at it five minutes, when he saw an account of 'Somerville, the Scots Grey', in which it was stated that he was a native of Berwickshire. This was not quite correct, my native county being Haddingtonshire; but it was near enough to suggest to Peter that this must be his brother Sandy, whom he had left at home herding the cows twelve years before. He wrote a letter to me, addressed to the regiment, on the instant, inquiring if I were his brother, telling me who he was, and that he was just landed in England after a long absence. This letter went to Birmingham, was sent after me to Coventry, and I got it at the very minute of starting with the mail coach to attend the Court of Inquiry at Weedon barracks. I opened it after being seated on the coach, and read it again and again. I neither saw peeping Tom on passing his corner, nor any street of Coventry, nor garden, nor meadow beyond; I continued to read this letter, and question its subject on all sides, to assure myself that it was not, like some letters I received about my Scots Grey case—a hoax. It was not. The *Tyne*, it was expected, would be paid off, instead of which she was ordered to be refitted for sea immediately. A squadron of ships was then fitting out under Sir Pulteney Malcolm, for what purpose was not publicly known. They put to sea. Peter once more on board without our meeting, as he and I had fondly hope to do.

CHAPTER XIX

The Court of Inquiry—Discharge Purchased

IN the county of Northampton, near the geographical centre of England, at the bottom of a gently-elevated hill, stands Weedon, too large to be called a village, too small to be called a town. On the elevated ground overlooking Weedon, there are extensive barracks, in which one or more full regiments of infantry are always stationed. On the south-east side of the elevated ground, towards the little town, there are artillery stores, containing shot, shells, rockets, arms of all kinds, and gunpowder; and underneath the hills—where none but a few persons possessed of secrets know—there are other stores of gunpowder and arms, and places which may be victualled with food.

At the Bull Inn, outside Weedon, the mail, upon which I was a passenger, halted; and Mr. Marriott and I got down. Here we met Mr. Wooler, from London[22]. Here, also, were general officers and their military attendants. All the house was in a bustle; business had come like a flood; and I, who was the chief cause of that business, was flooded into the back kitchen among boots and shoes, brushes, blacking, brooms, and men brushing the boots of generals and aide-de-camps, who were about to dress, to go in grand military form to open the Court of Inquiry upon me.

Mr. Marriot was in possession of my case, and was closeted with Mr. Wooler. Some of the servants seeing a soldier standing in the way, and not knowing what I was there for, called to me to lend a hand; and as it was more agreeable to be doing something than nothing, I stripped off my regimental coat, turned up my shirt-sleeves, and proceeded to polish the boots of two or three colonels or generals, who were about to begin to brush and polish me, in the Court of Inquiry. When I had lent a hand to brush their boots, I proceeded to my own. And then we went to the barracks, about half a mile distant, and the court was constituted. But no further business was done that day. Here are a few of the important particulars:

'Horse Guards, 12th July, 1832.

'Sir,—By desire of the General Commanding-in-chief, I have the honour to notify to you, that it has been decided that a Court of Inquiry, composed of the officers named in the margin (president, Lieutenant-General Sir Thomas Bradford, K.C.B.; members, Major-General Sir Jasper Nicholls, K.C.B., Major-General Sir Archibald Campbell, C.B., Colonel Burrell, 18th regiment, Lieutenant-Colonel Townsend, 14th Light Dragoons), shall be assembled at Weedon, Northamptonshire, to investigate the case of Private Alexander Somerville, of the Royal North British Dragoons, who has lately been tried by a regimental court martial, and corporally punished by the award of the said court, and on whose behalf a petition has been presented to the House of Commons for redress, in consequence of the said trial and punishment.

'A printed copy of that petition, and a newspaper (*The Times*), containing an extract of a letter from Alexander Somerville to a "gentleman in Glasgow", are herewith transmitted; and Lord Hill understands that these statements contain the principal, if not the whole, of Somerville's allegations against his commanding-officer, upon this occasion. Lord Hill desires that the court of which you are thus appointed president, may deliberately proceed to the investigation of all the circumstances of complaint set forth in the petition and letter alluded to, as well as of any further circumstances, though not stated therein, which the complainant may be desirous to submit for investigation, and which shall relate to his present complaint.

'The nature of the case will at once satisfy the court that Major Wyndham, of the North British Dragoons, is, upon his part, entitled to a full hearing in support of the measures which he thought fit to adopt towards Alexander Somerville; in other words, that whilst, on the one hand, Somerville is to be allowed every legitimate means of establishing his case, Major Wyndham is, on the other hand, entitled to the same privilege.

'Lord Hill understands that, in consequence of the importance which has been attached to this case in parliament, the Judge Advocate General is to officiate in person, at the ensuing investigation. Mr. Grant's presence cannot fail to regulate and facilitate the progress of the inquiry; and Lord Hill can have no hesitation in requiring that the court shall, upon any and every question not of a purely military nature, and upon which doubt shall arise in the course of the proceedings, conform to Mr. Grant's opinion. His lordship, however, thinks it highly desirable that a note of each point that shall be thus disposed of by the court, upon the authority of the Judge Advocate General, should appear upon the face of its proceedings.

'Major Wyndham and the complainant will probably each require the assistance of one legal or other adviser in court; and although it is not customary to permit the presence of gentlemen of the learned profession at military Courts of Inquiry, yet Lord Hill desires that, in this instance, the usage in like cases may be departed from; it being at the same time understood, that no legal adviser, or other adviser or advocate, is to assume the right of addressing a military court, and that the parties themselves only who are at issue, have that right, namely, Major Wyndham and his accuser.

'Major Wyndham will be ordered to produce to the court, of which you are president, the proceedings of the regimental court martial held in Somerville's case, should a reference to them be deemed necessary in the course of the investigation; but Lord Hill desires, that the production of the proceedings alluded to, may on no account be regarded by the Court of Inquiry as a right to take any cognizance whatever of the conduct of the regimental court martial, unless the Judge Advocate General shall, upon his own responsibility, declare that the last-mentioned court is by law subject to the review of a court not sitting under the obligations of an oath. This being purely a question of law, and not of military expediency, Lord Hill gladly leaves it exclusively to the Judge Advocate General's decision.

'The court, of which you are president, having received and recorded such statement as the complainant and the accused shall offer, and such evidence as they shall respectively produce, will carefully consider the whole case, and report, for Lord Hill's consideration, their opinion; whether Major Wyndham, in dealing with the case of Alexander Somerville, of the Royal North British Dragoons, acted upon any (and *what*) occasion in a manner unbecoming his station and character, as the temporary officer in command of that regiment.

'Looking to the nature of the discussions in Somerville's case, which have already appeared in various public journals, and which are but too well calculated to convey to the public mind an impression highly unfavourable to the mode of administering public justice in the army, Lord Hill is clearly of opinion, that justice and expediency alike require that this should not be an open court; and even the legal or other advisers of the parties at issue should be excluded, unless they expressly pledge themselves to the court, in writing, to publish no portion whatever of its proceedings, until the case becomes again a subject of discussion in parliament, after the court shall have made its report, and also until the Judge Advocate General shall notify to them respectively, that the case is to undergo no further investigation.'

(Signed)   'JOHN MACDONALD,
                              'Adjutant-General.
'Lieutenant-General Sir Thomas Bradford, K.C.B.'[23]

'EXTRACT FROM THE MINUTES OF THE COURT
'Present—The officers named in the foregoing memorandum, the Right Hon. Robert Grant, Judge Advocate General.

'Major Wyndham and Private Somerville appeared with their respective advisers. Adviser for Major Wyndham, Mr. J. W. Whately, solicitor, Bennett's Hill, Birmingham. Adviser for Private Somerville, Mr. Thomas J. Wooler, 51, Nelson Square, London.

'The advisers of Major Wyndham and Private Somerville having been apprised that, under the instructions of the General Commanding-in-chief, the court thought it necessary to require that, if they thought it necessary to attend the court, they should give a pledge for themselves and their clients, not to publish any part of the proceedings of the court until the case should again become a subject of discussion in parliament, after the court had made its report, and also until the Judge Advocate General should notify to them that the case was not to undergo any further investigation.

'Pledges were accordingly given.

'After a brief address from the president, explaining the grounds on which the court was assembled, the Judge Advocate General read the instructions before referred to.

'Also a petition to parliament, from Richard Smith (Samuel Smith), of 139, Fleet Street, London, praying the House to cause inquiry to be made into the case of the said Alexander Somerville; and a portion of *The Times* newspaper, dated the 10th of July, containing an extract of a letter from Alexander Somerville, to 'a gentleman in Glasgow' (Craig, of Airdrie).

'Private Alexander Somerville was then called upon for a statement of his allegations against Major Wyndham, and for a list of the witnesses he proposed to call to support them; but, Somerville not being prepared with a written statement, *and he having preferred that mode of grounding his case, to make a verbal statement of it*, the court yielded to his request, for time to prepare it; and, two hours having been mentioned, the court gave him the option of appearing before them again at the expiration of that time, or at ten o'clock to-morrow; which latter alternative being accepted, the court adjourned till ten o'clock to-morrow.

'*Thursday*, 19*th July*.—The court met, pursuant to adjournment. The president reminded Major Wyndham and Private Somerville, that their advisers could not be allowed to address the court personally.

'Mr. Wooler, the adviser of Private Somerville, then inquired, if he was not to be permitted to address the court on points of law, which might arise in the course of proceedings adopted; and Mr. Wooler was informed by the Judge Advocate General, that the court considered themselves as absolutely precluded, by their instructions, from allowing the adviser of either party to make any personal address to them, on any subject whatever. But, that if any observation should occur to Mr. Wooler, as being material to be made, it was fully competent to him to communicate such observation, either verbally or in writing, to his client, by whom the same could be brought forward to the court; and that the court would always afford time for the observation to be so communicated to his client.

'Mr. Wooler then begged to address the court, merely for the purpose of informing them, that *no statement would be produced; and that he had advised Private Somerville not to make any, either verbally or in writing*, inasmuch as Private Somerville was not before the court as an accuser, but was ready to answer any questions as a witness. He observed, that it was not proved to the court that Private Somerville was a party to the documents before the court, and that Somerville ought not to be burdened with the petition of

219

Mr. Smith, to the House of Commons, nor with the letter of Craig, which appeared in *The Times*; that he, Mr. Wooler, conceived that it was for the court itself to take up the inquiry, and investigate the case; and that such was the object of this inquiry, and the instructions to the court, as he understood them.

'The Judge Advocate General thereupon read extracts from the instructions, to show that it was intended that Private Somerville should appear as a complainant, and should support his complaint by evidence.

'After some farther discussion to the same effect, the court observed that it was necessary Private Somerville himself should state his intention.

'Private Somerville said that he declined making any statement, either written or verbal, as an accuser. The court was then cleared.'

I declined to put in a written statement, because I had placed myself in the hands of two lawyers, one outside the court, Mr. Marriott, and one inside, Mr. Wooler, who counselled me to abide entirely by their advice. But I could not refrain from telling Mr. Wooler, in private, as he was the first person whom I had seen from the office of the newspaper in London, which had made my case peculiarly its own, that I was aggrieved at the weekly publication of statements in that paper, which the public believed to be authorized by me, but which were not so authorized; which, on the contrary, with some small portion of truth in them, were amplified and exaggerated, to suit the political, personal, or commercial purposes of the paper, though I had, in several private letters, remonstrated against such acts of publication. I drew attention also to the letter written to Craig, of Airdrie, the correspondent of the Glasgow paper, in reply to what he stated to be a private inquiry on his part, for the satisfaction of a few friends, which I wrote as a private letter, unguardedly describing my case, as I would not have described it in a formal statement of accusation; which private letter of mine he at once made public traffic of in the Glasgow paper; from which it got into *The Times*, and was now included in the instructions to the Court of Inquiry. It was at my earnest desire, that Mr. Wooler urged upon the court, 'That Somerville ought not to be burdened with the petition of Mr. Smith to the House of Commons, nor with the letter to Craig, which appeared in *The Times*.' I earnestly sought to rid myself from the responsibility of those documents altogether; and it was only on my assuring my legal adviser, that if he did not repudiate them on my behalf, I would do so myself, that he spoke as he did. My wish was, to make a formal complaint in writing, and to call evidence in support of it. I was overruled by the very extraordinary advice, to tender myself as a witness, subjecting myself thereby to a searching cross-examination, which lasted many hours; during which, I gave replies which were taken as charges against Major Wyndham, and so dealt with by the court in its report, which I would certainly not have put into a written statement of charges.

The minutes proceed thus:

'After a short time, the court re-opened, when the Judge Advocate General again explained to Private Somerville, that the court having adjourned yesterday for the purpose of giving him time to prepare his statement, it was necessary for him to state distinctly whether he had prepared such statement.

'Private Somerville then said, that Mr. Wooler had fully stated what he intended to say; that he had thought that he was coming here only as a witness, and not as the accuser of Major Wyndham; and that, if he had thought otherwise, he should not have named any witnesses.' (This was written by Mr. Wooler, placed in my hands by him, and read by me as my reply, with the additional caution not to be induced, by any other question, to add to it.)

'The Judge Advocate General then, by desire of the court, stated that, as Private Somerville had declined to appear as a complainant, it was the opinion of the court that their instructions did not give them the power of proceeding with the investigation; but as Private Somerville, on re-considering the matter, and consulting thereon with his adviser, might change the intention he had expressed, the court would adjourn for two hours, to give him time to come to a final determination.

'Mr. Wooler then begged leave to ask one question; and leave being given, he requested to know, whether, in the event of Private Somerville still declining, as before, to proceed as an accuser, the court would dissolve itself?

'The Judge Advocate General stated, that in the event alluded to, the court had no other course to take than that of adjourning its sittings, and referring to the authority under which it acted, for farther instructions.

'The court then adjourned till two o'clock.

'The court having re-assembled, and the parties having been called in, the president addressed Private Somerville as follows:

'I desire to apprise you, Alexander Somerville, that the question I am about to put, is addressed to *you*, and you must, *yourself*, *reply to it*.'

The court had seen, by this time, that I was acting under an adviser whose opinions differed from mine, and whose personal behaviour in the court was, to say the best of it, very extraordinary indeed; but, as he threatened to abandon me and the case, and return to London, if I did not act upon his counsel, I assented. The question of the president was:

'Are you prepared to proceed as complainant in this case, according to the instructions which this court has received, and which have been read to you?

'Private Somerville thereupon delivered a paper, headed, "*The Protest of Alexander Somerville, Private in the Second or Royal North British Dragoons*", which was read to the court by the Judge Advocate General, and which is annexed:

'To the Right Honourable Sir Thomas Bradford, and the members of the Military Court of Inquiry, assembled at Weedon, on the 18th day of July, 1832, the protest of'—(etc. etc.).

'I have been informed, and understand, that the said Court of Inquiry was ordered on the question, whether I was punished for disobeying the orders of Lieutenant Gillies, of the said regiment, or for writing a letter to the *Weekly Dispatch*, on political subjects.

'I attended at the said Court of Inquiry, expecting to be called as a witness on the aforesaid question, as I have been informed, and believe, under the Right Honourable the Secretary at War, Sir John Cam Hobhouse; and, although disclaiming the expensive and onerous situation of public accuser, I am ready and willing to give testimony to the treatment I have received, and witnesses are in attendance to prove the fact.

'In the full and fearless challenge which I am prepared to give my oppressors, the Court of Inquiry has declined to examine me and the witnesses in attendance, and I have no means of obtaining justice, under the order of the commander-in-chief, except in protesting against any adjournment of the court, until the ends of justice are fully answered.

'A. SOMERVILLE.

'Weedon, 19th July, 1832.'

'The president then announced that the further sittings of the court would be adjourned until Monday, the 23rd instant, at eleven o'clock, and the court adjourned accordingly until that day and hour.'

My only *protest* was to my legal advisers, against being compelled to sign that which was in direct opposition to my wishes. I wished to put in a written statement of my case, and withdraw the newspaper rumours of it, which contained all the strong and somewhat vague assertions; but I was over-ruled and compelled, under a threat of being left alone at Weedon, to conduct the case myself, to sign that 'protest' of which I did not write one word; from which I vainly tried, finding that it must be signed, to expunge the bravado-like 'full and fearless challenge to my oppressors,' which I did not think necessary or well-timed. But I had no alternative; I must sign it, or take the case entirely into my own hands.

We walked to the Bull Inn, as before, amid people attracted to the roadside to look at the 'Scots Grey, as was making all the noise in the country,' who was, on the contrary, doing all within his power to keep the noise within bounds.

'*Monday, July* 23, 1832.—The court having assembled at eleven o'clock, the Judge Advocate General read the additional instructions from the general commanding in chief, dated Horse Guards, July 20th.

'Major Wyndham and Private Somerville were then called upon to furnish lists of the witnesses they respectively proposed to call.'

The court sat until half-past four o'clock, chiefly engaged in my examination and cross-examination; also in hearing part of the evidence of Lieutenant Gillies, one of my witnesses.

On Tuesday, 24th of July, the examination of Mr. Gillies was resumed at ten o'clock. Mr. Henry Simons, a civilian, who took lessons in the riding school, was also examined this day, on behalf of the other side, as it was necessary that he should return to his business at Birmingham. When that was done, Mr. Gillies was again examined by the court. Sergeant John Glen was also called by me on that day. Also Privates Robert Brown and Thomas Darling.

On the 25th, at ten o'clock, the evidence of Darling was resumed; and the day was occupied with it and that of Regimental Sergeant-Major Nelson, and Adjutant Ricketts.

On the 26th, Private Thomas Scott was examined by me; Mr. David Cope was examined by Major Wyndham; also Troop Sergeant-Major Aitkin, Hospital Sergeant Sykes, Assistant Surgeon Stewart, Privates Robert Robertson and Charles Buist; the two last were patients in the hospital when I was taken there.

On the 27th, Troop Sergeant-Major Gardiner and Corporal M'Lure were examined on behalf of Major Wyndham; and the major tendered himself as a witness. This was unexpected by the court and by me. The minutes introduce his evidence thus: 'Major Charles Wyndham, Royal North British Dragoons, then tendered himself as a witness; and, having been reminded by the Judge Advocate of the extreme responsibility under which he was placed, in regard to the answers he might give to such questions as were put to him, was examined by the Judge Advocate.' He was also cross-examined on my behalf. I have already given the most important parts of his evidence. He admitted nearly all that I wanted to prove.

On the 28th, Adjutant Ricketts was re-examined; on the 30th and 31st of July, and 1st of August, the court deliberated, and made up a lengthened series of charges from the newspapers, and from my verbal statements, under a long and harassing examination, which, in the absence of the written and concise statement, they were obliged to do; upon the greater part of which charges no evidence was offered; they accordingly set them down as 'not proved'.

The following are the principal paragraphs of the report, after disposing of those several charges selected by them:

'The court is of opinion, that Major Wyndham acted injudiciously, in entering into conversation with, or making inquiry of, Private Somerville, on the subject of the letter in the newspaper, while Private Somerville was before him, as a prisoner, charged with a military offence; and that this was especially inconsiderate at a period when, from the excitement which prevailed in the neighbourhood, and from the nature of the contents of that letter, the object and purpose of such conversations and inquiries were peculiarly liable to be misinterpreted.

'That Major Wyndham, when he heard a recruit offer the highly objectionable opinions, which are recorded to have been expressed to him by Private Somerville, respecting the duty and allegiance of a soldier, acted injudiciously, in not suspending all proceedings against Private Somerville, in relation to the military offence where-with he was charged, and laying before the general of the district, a full statement of the case of Private Somerville, and of the opinions so expressed by him, in order to obtain, from the general command-ing the district, instructions applicable to the occasion.

'That the method of procedure which Major Wyndham followed, in bringing Private Somerville to a trial before a court martial; the effect of which was, that Private Somerville was warned for trial, tried, and punished within the compass of a very few hours; and, especially, that he was brought to trial only an hour and a half after he received notice of it, were unduly precipitate, and, in that respect, not justified by the general usage of the service, though in accordance with the practice of the Scots Greys, [No] and, as the court believes, of other regiments of cavalry.'

The remainder of the court's opinion is embodied in the concluding paragraph of the memorandum, referring to the approval of His Majesty the King, which is the last quotation I shall make.

'Horse Guards, 9th August, 1832.
'The report of the Court of Inquiry, held at Weedon Barracks, on the 18th day of July, 1832, and continued by adjournments to the 28th of the same month, for the investigation of the complaints made by Private Alexander Somerville, of the Second or Royal

225

North British Dragoons, against Major Wyndham of that corps, together with the minutes of its proceedings, having been submitted to the King, His Majesty has been pleased to signify his approbation of the mode in which the court has executed its functions, and his entire concurrence in the observations and opinions contained in its report.

'His Majesty has further been pleased to express his deep regret, that an officer of the rank and distinguished service of Major Wyndham, and who had ever maintained a character so free from reproach, should, on the occasion and in the instances mentioned in the report, have evinced a deficiency in the care, discretion, and judgment, required of him, as an officer in the temporary command of a regiment.

'His Majesty has, however, been pleased at the same time, to express his satisfaction, that nothing has appeared in the course of the inquiry, to authorize any conclusion which would reflect discredit on the purposes, feelings, or motives of Major Wyndham; or which would subject his honour to just impeachment.

'By direction of the General Commanding-in-chief.

(Signed)   'FITZROY SOMERSET.'

On returning to the barracks at Coventry, I continued to do duty up to the 24th of August. Several parties called to see me, attracted by the celebrity which the case had now attained, but I declined to see all who were public or political personages. One of these was the late Henry Hunt[24].

Most people have heard of the annual procession through Coventry, of a lady on horseback, to represent Lady Godiva, who once saved the citizens from a grievous impost, sought to be inflicted by her lord. When the real lady rode through the city, all the male inhabitants were commanded to remain strictly within doors, none but females being allowed to see what a sacrifice the Lady Godiva was compelled to make for their sakes. There was, however, one Tom, who opened his window, just to have a peep as the lady on horseback passed, which so offended the citizens, that they placed his effigy in the window, where he stands to this day, known as Peeping Tom of Coventry.

In 1832, it was resolved to hold the festival in celebration of the passing of the Reform Bill, on the same day as the anniversary of Lady

Godiva's procession. From Nuneaton, Hinckly, Leamington, Kenilworth, and other places, processions long, dense, and noisy, with shouts and music, came and joined the political union of Coventry. It so occurred that I was on sentry at the front barrack gate, when the procession passed. Not one of the many thousands knew me personally, but each band ceased to play as it came near the barrack gate; each trade or section of a political union, halted in front of the gate, as prearranged by a master of ceremonies, and three cheers, loud and long, were given for 'Somerville *for ever!*' They had not the remotest suspicion that I was the sentry, with my carbine on my arm, standing in the gateway looking at them. '*For ever!*' they shouted in connection with my name. I had not been many months shouted for in that manner, when I was scouted, sneered at, maligned, libelled, and foully lied upon by some of those, who, at that time, led the multitude to set up an idol one year, and knock it down and trample on it the next; and all because I would not lend myself to any set of persons, or purposes, that did not accord with my own sense of right and propriety.

In one of *Cobbett's Registers* it was announced about this time, that he was coming to Coventry, on his journey to the north of England, and to Scotland, to lecture; and that he hoped to see me and talk with me. When he came, Mr. Horsfall, of the Half Moon, took me to Mr. Cobbett's lodgings, at one of the hotels. He had been overwhelmed with calls, and had given orders not to be interrupted, as he had writing to do; but on hearing who it was that now called, he set the orders and the writing aside. On approaching him, he shook me warmly by the hand, looked at me a few seconds, and said, 'You have at the least, an honest-looking Scotch face in your favour.' I sat down with him, and he proceeded thus: 'Now, you are going to London; let me give you a few words of advice. There are thieves in London who steal money; there are swindlers in London who make victims of the unwary; but there are worse people in London than thieves and swindlers; there are editors of newspapers; take care of yourself if you fall amongst editors. You are property for them. Each will try to get you exclusively to himself. They will traffic upon you. If one gets you in his den, and you do not always after go to that den, he will rush upon you some day and tear you to pieces. Take care of the editors: I know them well. Go to Mr. Rogers, of St. Giles's; Mr. Nicholson, of Fenchurch-street; Mr. Williams, of Watling-street; Mr. Swain, the tailor, of Fleet-street, and (another, whose name I have forgotten); and take this paper (he wrote their names and addresses), it is signed with my name, William Cobbett; any of them will give you good advice.'

About the 22nd of August, I was summoned to the officers' barracks, at Coventry. Lord Arthur Hill, the lieutenant-colonel of the regiment, whom I had not before seen, was present. This officer, though the name and title sound similarly, was in no way connected with Lord Hill, the general commanding-in-chief. The latter was the celebrated general of division, second in command to Wellington, in the Peninsular war; the former was one of the sons of the Marquis of Downshire. Lord Arthur put several questions to me, in a kind, gentlemanly manner, to one of which, whether I was desirous of obtaining my discharge from the regiment, I answered, yes. He said, that having heard this formally from myself, he would make application for it.

The rule of the service in purchasing a discharge, is, that the soldier must be recommended by his commanding officer before he can purchase. The purchase-money of mine, £30, had been lodged at the War Office for several weeks, and many applications on my behalf had been made for it. The last form being now complied with, it was sent down to the regiment on the 24th, to be given to me on the 25th of August.

At ten o'clock on that morning, I put off my regimentals, and dressed myself in a suit of plain clothes, which a tailor, one of several who competed for the 'honour' of equipping me, had made. I gave my regimental boots and shoes to my old schoolfellow, James Grieve, and also several other articles of my 'kit'. To most of my other comrades I gave something. They all shook me affectionately by the hand, and looked after me until I was out of the barrack gate.

Mrs. Shettle, of the Three Tuns, a house near the back gate of the barracks (and now one of the nearest licensed houses to the railway station), who had evinced much kindness, I may almost say, motherly regard for me, was, with her husband, kind enough to request that I would leave some article of my military equipments with them, as a keepsake. I gave them my forage cap. Fourteen years afterwards I found it there, better taken care of than I could have preserved it. After that lapse of time I called at the Three Tuns, and saw the same countenance beaming from the same seat, in its intelligence and benevolence—a countenance remarkable even amongst the finest heads of intelligent women. I sat down, talked, drank a glass of ale, rose to depart, and bade Mr. and Mrs. Shettle good-bye, yet they did not call to mind that they had before known me. Turning back, I said, 'I must introduce myself; I see you do not know me.' But that preliminary observation was enough. Both recognized the stranger; and then there was shaking of hands, and generous remembrances. And I was told how the forage cap had been treasured: how I had been often spoken of in the family circle, and so forth. I had in 1832 disclosed more of my sentiments, and more of the facts of my case, to this lady and her husband, than to any other persons in Coventry. This lady, like every other person who knew me intimately, knew that I despised the tin-kettle school of politics, and that I was misrepresented by tin-kettle politicians, because misunderstood by them.

On the 27th of August, Mr. Horsfall, of the Half Moon, who, at that time, was one of the proprietors of the *Quicksilver* London coach, to whom, and to every member of whose family, I had been indebted for much kindness, gave me a free seat to London, as a gift from the proprietors of the coach. I left Coventry at eight in the morning, and arrived in London in the evening.

22 *The Black Dwarf.* See Introduction pp. xii–xiii.
23 All the general officers named had been in the Peninsula, and no doubt shared the Duke's ideas on discipline. Robert Grant, however, who had been Third Wrangler and was later to be Governor of Bombay, represented the whig ministry. The office of Judge Advocate General was then political, not official, and Grant was M.P. for Finsbury and a junior minister.
24 'Orator' Hunt (1773–1835), then M.P. for Preston, who had supported Joseph Hume in raising Somerville's case in the House. Somerville does not mention the three cheers which, says *The Times*, greeted his return to the ranks.

CHAPTER XX

From London Home, and from Home to London—
1832, 1833 and 1834

THERE were two orders of minds with which I came in contact, at the time when I was discharged from the Scots Greys, that I found unwilling to understand me, or incapable of comprehending my motives in anything I had done, or refused to do, or then did, or then proposed to do. One of those mental orders comprised several kind, well-meaning friends. They had before them the facts, that I, a working man, with little school education, had become a soldier, improved my education, had occupied a dangerous eminence in the public view, under perilous circumstances; defended myself before a court martial, in the absence of all earthly friends, when every word of defence uttered, was an aggravation of my alleged disinclination to obedience; that I had suffered the most cruel and excruciating punishment which can be inflicted on the human body, with a firmness and propriety of bearing which even the commanding officer bore ready testimony to, at a time when not inclined to say much in my favour. Those and other things led them to believe that I must have self-confidence, forwardness, and 'face' enough, for any public exhibition of myself. They could not comprehend how a person 'who had been in the newspapers so much', should have any objection to go to public meetings of the political unions, to receive votes of thanks, carried by acclamation, 'for having helped to carry the Reform Bill'; which acclamation was, in their ears, and the clapping of hands, in their eyes, the most agreeable of sounds and sights.

The other order of minds comprised those who could not assign to me any other motive, since the public had subscribed money to purchase my discharge, and to add to it a gift to me, but that I had, from the beginning of the case, before I was punished, and when I was punished, designed to make it a means of obtaining money. Some of these persons could not see why I should endeavour to stop the collection of money on my behalf, or refuse it by any means through which it could be obtained. Others of this order of persons set down my remonstrances against the collection of money on my behalf, to hypocrisy; to a deep plan of victimizing the public. One set of those persons published that I had remonstrated with them, and with others, against the proposition to give me money; but that I was well entitled to it; that it was the spontaneous gift of the public; that less than public duty would be done, if a liberal subscription was not made; and that it was not for me to interfere in the matter; that I must leave this part of the case to those who believed I had done a public service. Yet that same set of persons published, in the same paper, at no distant time, when they knew nothing more of my motives, except that I would not allow *them* to make traffic of me, that I was an 'imposter', a 'victimizer of the public', and so forth.

After deducting £30 for my discharge, £40 for lawyers' fees incurred at the Court of Inquiry (this sum was paid to Mr. Marriott; Mr. Harmer[25], who sent Mr. Wooler from London, made no charge), and other expenses incidental to the business, I received about £250. The only remarks which came to my ears on the subject of money, at that period, were to the effect that people wondered why I should be resolute in not allowing those who were willing to carry the public subscription farther, to go on. The first act of mine, which that order of minds last spoken of could not comprehend, was my reply to an application made on behalf of Madame Tussaud, to have a wax figure modelled, and placed in the exhibition then forming. I was offered £50 in cash, to allow them to place in the exhibition, 'Somerville, the soldier'. I said, 'It must not be done.' I was told that it might possibly be done without my consent; to which I replied, that if done, it would be without my consent, and that, whoever did it, might rely upon my taking measures to prevent its exhibition.

The next affair which some of those parties could not comprehend, was my answer to a proposal that I should have a benefit at one or more of the London theatres. Several of the performers engaged at the New Strand Theatre, amongst whom I remember Mrs. Waylett, the late Mrs. Honey, Mrs. Chapman (sister of Miss Ellen Tree), the late Leman Rede, and Mr. Chapman, more particularly, offered their gratuitous performances (so Mr. Rede informed me) for a night. Mr. Rede offered to write an address. I was assured that probably not less than £100 would accrue to me. But I gave a firm 'No!' to the proposal.

Another was, to lend my name to a literary speculation of some kind. I was ambitious to be connected with literature; but as the parties proposed to write in my name, I declined their offer of payment in terms which they, looking on me as an adventurer getting money wherever I could get it, could not understand.

There was at least one more proposal, that I would allow my name to be used in a newspaper, which I firmly declined, somewhat to the annoyance, I believe, of those who made the offer; respecting which, I shall not now do more than make this allusion to it.

Another was, to allow certain parties to organize a system of collecting subscriptions for me throughout the metropolis and the kingdom; to which I also gave an instant and positive negative.

It was not so easy, however, to put a stop to some of those who took up that business on their own account. One of these, named ——— ———, a journeyman pencil-case maker, notorious for his political orations at the Bull Ring, in Birmingham, and much more inclined to the making of political speeches in public-houses, than the making of pencil-cases in his workshop, took upon himself to patronize me. During a fortnight, he, with some others, visited the manufacturing towns in the neighbourhood of Birmingham, and many of the public-houses where trades' clubs assembled in that town, and collected money, 'to purchase the discharge of Somerville, the soldier.' I knew nothing of their doings, nor of the persons, at that time, and so could not interfere; but as they were known to some of my friends in Birmingham, a public caution was given that they were doing that business on their own account.

Prevented in Birmingham, ——— ——— proceeded into the Staffordshire potteries, and carried the trade on there. Ultimately, he and a few others made their way to London; and having some papers in the form of credentials, and speaking the Warwickshire dialect, it was readily believed, in London, that they were appointed on my account to go through the public-houses, and make speeches, and collect money. They were in London, thus employed, when I went there at the end of August. On my threatening some of them with a prosecution, for obtaining money under false pretences, they decamped, and I saw no more of them, except ——— ———. He came to me, and begged that I would make no public exposure of him; that the others had the money, and had run off with it; that an exposure would be his ruin in Birmingham; that he was now left penniless in London, was desirous of getting home to his trade, and wife and family, but knew not how to get there.

He impressed me so deeply with a sense of his honesty, his misery, his misfortunes, by the others misleading and deceiving him, that I went and borrowed £5, having no money in my own hands, and gave him it all, besides clean linen to go home with. Instead of going direct home, he proceeded on tramp, as I subsequently ascertained, working his way to Birmingham through the towns and villages, gathering the people together in the streets, addressing them in pathetic appeals for 'poor Somerville', and showing a pretended written authority to collect money.

When I was in Birmingham, about a month afterwards, on my journey to Scotland, I staid a few days, paying my respects and gratitude to those who had befriended me. In a cheap unstamped newspaper, then published there, I was surprised one day to see a printed notice, stating, '*We* understand that this man (myself) is now in Birmingham, and we hope he will call on —— —— (the name was in full), and make the *amende honorable* for his shabby treatment of him'; or some such words. I submitted it to two or three gentlemen who knew the man, and they counselled me to take no notice of it; that it had been put in print, anticipating that I might possibly say something about him in Birmingham, that he might have something mysterious to refer to in return. They told me that I would have done right had I given him into the hands of the police in London. I never heard of him afterwards. I would not now refer to the affair, were it not to give one out of many instances which I might give, of impositions committed on the public in my name, at that time, by persons who, to make themselves look fair and blameless, turned round with some insinuation or attack upon me, as soon as they discovered that I would not connive at what they were doing.

I had not, up to this time, seen any great public dinner or festival, nor heard great men make speeches. During my stay of six weeks in London, one of these dinners, at which between two thousand and three thousand people were present, occurred at Hackney, to celebrate the legislative formation of the Tower Hamlets into a borough; Dr. Lushington, Sir William Clay, Colonel Stanhope, Thomas Campbell, the poet, and a few others, were the speakers. I had expressed a desire to be present at such a festival as that. Certain parties were as desirous that I should accept a ticket at their expense, and allow them to take me there, to be introduced or exhibited. I declined to go on those conditions. I went quietly alone; sat in a place as little exposed as I could find; listened to the speeches, with intense interest to the poet, of whom I had heard much, but had not before seen; and when discovered by those who would, with or without my consent, drag me into public view, to be 'introduced' to the meeting, I left them and the meeting, much to their surprise, as I have been subsequently told. They could not comprehend my motives. And yet it seems to me a natural consequence, that a person of my limited education and knowledge should shrink from such a public appearance.

So also at a meeting of the London Political Union, in the public room in Theobald's Road. I was attracted to it, to hear the speeches of Mr. John Lawless, from Dublin, and other crack men of the day, at that time in London, from the provinces. I was observed; some one called me loudly by name; there was shouting and clapping of hands, and a cry for me to go to the platform. I at once left the body of the hall, as some thought, to go on the platform. Those who came to escort me thither, found me in the passage, forcing my way to the door. I left the place despite their attempts to detain me; and it was not long until I found some of them saying in print, that I was an 'ungrateful person', and altogether unworthy of their good opinion, because I would not go with them upon a platform.

With those two exceptions, I attended no public meetings in London at that time; and in no case whatever did I accept an invitation to any private house. I have read in newspapers that I lived in London, in the houses of private friends, at the expense of private persons, at this time. I not only did not live with them or upon them; but in no case whatever, during those six weeks, did I visit at any house, public or private, as a guest. There was not, in all the metropolitan wilderness of streets and houses, and it is a wilderness to those who are alone, a more lonely being than I was, at that time. I saw my name every week on the bills of newspapers, saw and heard people reading those bills at street corners; heard my case and myself discussed in the parlours of public-houses, occasionally by persons who professed to know me intimately; none of which persons I had before seen in all my life. I felt that I was not the kind of man that everybody expected or believed me to be. They depicted to themselves a person of flashy exterior, fluent in address, able and ready to talk and speak anywhere, at any time; and so well skilled in the ways and usages of free and easy society, as to take a hand at cards, play billiards or bagatelle, or crack jokes, crack nuts, or crack heads with equal readiness. I knew of no quality which entitled me to respect, except that I had a strong right arm, a determination not easily turned aside, and that, had the month of May become one of civil war and bloodshed (as it seemed very likely to be), and the Duke had attempted to ride from the Land's End to Inverness, and, with ten thousand men, put down the political unions, and allay the cry for reform (as it was said he threatened to do), I knew that that arm, and the determination not easily turned aside, with the other military allies, as determined as myself, would have been raised in defence of the House of Commons, whose majority was for reform and for the people. I found that those who should have known me best—who, in their newspaper, professed to be in the closest intimacy with me—gave me credit privately for no higher quality than that of petulant insubordination to military orders. That one act of disobedience, which of all occurrences of my life I most regretted, was the only thing which they saw worthy of respect in me. I was introduced to the chief proprietor of their establishment, who gave me an audience of nearly ten minutes, not quite so much, who never again spoke six sentences to me, to whom I had not the opportunity of speaking ten words; and this was the entire amount of our intimacy or knowledge of one another, though, so long as it served to advertise and sell their paper, and raise its sale progressively several thousand copies per week—for never in the history of the newspaper press did any single case do so much for the circulation of a newspaper, as mine did for that paper—so long as it served to advertise the paper, they advertised me, though, in reality, no person in the proprietorship, or in the management, knew anything about me. The only individual connected with them who had any means of knowing me personally, was Mr. Wooler, at the Court of Inquiry, at Weedon; and, for reasons not necessary to be repeated here, he was not likely to report favourably of me in London.

As already said, I was one of the loneliest beings that wandered through the metropolitan wilderness. There was not one man or woman, out of the million and a half of people in Middlesex and Surrey, to whom I could confide my thoughts; the few to whom I made an advance, seemed to look upon me with feelings of disappointment, as a man so different from the ideal 'Somerville, the soldier', whom their newspapers, and their own imaginations had made, that I felt disappointment too, and shrunk from them.

One day I got a letter with a well-known post-mark on it. I had renewed, and made a formal proposal to the nameless one; and I expected an answer, not of yes or no, but of hope or absolute denial. Uncertain then if I should remain in London, or go to Scotland, I waited for this letter, to be determined by it. For three hours at least, I could not muster courage to open it. I walked from the Strand to the Surrey side of Waterloo Bridge, and back to the Strand, and again from one side to the other, until I had paid all the money I had with me, in pennies at each end of the bridge, not thinking on what I was doing; thinking intensely upon what I would do in case the letter had no hope in it, and on what I would do if it were what I so earnestly wished it to be. At last people stopped to look at me, their attention directed to the questionable nature of my promenade by the gate keepers. Some thought I was engaged to walk between the Strand and Waterloo Road, so many times in so many hours, for a wager. Others connected my perambulations with the traditions of suicidal leaps from the bridge into the deep river. Nothing was further from my mind than a plunge in the river. At last, I made a desperate resolve; halted suddenly at one of the recesses; opened the letter and read—read, that it *might* come to pass that my hopes would be realized; and, that if Providence had designed *it* to be, *it* would be.

I turned round, and people who thought me insane and within a second of going over the parapet of the bridge, stood close behind. Some of them spoke. I laughed when I heard their remarks, and they probably thought me not the more sane because I laughed.

Providence! I felt as if I were now the general in command of all possibilities, and that Providence had only to be dealt with like a quarter-master general, who had charge of ammunition and stores. Providence would help me if I helped myself, as the proverb says.

Impious vanity! Never was mortal man more in earnest than I was to succeed in that object; and yet I did not succeed. But it was possible that *im*providence might be an ingredient in non-success.

My resolution was at once taken to leave London. At Birmingham I was solicited anxiously, and was pressed until it was painful to refuse, yet I did refuse, to go to the political union for one night. I felt that I could not make a public appearance, and so did not. I was not at any meeting of the Birmingham political union, either before I was discharged from the army, or after, neither at the usual place of meeting, nor at any other. I have read in newspapers that I was; and have even read a speech attributed to me, which circumstance is the only excuse I have now for taking notice of this topic.

At Glasgow I was as anxious to avoid a public appearance, as at Birmingham and London, but was not so successful. One morning, when the factory workers were out of the mills at the breakfast hour, I was in a stationer's shop, the door of which many hundreds of them passed. The fact of the 'Scots Grey that got his licks' being there, became known, and a crowd of people gathered around the door, until the street had a multitude in it. I was obliged to go out and take off my hat to them. They shouted with an enthusiasm which made me blush, and wish I was beneath the stones of the street; yet, upon reflection, I saw such a hearty good will about them, that I felt what must now be confessed, a gratified vanity.

Within an hour I was seated under the hands of a hairdresser. He was full of what he had seen when the crowd was at the stationer's shop, and gave to me, and other customers present, a full description of 'that chiel, Somerville.' He told what he thought of him; and each told what he thought. Taking the average of what they said, I had no reason to feel flattered.

I had been detained fourteen days for the meeting of the political union. When the night came, the place was not only crowded, but the streets leading to it also. I had again, and again, begged to be allowed to write my thanks to the public of Glasgow, and publish the writing, so that I might be saved the humiliation which I dreaded, of going before a great public meeting, to exhibit myself as a coward, afraid to *look the people in the face*. Mr. ——, in whose hands I was, would take no denial. As the hour approached I felt myself more incompetent to the task than ever, and evinced signs of a determination not to go with him. He impressed upon me the great injustice it would be to him, who had announced me in his paper, and at last asked me, 'what did I think he had kept me in his house for during a fortnight?' This stung me to the heart. I said, 'Go on, take me where you like.' We went through the crowds, my knees inclining to smite each other; yet the weakness counteracted by a feeling, which inclined me to smite my head against a stone wall, had one been near enough. Having been housed and fed up for the exhibition for a fortnight, and the terms being, as it now appeared, a public show, with my keeper leading me by the arm, I could not resist.

Making way, with great difficulty, to the front of the most crowded auditory which had ever been crammed within the walls; while some one else was speaking, my keeper, without waiting for that speaker to be done, holding me by the arm with one hand, lifted his other hand, and, with a voice well known for its strength and loudness, in Glasgow, cried, 'This is the man!' What more he intended to say, I know not. Every person present sprung to their feet, and burst forth in shouts and clapping, which seemed to have no ending; it was renewed again and again, until I fell back into a seat, my limbs powerless, my head swimming, from which I was only relieved by hiding my face in my pocket-handkerchief, and wetting it with convulsive tears.

When silence was obtained, it was suggested that the business then in hand should be finished first. When that was done he again rose, and began, 'This is the man!' and again the people rose. But I was now more firm. When he had made a speech, and a vote of thanks had been carried by acclamation to me, for the services which they were pleased to say I had done for the success of the Reform Bill, I said a few words of acknowledgment and thanks, which I believe the tory newspapers reported more correctly than any others did, though not intending to pay me a compliment. They said, 'After the man had been exhibited, he stammered out some ungrammatical sentences, and there was an end of the exhibition.'

I never saw the gentleman, who had kept me a fortnight for the show, after that night, for eight years. But I was obliged to hear what good-natured friends told me, that, with all that recklessness which led him to reprint some feeble verses of mine, and call them 'worthy of Byron', and hail me, before he had seen me, as 'another Byron', 'another Burns', and all that fudge; with the same recklessness, he began to write me down, as soon as the exhibition was over, and never allowed an opportunity to slip, to do so, from that time forward.

I left Glasgow next day. When the late Mr. Thomas Atkinson, of excellent memory, and some other friendly gentlemen, discovered that I had left Glasgow without calling upon them, they wrote to me, at Edinburgh, regretting the circumstance. I had not been allowed to go out without my keeper. Mr. Atkinson said that he was sorry I had placed myself in the hands of an individual, and expressed a fear that I would have reason to be sorry for it, as he had once been befriended by that personage. For himself, he said, he was on the verge of the grave; he felt as if one foot was already in it, but as the other foot was still out, he would hold on until he wrote on paper some things which he would have told me by word of mouth, had I called upon him, as he had expected me to do. Some of his prophetic words came too true, and sooner true than even he expected. He died soon after.

I must now, in my narrative, hasten to join Peter and James, who are waiting for me, at Edinburgh, to go, all three together, to Thriepland Hill, where, in the old thatched house, our old father and mother and youngest sister are anxiously awaiting us, and mourning our delay. With a knowledge of this, and with an earnest affection which daily yearned in me, to get home, to see the fireside once more, with Peter beside me, who had been so many years lost, it was no small sacrifice to allow myself to be detained in Glasgow a whole fortnight. Nothing but the allegation, that the paper which was said to have been devoted to me, would suffer if I did not remain with him who owned it, would have induced me to make such a sacrifice.

When I left London, on my journey to Scotland, it was at eight o'clock in the morning. On that day, at twelve o'clock, Peter, my sailor brother, arrived in London, to see me. Sir Pulteney Malcolm's squadron had returned to Portsmouth; and Peter, having had several years of foreign service, readily obtained his discharge from the sloop of war, on its being applied for, though the ship was not formally paid off at that time. I had applied at the Navy Office during the six weeks which I spent in London, and had written to the ship several times, inquiring if there was any probability of his returning to England soon; but the squadron being at sea, and under secret orders (probably the Belgian revolution, and the Netherlands war which had ensued, and was then carried on by bombshell and mortar practice at Antwerp, was the cause of the British government sending this squadron of ships to sea, to hover on the coasts, under secret orders); from these circumstances, I got no satisfactory intelligence.

Peter, finding that I had gone to Scotland by a route upon which it would be difficult to overtake me, went direct by sea from London to Leith, and so reached Edinburgh while I still lingered among friends, first at Coventry and Birmingham, and next in the neighbourhood of Liverpool. Had I known that he was not on board a man-of-war, I would have soon made my way to him. As it was, we were, unknown to me, approaching each other.

Nothing occurred on my journey from London to Liverpool which

I need remark upon, except that at Manchester I saw a railway, locomotive engines, and railway trains, for the first time. Upon the railway, not then out of the second year of its age, I proceeded to Liverpool. The opening of that railway is an epoch in the history of the world. In memory, I see my first whirl upon it, standing so prominently out among other recollections, that it seems like an epoch of my life. All sights which I had seen, in London or elsewhere—the beautiful, the grand, the wonderful—shrunk into comparative nothingness, when, after reaching Liverpool, I went into the country a week, in the neighbourhood of Prescot, and saw (each day I sought to see it, each hour of the day I could have stood to see it again) the white steam shooting through the landscape of trees, meadows, and villages, and the long train, loaded with merchandise, men and women, and human enterprise, rolling along under the steam. I had seen no sight like that; I have seen nothing to excel it since. In beauty and grandeur, the world has nothing beyond it. In wonder alone, the electric telegraph outstrips the railway; but they belong to the one family of wonders. I used to stand and look at it, and dream as I stood; and when I ventured to relate any of those dreams, people used to say that I was very dreamy indeed. Related now that sixteen years have passed, those thoughts would seem very sober realities.

The Reform Bill had just then passed into law. Some people saw no good in the Reform Bill, but much evil; some saw no good in the railways, but much evil; others saw no evil in either, yet not much good; the greater number saw boundless good in both. But many of those who saw boundless good in the Reform Bill, turned in the second, third, fourth, fifth, sixth, seventh, eighth, or ninth years of its existence, and did all they could, by fair means and unfair means, by their own votes, and by their influence over the votes of others, to oppose the principles of the Reform Bill, and the faithful adherents of it: they promoted the political principles opposed to it, and supported its opponents, because the boundless good which they expected to come out of it, did not come in the second, third, fourth, fifth, sixth, seventh, eighth, nor ninth years of its existence. The same order of minds who foresaw boundless good from the establishment of railways, and who did not see it come in the shape, and within the time, that they expected it to come, would have put their backs to the locomotive engine, and would have prevented another train from starting, had they been strong enough.

To those who advocated the reform of 1832, it may be almost deemed a triumph, to have lived to see that it has done no harm. The opposition to it was not founded upon the probability of its doing no good, but on the certainty of its doing positive and irreparable mischief. He must be a bold reasoner, or a man too weak to reason, who says it has done no good. He must be a bolder or a weaker man, or one in whom both qualities are compounded, who says that the Reform Act has done evil. The first principle of magnitude—the greatest of all, indeed, solved by the establishment of the Manchester and Liverpool Railway, was this, that the *innovation* upon old customs was safe. The railways have proved that, and much more. The greatest principle established by our experience of the Reform Act, which gave Manchester two members for the first time, is that *innovation* upon old customs, of admitting a large number of the population to share in the privileges of the constitution, is safe. The Reform Act has proved that, and much more.

And if the doors of the constitution were opened again, I have no fear but all the predictions of mischief to follow, would be like the predictions before the enactment of the Reform Bill; there would be no wrong, nor danger of wrong. Like the hopes formed of the Reform Bill by the sanguine, and those who do not accustom themselves to the use of reason, or who, being weak in the faculties which deal with *cause and effect*, cannot understand the operation of reason, there would be expectations formed only to be disappointed. No acts of parliament can make a population well clothed, well supplied with food, well lodged, and happy; but acts of parliament can remove the artificial hindrances to those desirable ends, and promote their accomplishment. Comfort and happiness depend on the self-exertions of those who seek them, and cannot be conferred by others. But so long as men are excluded from the political privileges of their birth-right as men, it is natural for them to think that they could make themselves more comfortable and happy, if they had the exercise of their natural rights.

The time when I first saw the railway uniting Liverpool and Manchester—spanning the bog where human foot could not tread—stands as I have said, in memory, like an epoch of my life. I looked upon that most poetical and most practical of the grand achievements of human intellect, until people thought I stood and slept; and, when they heard the dream, they said it was very dreamy indeed. I should fear to tell the dreams which I have now beside the electric telegraph, and on the railways, and within the regions of the god-like inventors and makers of machinery. There is a time coming when realities shall go beyond any dreams that have yet been told of those things. Nation exchanging with nation their products freely; thoughts exchanging themselves for thoughts, and never taking note of the geographical space they have to pass over, except to give the battery a little more of the electric spirit, if the distance which the thought has to go be many hundreds of miles; man holding free fellowship with man, without taking note of the social distance which used to separate them, except, perhaps, the lord (landed lord or cotton lord) shall use a little more of the moral electricity, when conveying a thought to a working man, at the opposite end of the social pole, who used to be very far distant; that lord may put on a little more of the moral electricity, which shall then be discovered, to carry the instantaneous message of one feeling, one interest, one object, one hope of success from the lordly end, to the working man's end of the social world. Universal enfranchisement, railways, electric telegraphs, public schools (the greatest of the moral levers for elevating mankind named last—because last to be advocated, which should have been first); these are some of the elements of a moral faith, believing in the universal brotherhood of mankind, which I daily hold, and never doubt upon; which I believe will as certainly be realized, as I believe that *good*, and not *evil*, was the object of all creation, and is the end of all existence.

I took a passage by a steamer, called the *Manchester*, at that time a new and crack packet, running between Liverpool and the Clyde. After twenty-four hours of stormy weather, she got alongside Greenock quay. It being Sunday, and the hour when church and chapel attendants have nothing to do but think on the forenoon lecture, anticipate the afternoon sermon, or shiver on the quay if the day be cold, and look at the ships, beating against the wind, in the Clyde, or perchance go into 'some decent spirit-dealer's shop and get a dram'— it being at that hour, the number of people assembled, to see the Liverpool steamer come in, was greater than usual. It was greater also than it would have been even with these people, in consequence of some friends of mine having let it be known, that *their* friend, the Scots Grey, was expected to be on board. They did not see me get on shore. I stood by their side, and heard one of them say, 'I doubt he is not here'; and other persons, who probably expected to see me in a soldier's uniform, said, 'No, there is no Scots Grey coming out of her yet.' At last the two brothers, E—— F—— and J—— F——, who had waited for me all the day, saw my face, and said, 'Here he is!' And there I was, and happy to meet them. They were natives of Berwickshire, but were then resident in Greenock. I had corresponded with them from a feeling of friendship, arising out of intellectual similarities of nature, and also arising from another delicate, and, at that time, sweet and hopeful circumstance, not necessary now to be named. I staid with them one night, and, next day, J—— F—— accompanied me to Glasgow. I was urgently requested to stay a few days in Glasgow, to pay my respects and gratitude to some persons there, who had made themselves active in my behalf, and to appear at a meeting of the political union as already related. I complied.

I wrote to my brother James, in Edinburgh, stating that I was detained in Glasgow, and that, being anxious to see him, I wished him to meet me at Glasgow. He came, and found me where I was then staying; and, after an affectionate greeting, a few inquiries about friends, and some other matters, he said that a gentleman who travelled with him from Edinburgh, had a very strong desire to see me, that he was at the inn where they alighted, and had not come to me, as I was in a private house. I at once put on my hat, and went with him. We entered an apartment at the inn, where sat a personage with a weather-beaten face, whiskered, respectably dressed—something like the mate or master of a ship that has been on a long voyage. We bade each other good morning, and made several observations about weather, politics, country news, and so forth, and still it did not occur to me that this bearded, weather-beaten, naval-like personage was more than a fellow-traveller with James from Edinburgh.

James, at last, said to me, 'I suppose you do not know who this is?' I looked at the stranger, and said, 'No.' 'Did you never know,' James continued, 'any one in the east country of the name of Peter Simerel?' 'Peter Simerel,' I replied, 'there were no Simerels but ourselves in the east country, that I know of; I do not remember of a Peter, but'—I was going to say—'*our* Peter.' I did not get it out. It was our Peter. When he found me trying to recollect him, and could not, the tears rolled out of his eyes, over his weather-worn face, and he cried, '*Sandy!* don't you know me?' I, like him, hardly able to make myself intelligible, cried, 'Pate, I did not know you.' After a time, we all three fell into a fit of laughter, and laughed at ourselves, because we, who had not met since some of us were children, had met now as if we were still children.

But even after this fit of laughter, we had some more of the pathetic. Perhaps the manliness of none of us was the less, that it dissolved under the superior influence of feelings arising out of that unexpected meeting. I was obliged to remain in Glasgow a few days longer, as it had been announced that I was to appear at the political union with Mr. ——, and he would take no denial. My brothers returned to Edinburgh. As soon as I could escape, I followed them.

From Glasgow there were forty-four miles of road, and five hours upon a coach, and I was in Edinburgh. From Edinburgh there were twenty-eight miles of road, and less than four hours upon a coach, and I was at Dunbar—James and Peter with me. We had six miles to walk to reach Thriepland Hill. There were earnest hearts there, longing for our coming, we knew, and we lingered as little as possible. Still we could not pass every kind friend who came to bid us welcome; nor every well-known road-mark, which our own memories welcomed. Few of those who met us, knew Peter, he had been so long absent; most of them knew James; and all of them knew me, personally, or by hearsay—the affair in the Scots Greys having excited much attention in my native neighbourhood. My friend, Mr. Hugh Brown, met us from Innerwick, and as I owed him much gratitude for the interest he had taken in my military difficulties, in reading the newspapers to get at the facts, to communicate them to my father and mother, who were not in a position to see newspapers, we paid a brief visit to him.

Then, as we got upon the old familiar roads, though it was dark, the time ranging between seven o'clock and ten, at the end of October, we had so many recollections to tell to one another. Peter remembered something which had happened to him, in riding from Branxton to Dunbar, and back at night on the master's horse; and I remembered, that on coming out of Dunbar once when a boy at night, on a horse, when passing under the dark trees at the lonesome Calky Ford (the spot where the heat of Cromwell's battle of Dunbar was fought), a place that had an ill name for highway robbers, and not too good a name for witches and ghaists, I heard something stir, and then cry, and I put heels to the horse, and went off at the gallop; and I remembered and told how there was still something crying behind; how the horse galloped faster and faster until I approached Dryburnford Bridge, when the thought came into me that perhaps

Cutty Sark was behind, and that, like Tam O'Shanter, I must 'win the key stane o' the brig,' else we would be caught; but that to my horror it would not enter upon the bridge. It halted, reared, and backed with me, as if the witch had got it by the tail, or, as if waiting for the witches to come up to get hold of me, though the fact was, that the poor animal wished to drink in the stream, to which it had been accustomed to go, instead of crossing by the bridge.

Such reminiscences we told, until we came to the Place Dykes, where we saw through the dark the place of the old castle, indicated by the solitary light of Sandy Cowe, who, by the old feudal ruin dwelt alone, rearing garden plants, on ground which was once the glacis and fosse of the Norman castle of the lords of Innerwick; from which ground, disturbed by the spade and the ploughshare only—to be disturbed by the spear and the engines of war no more—he sent the seeds and plants throughout the country, to replenish the kailyards of the peaceful hinds, the ploughers of the farm fields of Lothian. Looking across the blackness, and listening to Thornton burn murmuring in its bed deep below us, far deeper than we could see, and no louder than we could faintly hear—we said it seemed as if past times and things had gone to sleep, and were dreaming in their deep slumber, and had left but a feeble light burning to show us, when we came, where the past was sleeping. And in that mood of thought, as we journeyed along the Thornton road, my memory took me into the burn below, among things which had long slumbered; and deep as the ravine was, and thick the darkness, it was light and sunny on the water-pools with memory there. The bummelberries hung over the rocks in ripe clusters, and the trout in the shady places underneath retreated from danger, or lay in the shallows in sunniness and safety, while I loitered, and waded, and slowly made my way down to William Thomson's mill, on some errand concerning oatmeal, or one of his famous breed of young pigs.

We reached the place where the path, ancient as the Edwards of England, and of our own Bruce and Wallace, led over the Law and Eden-Ken's brig, and upward by the King's stones, but no bridge was there now, and we had to go round the cart road. Tradition says, that the Scots were once posted behind the Law, to intercept one of the invading Edwards, in his attempt to cross the burn and its rocky banks, expecting that he did not know of the bridge. But seeing him advance directly down upon it from the top of the Butterlaw Bank, the sentinels cried out, 'Edward kens the brig!' which alarming cry communicated a panic to the Scots, who retreated. The untimely alarm, the panic it caused, and the disaster, fixed the name, which was abbreviated to 'Eden-ken's brig'. The King's Stones had been blasted with gunpowder to make clearances for agriculture, before I was old enough to remember them. But I was a boy grown, when, to prevent travellers from using the ancient pathway, the venerable grey bridge was blown down with gunpowder. The first impulse of indignation which I felt in my life, at anything like an outrage on public privileges, was felt at the destruction of Eden-Ken's brig. The first time that a desire was kindled in me to take a pen and write, was the desire to avenge its fall. The first attempt I made at rhyming, was to record its fate. Almost the first political reflections which passed through my mind, when I was some years older, were reflections on the character assumed by the party called tories—that they venerated and preserved old things—and the character imputed by them to all who were not tories—that these delighted in pulling down and destroying old things. I had seen all power vested in, and used by the high tories exclusively; nobody else had any power in those parts of Scotland. Many aggressions were made on the public rights of the humbler people, and no one dared complain. Some of those aggressions were so wanton, and without the shadow of justification, that I had, by a process of natural logic, years before the political term, 'destructive', was heard of, associated the name of toryism with destructivism[26]. This arose from the fact, that a few individuals who had much power vested in them, as land stewards, elders of the church, clergymen, and squirearchal magistrates, boasted of being tories, and the enemies of all radicals.

A better acquaintance with political men has led me, and, probably, their farther acquaintance with one another, and the world they live in, has led them to estimate actions by their own worth, rather than by the social position or political connections of those who commit them. I once thought that if I grew to manhood, I would punish the bold ruler of 2,000 acres of land, and of two or three score of people, who, unchallenged, no one daring to say he had done wrong, destroyed our beloved Eden-Ken's brig; and with that thought, when a boy, I would sit on the broken arch for hours together, building a castle in the air, in which was inwoven the shadow of my being a lawyer, who would compel its destroyer to rebuild it, or of being rich enough to rebuild it myself; or, at least, of being strong enough and bold enough, not to be afraid of telling him he had done wrong, and of making him

confess it. I have been neither a lawyer with law, nor rich with money
or with stones; nor have I had the power to upbraid him (its destroyer)
with wrong doing, and make him confess it. I have met him in the
streets of Edinburgh, with a poor horse dragging a load of coals, himself poor, and have given him a job to do. My brother James has given
him many jobs to do. And so the world goes on. Men come to the
level of the ground, as well as old bridges; of the two, the wreck of
the old man is the most melancholy.

We were up the Butterlaw bank and into the Horse Hill planting,
before we ceased to speak of Eden-Kens, and the old recollections it
brought to our minds. There was the Rig on our left, where James had
herded the cows, where Peter had herded after him, and where I herded
after Peter. There were trees on which all three, with years between,
had carved our names; rabbit holes, where all had catched rabbits; a
trickling spring, where all had stemmed pools and placed our water
mills.

As we went along the loaning, Peter told how, when it was daylight
to-morrow, he would go and see Thorntonloch, by the sea-side, where
he was born; and, on another day, Springfield, where I was born; and
the Dean Mill, where old Thomas Sanson lived. And James said, they
would go and see Closehead, where young Thomas Dudgeon lived
when they were boys—poor Tom! who, when a sailor, was drowned
in the Tagus, at Lisbon. And, when at Closehead, they would be, they
said, where James had carried me on his back when I was the baby,
and Peter was not yet sent to school.

But we were now almost at the gate, inside of which, and of the
round stone pillars, and the thorn-bush, and the beech-trees, and the
railing, stood the humble thatched house for which we were bound.
Peter had gradually fallen into silence; and now he stopped short, and
stopped us, and said, 'Heave to, till I overhaul myself! I have cleared
for action more than once, and have stood by the helm in some
roughish gales, in my time; but I never felt my courage go, as it is
going now; let us take an observation before we go in.'

There were two houses; ours was the one next the gate. Within,
were three persons—our mother, father, and youngest sister. It was
now ten o'clock, an hour-and-a-half past their usual bed-time, two
hours past the ordinary time of family prayers. But they expected us,
and had waited until they thought we would not arrive that night.
There was a streak of light, which enabled us to see between the folding

window-shutters. Peter and I got within the railings, and looked in. We could hear, though not distinctly see, that our father was performing family worship.

'Do you think,' said Peter, 'he will have us at the *questions*, to-night?' 'Questions!' I replied; 'your absence for so many years, in so many latitudes of the world, will lay you open to a few questions; but our father likes to hear about foreign places—tell him all about Brazil!' He rejoined: 'I wish there was nothing but the latitude and the longitude, the altitudes of the Andes, the geography of South America, the products, the rivers, and such trifles as these;—I mean the *questions* beginning with "*What is the chief end of man?*" I bought a catechism at Edinburgh, to overhaul them; but I have had no time yet; and so many years abroad, has put me rather out of my reckoning with some of them—"*Effectual Calling*," for instance; I fear I should get aground there, if I were not in shoals long before!' 'Don't fear,' said I; 'we shall not be put to the catechism to-night.' He continued: 'But if you see any signals in that direction, put off to sea—somewhere, anywhere, any parts of the coasts of America, the West Indies, or Africa—launch me, and get me afloat, and I'll give you yarn enough to keep us from running into the catechism, until I have taken soundings in it; when I have had a day or two of calm weather at it, I shall not care so much; only, do not let me get into shallows too soon; the "*Confession of Faith*", too, keep me off that coast, until I work my reckonings again.'

We heard a movement of seats, and voices in conversation. I heard our mother say, she would not give up hopes of our coming, yet; for she had no doubt that I had called to see Hugh Brown; and they were greatly obliged to Hugh Brown for his kindness; many a night he had come all the way from Innerwick, to bring them the newspapers to read about me. But our sister said, she feared we were not coming that night. James told us we must not stand longer outside; we must go in. We bade him go first; and Peter whispered to me, that, had we been about to board an enemy, he would not have let me go before him; but, as we were going to board the old fire-side at Thriepland Hill, he could not, for the life of him, go before me.

We knocked at the door. It was opened, and we entered.

On the Sunday following, we went all to the meeting-house together, at Stockbridge. This is a solitary, yet centrally-situated chapel, to which a congregation of Presbyterian seceders come from a wide district, agricultural on one side, and moorland on the other, a congregation that would be called large, even in a populous town. It is ministered to by my respected friend, the Rev. David Inglis, one of the most useful ministers in the Presbyterian Secession Church, and best of men in that or any church. Our father was not a little elated on going to, and returning from church, with his three sons, on that day. And I was not a little pleased to see—I need not now write whom.

Peter had not been long at home, until he was carried in sight of one of the shoals which he had desired me to pilot him from; but it did not extend farther than the question of what had he done with the *Marrow of Modern Divinity*, and the volumes of sermons which had been sent to him to Woolwich, some years before? He carried our poor old father through so many scenes of adventure, on sea and land, on the coasts of Africa, in the West Indian Islands, round Cape Horn, and through the interior of Brazil, that the father could not do otherwise than listen to the adventurous son. He soon became the leader, and would renew the conversation, by saying, 'Come, Peter, take us to the native land of the potatoes again'; for it delighted him more to hear that Peter had seen the potato plant growing naturally, on the slopes of the Andes, than that he had been a worker at the gold mines; and he would remark, 'Oh, man! that would make a rare book; if you had only had schooling enough, Peter, you might have been an *outher*.'

After a visit of eight days, I returned to Edinburgh, and obtained employment as a wood sawyer. I was not without advisers, who, knowing that I had £250, pointed to the folly, as they called it, of my working in a saw-pit, at work the hardest which manual strength performs, while I had so many chances of making a profitable business with the money. But I sawed on, and heeded them not. During several months, the money remained unbroken, excepting what I drew from it to lend. Of the various kinds of labour at which I had been employed —ploughing, hedging, ditching, draining, gardening, stone-quarrying, road-making, and wood-sawing—the latter was the best paid. I chose it now, because I could choose nothing better. In London I had been advised to invest the money, and the use of my name, in a public-house. I did not approve of that project, for various reasons; partly because I saw nothing enticing in the social life of a publican, partly because I knew nothing of the business, but chiefly because I had no faith in those who advised me. In another town in England, I had an offer of an opening in a malting business; that I also declined. In Glasgow or Edinburgh, nothing better than becoming landlord of a public-house was immediately open to me, and I chose to strip to the shirt, and go into the saw-pit, from six in the morning (with candle-light) to seven at night (with candle-light), for several months during the winter, rather than take a public-house. I had some indistinct purpose before me, of entering into the trade of a furniture dealer at the following Whitsuntide; and with that in view, I occasionally turned an inquiring eye into the mysteries of bargains in old and new furniture. But I did not fall in love with this project, and so sawed on, living on the wages I earned, and withdrawing none of the money from the bank, except, as I have already said, to lend—except to lend again and again, as I had already done.

There was a moral space, a chasm between me and that money, which made it different from any other money; I had not worked for it. I never loved it as my own. I never had confidence in it. There was a prophetic dread of it, and of some of those who had given it, always about me, that the time would come when I would be upbraided for having received it. Perhaps this feeling, associated with a desire to let my want of affection for the money be seen, made me the more ready to lend it, without being exact as to the kind of security I got. At all events, those who could urge some pretensions of services done to me, borrowed easily enough. My brothers warned me that I was losing it; but they did not see it with my eyes, nor feel it to be an alien treasure, as I felt it.

At last, during the spring of 1833, I became connected with parties who were to open an extensive coffee-house, with me jointly. After a loss of time and some expense, I discovered doubtful circumstances about them, and withdrew. Other parties, about the same time, proposed a partnership of a more agreeable nature. This was, to start a literary journal; and as they all had, or professed to have, money in their own hands, or obtainable from connections, I did not hesitate to furnish the preliminary supplies. Type and other necessaries for printing, were ordered. As my name was best known, I undertook to write to several literary men for contributions. Ebenezer Elliott sent us a poem. The late Thomas Campbell sent a letter promising a poem; Professor Tennant, of St. Andrew's, sent a poem; Thomas Atkinson, of Glasgow, lamented that he was on the verge of the grave, and that he had not seen me in Glasgow. Others contributed. The publication never made its appearance. I found none of the partners bringing contributions in money: one brought verses; one, a treatise on banking; a third, a story; all of them brought tales—tales in manuscript to be printed, and tales told by word of mouth, to satisfy me about the expenses they had incurred in my name.

I did not let my brothers know of those preparations to go into such a perilous adventure. James's taste in literature I knew to be fastidious, and too refined for him to have faith in me or my partners; and his knowledge of mankind and of business, extended so much further than mine, as to render him suspicious of them. Meanwhile, one of them undertook to initiate me into the mysteries of buying and selling tea, coffee, wine, whisky, porter, ale, and other commodities of a trade peculiar to Scotland, which is neither grocer, spirit merchant, nor tavern-keeper, but a little of each; and as I now thought that, with such professional assistance as was offered, and pecuniary support as was *promised*, I might unite an agreeable employment to a profitable one, I abandoned the sawpit and the saw, took a shop, and, in six months, had not one shilling that was my own.

I left Edinburgh in debt. The debts owing to me were more than double the amount of those which I owed; but they were of a very different kind. With few exceptions, and these of trifling amount, the debts I owed were contracted by my putting my name as security for that which I got no value for; while all my credits, without one exception, were for money lent, goods given, and service done, for most of which I held no good legal bond.

All those things must make me look very silly in the eyes of people accustomed to business transactions from their childhood. I am silly enough in my own eyes, when I look back upon myself, look back to Edinburgh, look back to 1833. But facts are the subject of the present narrative, and there they are.

On leaving Edinburgh, I had not quite seven pounds in money, and part of that was borrowed from my brother. But I felt more at ease with the wide world before me, and my own world of life to begin again, than I had done at any time since I had enlisted as a soldier. I had health and strength, and could work, and I was not afraid of the world. Had I laid my purpose to take as much away with me as I could obtain possession of, I might have been outward bound from Edinburgh much better provided. I had the means in my power to have done so. I might have remained, and, with a little perseverance, have got over the temporary difficulties of the ill-managed literary project. But what with the bitterness of a broken hope long cherished—in soft language, called love—and what with the disappointment of not finding every one with whom I was associated as single in purpose as I took them to be; and what with my not feeling satisfied to follow the business I was in, now that the literary project had gone to the ground at so much cost to me, I determined not to remain where so many people knew me, who were inclined rather to laugh at the most delicate of my troubles, than to sympathize in them. I sold all and paid all, so far as I could sell and pay; and went out with five pounds odd shillings of my own, the remainder of seven pounds borrowed from my brother. Thus I once again faced the world, to begin a new chapter of my life.

[25] Alderman Harmer, the founder and proprietor of *The Weekly Dispatch*.
[26] A hostile political label for chartism in the 'forties.

CHAPTER XXI

Marriage

THE 15th of March has so frequently been an eventful day to me, that, if disposed to write about destiny, I might refer to it for illustrative occurrences. On that day, in the year 1811, I was born. On that day, in the year 1834, at which my narrative has now arrived, an incident which led to the most pleasing and most important event of my life occurred, as I shall presently relate. On that day, in 1836, I did something in Spain, which obtained for me the good opinion of all the soldiers in the ranks, and all the officers commanding them, who knew me. On that day, in 1837, still in Spain, the heel of my boot was cut off by a grape shot, while a stone, thrown up by a cannon ball, struck me on the head; and, though knocked down by the stone in the front of a thousand men or more, all rushing forward to take a fortified hill by storm, from which cannon and every kind of fire-arms were flashing, thundering, and discharging the missiles of death in our faces, I was on my feet soon enough to be the third person who mounted the first fortification—having intended, as it was my birth-day, to be the first to mount. Having fired my fusil, I was reloading it, when a bullet, in return for the one which I had just sent off, took the ramrod out of my hand, carrying it between my arm and body, taking a bit of cloth and a bit of skin with it. The ramrod, bent double, was picked up by some soldiers in the rear. On the 15h of March, 1842, I wrote an article for a newspaper, which attracted so much attention, as I have since ascertained from the chairman of the Anti-Corn-Law League, that he and other gentlemen in Manchester were induced to make inquiries about its authorship. Unknown to them, Mr. Cobden was at the same time making the same inquiries in London. It resulted in my introduction to an employment, as honourable as anything was in which I had been engaged before, not less so than the most dignified employment known to human enterprise—working with a spade or a plough, or other implement, or with one's own hands, without an implement, for one's own daily bread; it was as honourable

253

as that employment, and more useful. It was to effect that which the use of warlike implements and the politics of war can never effect, the goodwill and harmony of nations. I might select some other noticeable incidents from the thirty-eight fifteenths of March, which I have lived over; but I shall only revert to that date in the year 1834.

I was in London. In the forenoon I entered a house not far from Finsbury Square, where newspapers were kept for the use of customers who breakfasted, dined, or refreshed themselves. The paper I wanted to see was in the hands of a gentleman who kindly offered it the moment he heard me inquire for it. I begged him to retain it until he had finished what he was reading. He politely urged me to take it. The willingness of each to oblige the other, led us into conversation. Our conversation turned upon the topics in the newspapers, and from these alighted upon a piece of veneer of fancy wood which lay at his side. He explained the beauties of the wood, and its uses in fancy cabinet work, by which I ascertained that he was a cabinet maker. We spoke of the excellence of veneers now that they were cut by the circular saws at the mills. compared with what they were when cut by sawyers on the sawpit, which led him to know that I had been a sawyer. From speaking of what I had been, our conversation came to what I was; and, in its course, touched upon my having been a soldier. He told me how pleased his wife would be, if I would, on the following Sunday, come and dine with them. I accepted the invitation. I found a large family of young, happy, healthy, kindly, well-bred little boys and girls, and a mother—such a mother as such a family must have, to be what they were. The children, at that time old enough to remember in subsequent years, have told me that they recollect me, and the time, from the broad Scotch that I spoke. I remember them and the time from the delightful conversation we had. Their mother, a Londoner born, told me much that I did not know; and displayed that vivacity, intelligence, and generous hospitality—the hospitality not of the table alone, but of manners and conversation, which leave no doubt upon the visitor's mind, that he is welcome—a hospitality peculiarly characteristic of the genuine native of London. I visited again, and many times, always welcomed when I went, always requested to return soon, when I came away. I left London, and was absent three years, two of those years in Spain. They did not know where I was during those two years; but, on returning to London, and finding them still the same kind friends, they assured me that had they known where I was, they would have read the accounts of the campaign in the newspapers with a very different interest. I continued to visit, occasionally, during the three years, the children from oldest to youngest, ready to run to the door when they heard my knock, the faces smiling, and the fireside warm, and a seat ready always. All who were above mere childhood contributed to the family resources, by working; all, down to infancy, contributed to the family happiness. The girls always tidy, always doing something useful, always with smiles upon their faces, moved about like household angels, as they were. I said to their mother one day, 'When those girls are old enough, I must have one of them for a wife.' It was agreed, that if I waited two or three years, until they were grown out of childhood, and, if I could persuade one of them to have me, there would be no objection. Having the father and mother on my side, and having nursed my chosen one on my knee when she was a child, the task of winning her was not so difficult as some such tasks have been to some wooers. One day, the 10th of January, 1841, after years of familiar friendship had passed, we repaired to a quiet church in the city, where her father and mother were married, and there, on that sacred spot, memorable to them, they gave her to me. The highest testimonial of respect that I ever received, and the richest pledge of it, was from that excellent mother on that day, in these words: 'She is the first of my children married; she is so young, that I could not have consented to her marriage with any man but yourself. We have known you so many years, that I can entrust you with anything. What higher proof can I give of my esteem and confidence, than to give you my child, so dear to me as she is?' Every day and year since has ripened our confidence and affection; and of all the blessed days in the calendar, I have most reason to say, 'Blessed was the 15th of March, 1834, on which I asked for the newspaper to read from a kind man, who offered it to me before he was done with it.'

The next events in 1834, which I was concerned in, and which are in any way interesting, are those for which a new chapter is necessary. They are historical. I must begin at the beginning.

CHAPTER XXII*

Political Discontent, Plots and Conspiracies in 1834

BEFORE proceeding to relate what I know of the political conspiracy, which was formed under cover of the trades' unions of 1834, it is necessary that I should glance backward to the reformed parliament, which was elected in December, 1832, after the passing of the Reform Act, and to the reform ministry; and trace the sources and the operation of the unpopularity in which the ministry and their parliamentary supporters lived, moved, and acted, in 1834. The expedition and simplicity of the new elections, finished in one or in two days, compared with the rioting, drunkenness, and expense of the elections which lasted fifteen days, convinced even the prophets of evil that a reform had been effected. The elections were numerically in favour of the reform ministry, to an extent hardly anticipated. Of the 658 members, 400 were ministerialists; and only 150 were tories and conservatives. The Irish repealers, ultra-liberals, and radicals, who could not be classified by anticipation, numbered over 100. By another analysis, the *reformers* numbered 509; and the *anti-reformers*, 149. Experience proved this estimate to be incorrect, though probably it accorded with the intentions or professions of the members when elected. The measures brought before parliament by the government were too liberal for many of the professing reformers, who thenceforward allied themselves with the conservatives; and too stringent or illiberal for others, who, in consequence, voted against ministers, or absented themselves on occasions important to the ministry.

* This portion of the Autobiography was first written at Dublin, on the 21st of January, 1847, sealed up, and sent to the careful keeping of friends in London. Famine, fever, and the worst ills of the worst times of poor Ireland, were then at their crisis. I was sent from England by the proprietors of the *Manchester Examiner*, to travel through that country, to examine into its actual condition, without regard to political or religious parties, and to report to that paper what I saw. This task I fulfilled. But upon my first arrival in Dublin from England, I was taken suddenly and seriously ill while visiting some of the deplorable abodes of poverty and disease in that city. When I recovered sufficiently to be able to write, I reflected on the chances of recurring illness and death, while travelling in the fevered, famine-stricken, crime-committing districts of the south and west of Ireland; and that if I did not write this chapter then, I might pass from the world without its facts being known—without the lesson to working men contained in the facts being written.

In no previous parliament has such an amount of business been transacted as in this. The previous sittings of the House of Commons had averaged five hours each; in this session, they averaged above nine hours. More than 11,000 speeches were delivered.

The leading subjects were, First—A measure to reform the Irish church, by which the bishops were reduced from twenty-two to twelve, and church-rates were superseded. This measure alarmed many churchmen, who otherwise supported government, by which the anti-reforming opposition was rendered stronger in numbers as well as in hostility. But the measure was carried.

Second—A measure by which one million sterling was lent to the clergy of Ireland, whose tithes were in arrear. This was supported by the anti-reformers, but opposed by many of the ultra-liberals, rendering the ministry unpopular with them and with the unrepresented classes of the people.

Third—Acts were passed reforming the grand and petty juries in Ireland, which, though meritorious, did not affect public opinion in England.

Fourth—The Scottish Burgh Reform Act passed, offending the anti-reformers, giving high satisfaction to all other parties in Scotland, but not appreciated as a popular measure by the general body of the English people.

Fifth—Twenty millions sterling were voted as payment to the owners of negro slaves in the West Indies, and a bill enacted for the liberation of the slaves accordingly. A majority of parliament—a majority of the religious philanthropists, and philosophical liberals, were in favour of this bargain for humanity. With the millions of working men and women in Great Britain, all so highly taxed, many of whom did not eat and drink so well, nor work so little, as the negro slaves, this free gift of twenty millions sterling to the slave owners, who, while they received it, and long after, had a monopoly of the sugar market—they, in most part, living in luxurious ease in England, and never attending, as business men should attend, to the profitable cultivation of their sugar plantations—with the millions of our own working population, who paid dear for sugar and coffee, and were able to consume but little of either, this grant out of the taxes was exceedingly unpopular. In the next year, when the government prosecuted and transported six poor Dorsetshire labourers[27], for combining to raise the agricultural wages of their district—upon which wages they could not procure such good food nor such full meals as were allowed to negro slaves—this was remembered against them by the formidable trades' unions, which gave them such a year of disquiet.

Sixth—A series of measures reforming, or, at least, altering, the government of India, renewing the company's charter for twenty years, and throwing open the trade to China, were passed. The last, though a measure of great national importance, did not add to the popularity of the ministers with the general body of the people, who did not understand, or care to understand, the great principles involved in the abolition of monopoly.

Seventh—The charter of the Bank of England was renewed, after several discussions on the currency, which, though of national import-ance, did not attract much notice beyond the doors of parliament. The ministers would neither have gained nor lost popularity by that question, had they allowed each member to speak and vote in the usual way. But a speech of Mr. Cobbett, and a vote of the house taken upon that speech, were, on the motion of the Chancellor of the Exchequer (Lord Althorp), expunged from the minutes of the proceedings of the House. Out of doors, people who neither believed with Mr. Cobbett, nor cared to understand the currency question, understood that a veteran reformer had been morally chastised by a union of ministerial whigs and opposition tories, for his reflections upon Sir Robert Peel, the leader of the tories. This occurred on the 16th of May, while a jury was sitting to inquire into the cause of the death of a policeman, named Robert Colley, killed in Coldbath Fields, on the 13th, in an affray, in which the police, by order of Lord Melbourne, the Home Secretary, were employed in dispersing a political meeting. Much violence was committed by the police, as well as by the mob, whom they attacked. The policeman was *stabbed with a dagger*; and the jury, after sitting twelve days upon the inquest, returned a verdict of *justifiable homicide*; on the 30th, this verdict, on the motion of the Solicitor-General, was set aside by the Court of King's Bench. This added to the public excitement. With the multitude, and the orators who led it in its public meetings, smoking-parlours, tap-rooms, or workshops, the Home Secretary was the most accursed of ministers, or of public men. He was not less popular in the following year. Nor had the dagger which killed the policeman ceased to be referred to, in connection with his name.

While that jury was sitting in Calthorpe Street, attracting the nation's eyes to itself and to the meeting which the police had been unwisely employed to disperse, public meetings were held in the large towns, to memorialize the king to dismiss his ministers. Mr. O'Connell and Mr. Attwood were conspicuous at a vast assembly held for that purpose, on the 18th of May, at Birmingham. And the anti-reformers were also agitators now, though not openly. They operated upon the working classes, urging them to resist the tyranny of the whig reformers, pointing to Coldbath Fields and to the Irish Coercion Bill. Their purpose was to get the whigs out of office.

Eighth—The Irish Coercion Bill was the first of the unpopular measures of 1833, in regard to time; but, except in Ireland, it was not instantly decried. Now, it was the popular theme of accusation against the reform ministry, among all the unrepresented people of England, and among a majority of the liberal electors.

Ninth—A subordinate member of the government, Mr. Robert Grant[28], brought in a bill to remove the Jewish disabilities. It was defeated, and an outcry raised against the ministry, by the churchmen and some others, which did them more harm with the religious electors, than the dispersion of the Coldbath Fields meeting had done.

Tenth—The Court of Chancery was reformed, and many offices abolished; by which more than a proportionate alarm was raised among the legal functionaries, affected, or afraid of being affected, by the reform. They added their efforts to increase the unpopularity of the ministry.

Eleventh—The total repeal of the duty on tiles; the repeal of two shillings stamp duty on advertisements; the reduction of assessed taxes on shops; the reduction of duty on marine insurances; the repeal of the stamp duty on receipts under £5; the repeal of the duty (additional laid on in 1821) on raw cotton; the reduction of half the duty on soap; and a variety of good measures, were carried; most of the latter for the improvement of the administration of the law. But it is questionable if all those good acts of the ministry, in the session of 1833, added to their popularity, or warded off any odium, except among the philosophic few, or the moderate thinkers. To the general body of the people the reduction of taxes gave offence, because it did not go far enough; and the amendments of the administration of justice gave offence to those who felt any personal interest in the measures, by going too far.

Finally—There was the subsidence of enthusiasm on the part of the nation, to render the reform ministry unpopular. It came into power amid acclamation. The excitement of the nation was strained beyond the power of nature to endure. From the fall of the Wellington administration, in October, 1830, to the end of the election of the first reformed parliament, in December, 1832, the political drama deepened in interest at each act; and the changing scenes had been so crowded upon one another, that the stirring politics of 1833 became a sleepy afterpiece; a dull play, which the outworn auditory would not be pleased with. This was no fault of the political actors who had done so much to please; it was their misfortune.

The fact of its being their misfortune became more manifest in 1834. That year opened with the electoral classes making large demands for more reform, and with the non-electoral classes complaining loudly that they were betrayed, and marked as a slave class by the Reform Bill, and that the whigs were the most treacherous of all statesmen. Before the year ended, the king dismissed the ministry from his councils for being too liberal, though their measures (of which the new poor-law was the chief) were more unpopular in England, than anything which they did in the previous session. This narrative does not lead me farther into the parliamentary history of those times. I am only justified in relating what I have done, of parliamentary history, because I have good cause to believe, and no cause to doubt, that, in the month of April, 1834, I saved one or more of the cabinet ministers from assassination, the government offices from capture; and, because, in relating how they were endangered, how they were to have been surprised and overcome, how the palace and the king and queen were to have been taken, how the soldiers were to have been outwitted, how the Bank of England was to have been captured, and all London held by the insurgents (England to yield in its turn to the insurrection); it is necessary that I should shew the political circumstances by which the ministry was then surrounded, and the popular sentiments then entertained, for or against them.

To make this relation of ministerial circumstances complete, I must also refer to the trades' unions, premising that the political conspiracy was concocted under cover of the unions, and was probably known to very few of the provincial leaders of those bodies, certainly not to the general members.

The object of most of the unions, if not of all, formed by the trades, previous to the years 1833 and 1834, seems to have been confined to the attainment of trade advantages. The object of the unions was now to support one another by turns. Some trades were to work while others were on strike; those working, to support those not working, the object of not working being to enforce a higher rate of wages. When that higher rate of wages was obtained, they were to resume work, and allow some other trade to strike. This arrangement was broken by the tailors of London, who struck work without the consent of many of the trades earning lower wages than they, and which, called upon to contribute to their support, did not respond to the call.

Mr. Wade, in his *Chronological History of England*, states, under date of 1834, that 'the unions of operatives were not less active at Paris, Lyons, and Brussels, than in London, Dublin, Manchester, and Leeds. As workmen can only form effective combinations against their employers when their services are in urgent request, the existence of the numerous associations to keep up the price of labour is evidence of the industrial activity now pervading Europe.

'Up to the year 1824, the law of England made it a crime for workmen to combine, even in the most peaceable manner, for the purpose of obtaining a rise, or preventing a fall of their wages. But in that year parliament abolished this invidious restriction, and workmen were allowed the same liberty in fixing the price of their labour, that capitalists exercised in fixing the price of their commodities. The old law was inefficient, as well as inequitable. It did not, in fact, prevent the offence it prohibited. Trades' unions were formed and maintained, in the face of it. They existed in the metropolis, and all the chief towns; and their chief tendency was to render proceedings which would have been open, secret, and stealthy.

'Besides keeping up the price of labour by the only just mode of sustaining its value—that of refusing to sell it—the unionists adopted regulations which infringed the liberty of others, they sought to exercise themselves. The number of apprentices to be taken by masters, and the time of their servitude, were to be regulated by the union; the employment of any but regularly associated workmen was, if possible, to be prevented. They even claimed to regulate wages by the rate of profits derived from capital, and from mechanical improvements.

'It is impossible to say how far these interferences with the liberty of others would have proceeded, had they met no resistance, or not been defeated by their own inherent unreasonableness. In the course of the present year, it will be seen that there was a succession of *strikes* amongst the most numerous and useful classes of workpeople, both in London and the country. Consumers of products of all kinds, and of all ranks and degrees, appeared in danger of being reduced to their natural resources. The gasmen of London would not allow light; the tailors, shoemakers, builders, and shipwrights refused their aid; and the weavers and spinners of Yorkshire, Lancashire, and Glasgow, in quick succession, became refractory.'

Though the legislature wisely repealed the laws which had rendered combinations and trade-societies secret, they did not become open when the repeal of these laws gave them liberty to exist, and freedom of action. The unionists continued to have their secret oaths, their skeletons, with blue lights burning within the skull; chains to rattle over the head of the novice, and brimstone to burn under his nose; the Bible, and key, and knife; the asseveration, of awful solemnity, amid the symbols of superstition and despotism, that he, the novice, would give his heart to be cut out of his body, his body and soul to be burned in brimstone for ever and ever, and so forth, if he adhered not in all things to the laws of the union; to the laws of those enlightened reformers, who, in a tawdry imitation of the pomp and mystery of the worst times of priestly inquisition and sovereign despotism, with their javelin men, halberdiers, block, and hatchet, and executioner, administered the mummery, and exacted contributions in cash—the mummery, a delusion; the contributions in cash, a reality.

Of all the trades' unions which, in 1833 and 1834, turned out on strike, defensively, for their own rights, or, aggressively, against the rights of others, none was more generally sympathized with in London, nor so liberally supported by the voluntary contributions of the metropolitan working-men, as the union of the trades in Derby. The employers in that town combined against all workmen who were members of unions, refusing to employ any man until he signed a declaration of non-membership. I have just had access (February, 1848) to an account-book, in London, in which all the sums of money collected in pence, in the metropolis, for the relief of the men on strike at Derby, are entered, with the receipts of those to whom the treasurer in London paid the money. The amount of those subscriptions, collected in pence (in addition to greater sums collected by the trades of London for themselves), and the amount of money contributed by the working classes, for various purposes, since then; afford proof not to be doubted, that working men, by associating together for the attainment of practical objects, have the power within themselves of rising socially, morally, and politically; of advancing politically, because of rising socially and morally.

But the kind of persons selected to receive those subscriptions, of 1834, in London, and remit them to, or disburse them in Derby, and the kind of persons selected, in most cases since, are a proof of the little discretion possessed by associations of the working classes, in the selection of office-bearers. The men of reflection, of wise consideration, of business habits, of business thoughts, were, in every case, in 1834, and have been and are, in most cases since, overlooked, or set aside, or violently thrust out of association, or socially trampled upon, if they do not submit to be thrust out—trampled upon by the violent and the unscrupulous—while the persons selected for office-bearers, leaders, or guides, are the mere talkers.

These men, voluble in tongue, were sent up to London from Derby, and elsewhere, or who, being in London, were chosen, or were permitted to force themselves into the offices of trust. One of them, after acting for the Derby working men and women about three months, finding that the strike which the London tailors had unadvisedly entered upon, was likely to curtail the payments made through him from the metropolis, took all the money which he then found destined for Derby, and something more, and disappeared. His employers, the working men and women, trusting in him, looked for the fulfilment of his trust, but looked in vain. He declined to work for them, and left the country on *strike* against them, and against honour and conscience. Another, the chief leader of the tailors, finding that funds did not flow into his treasury so fast as he had expected, and taught thirteen thousand men, who had been earning the average of thirty shillings a week, to expect when he induced them to strike work, cleared out the treasury, filled his pockets and a carpet-bag, and took shipping for the Continent. His defrauded constituents, however, had their eyes upon him; they pursued; the packet was still on the English coast; they took a boat, got on board, got hold of the orator, laid him on his back on the deck, and took all the money they could find, except as much as would carry him into another country, to hide his shame, and save them the shame of returning with him, and prosecuting him in London.

Thus the London tailors (whose great strike of 1834 had less of public sympathy than any other in that memorable year) were compelled to return to work at lower wages than they earned before they struck, and, in addition to their humiliation and suffering, were compelled by the masters to sign a declaration that they were not longer members of a trades' union.

The bakers managed differently. They accumulated a fund to sustain them on strike; but finding that the unions, after the fall of the tailors, were going down, they resolved, in a public assembly, not to strike work, but to spend the funds, that their executive might have no temptation to dishonesty; and, as the readiest, and most generally agreeable manner of getting rid of the funds, was to have a series of jollifications at public-houses, they proceeded accordingly, and so saved their office-bearers from following the example of the officers of certain other trades.

To the credit of the more rational and manly of the journeymen bakers, that vote of a majority which devoted the funds to dissipation, and the act of dissipation itself, were felt to be a reproach on their trade, which some work of good intention, well performed, must wipe out. They instituted, and have carried on with success, a mutual assurance and benefit society, to which they invited the co-operation and friendly intercourse of the employers, instead of suicidally waging war with the master class, against capital, which is only a war against wages, and against themselves.

My *present* purpose is not, however, to write a history of trades' unions. They are referred to here as examples of the management, or governing wisdom and honesty of those great confederations, so formidable in their complaints against national misgovernment, and under cover of which our tried political institutions were so nearly exchanged in 1834, for something untried and unknown; those who were to take the governing power of the untried and unknown accidents being the men of whom these trade leaders are specimens.

It is in like manner necessary that reference should be here made to another variety of leaders whom working men have followed; namely, those who were not members of trade unions, being 'born gentlemen', too high to live like working men, yet too necessitous to exist without living at the expense of some one, and who, finding the working order the most easily deluded, and most easily fleeced of all orders of men, lived on them. It was early in the spring of 1834, when the unions were in their meridian, that I, for the first time, heard some of these orators deliver speeches. One of them, then new to London, but since successful in obtaining an influence over the least thoughtful and discreet of the working classes, attracted my notice, drew to him my listening ear, excited me to an anxious and searching reflectiveness by his first speech, more than all the other great speakers of that day did. I heard the voices of a greater number of working men applaud him, and saw more hands with the signs of work upon them clapping for him, than for any of the other orators. And that sentiment of his which was most enthusiastically applauded, was this, that no matter *how far* the other reformers then on the platform would go, in effecting great political changes, *he would go farther*. This was repeated in various phrases. It was the burthen of his oration. It did more than any speech I ever heard, to make me reflect.

It was about this time, that some labouring men were tried at Dorchester (at the spring assizes of 1834) for being members of a union, and administering illegal oaths. They were indicted upon an obsolete statute, which was enacted for the suppression of mutiny in the navy, and sentenced to seven years' transportation. A strong feeling arose throughout the country, from the first report of their conviction, that they had been harshly dealt with, as examples to other unionists rather than as criminals. This feeling deepened when they were hurried out of England, as soon as it was found that petitions to the government in their favour were preparing in almost every town in the kingdom. I never signed petitions with a stronger impression upon my mind, that I was performing a bare duty to unfortunate fellowmen, than the petitions I signed in favour of those poor labourers. The law, in their case, grappled with a giant's strength upon the feeblest, and most innocent of all the unionists; while those that were formidable, comprising the well-paid trades, led by men neither ignorant nor hungry like the Dorsetshire labourers, were left untouched. The government seemed too weak to grapple with the great unions; at least, the great unions thought so.

Preparations were made for a grand assemblage of all the trades in London, to meet in Copenhagen Fields[29], on the morning of the 21st of April, and march through London to the Home Office, at Whitehall, to present a petition, praying for the release of the Dorsetshire convicts, and then proceed over Westminster Bridge to Kennington Common. No one who listened to the vehement and reckless speeches of the London leaders, or reflected on their policy of intending to overawe the government on that day, by a show of vast numbers, could have any other opinion than this, that they cared less for the fate of the poor labourers of Dorset, than they cared for a display of their own leadership. That kind of reasoning which is called common sense, would have suggested, that the more reserved in a display of physical strength, and the more mild in words the petitioners were, in soliciting the pardon of the Dorset unionists (since the members of all unions were so much dreaded), the more likely they were to succeed. Such thoughts occurred to me. Such thoughts might have occurred to tens of thousands of the ordinary trade members, who walked in procession, had they not been misled by those who had ulterior objects.

The preparations for the grand display proceeded; deputations came from the provincial unions; the union parliament at the H——P—— held its nightly sittings, and had its daily and nightly committees; secret deputations proceeded from it, to secret committees sitting elsewhere. When the time between the preparations and the event was only eight days, news from France told how the trades' unions of Lyons had risen against the law—had rescued a member from trial—had resisted the military who were ordered to re-capture him—had received the military bullets and bayonets bravely—had returned the fire of battle upon the garrison, had defeated it, and then held the town and the authorities at discretion.

'Slaves, that we are!' said some; 'knaves, let our names for ever be, if we suffer our brothers of union to be transported! Death to the tyrant whigs! death to ourselves! destruction to London and all that it contains, if we be not amply revenged for their wrongs, and all our own!' Such were some of the interchanged sentiments, and impromptu resolutions, at the meetings of the secret fraternal committees.

The news from Paris, under date of the 12th, conveyed the intimation that Lyons was subdued, and law and order had resumed their reign. This was not believed. It was alleged to be forged news, to deter Paris from moving. The next mail, giving the fact that the military were subdued in Lyons, and the populace triumphant, confirmed the suspicion of forged news at Paris, and led to the anticipation of a Parisian insurrection being imminent. Private information arrived, that the 'men of Leeds' were preparing to attack the mills; and that at Oldham two unionists apprehended by the police, had been rescued, a factory demolished, blood spilt, life sacrificed, and the authorities set at defiance.

266

At the same time, the secret committee received information that Birmingham, Manchester, Derby, and Nottingham were 'ready to rise', all being prepared; that they waited only for London to lead; and, almost at the same time, the news came that 'Paris had risen'.

Another post from France brought the intelligence that Paris had not succeeded; the insurrection was only a riot, speedily suppressed by the military; and that, after four days of street warfare in Lyons, one thousand seven hundred of the military, and five thousand of the inhabitants slain, and nearly one-half of the houses and property of the town destroyed, the military power was triumphant, and martial law was established in Lyons.

Those failures, and their terrible results in France, were anxiously deliberated upon in the secret committee of London. But they had no terrors. Lyons was only a provincial town, it was contended, and would have conquered if Paris had risen. Paris had not risen because the insurrection had begun in the streets, and especially in the streets of the poor inhabitants; as hopeless a case as if London was to begin in Spitalfields, and break the windows of Brick-lane. 'No,' said the chiefs who were to take London and England, and all the British empire, and give them a blow that they would feel; 'it must be a blow to the *hearts* of the *tyrants*; a blow at the heart of tyranny; a stroke on the head, that shall not only do its work effectually and at once, but be a signal to the whole people to be up, to strike all the tyrants throughout Britain.'

Such were the designs deliberated and fixed upon during the week preceding the great day, the 21st of April. When further explained, those designs comprised the plan of a select few of nerve and resolution accompanying the deputation, and in part forming it, which was to carry the petition into the Home Office, to present it to Lord Melbourne. They were, at a given signal, to fall upon him and his attendants; seize the sentries at the door, disarm them; admit other leaders from the outside; take all the government offices, and as many of the ministers of government as they could find. The military, on the alarm being given, would rush from the barracks in St. James's Park, to rescue the government offices and the ministers; the thousands of men 'who had learned to march' between Copenhagen-fields and Whitehall, and who would all have learned how to fall into their places on the field, and what colours there were to follow and rally under, would rush into the barracks, which would, by that time, have few soldiers in them; overpower the barrack guard, take their arms and accoutrements, and also those of sick men, military servants, and others, and at once fall upon the palace, disarm the palace guard, capture the king and queen, the lords in waiting, and the maids of honour; hold them in captivity until the military capitulated, and laid down their arms; then arm a *People's Guard*, when the military were disarmed, and continue to hold the royal family, and as many of the nobility and the directors of the Bank of England, as it might be convenient to retain *in hand*, as securities against such regiments of the army as might not be disarmed. The Bank of England was to be taken much in the same way as the palace; but if it was not surrendered readily, the *People's Guard* was to see that none of the gold was carried out, and so let it remain until the more urgent business was settled at the west-end. All the other banks in London were to be similarly held, by similar guards, until the people's government ordered the money in the banks to be brought forth and used for the benefit of the people. The East India House would also be attended to in like manner. And on the signal going throughout the kingdom, of the great stroke being given, of the treasury, the palace, and the banks being taken; of the king and queen, the lords in waiting, and maids of honour, being prisoners; some of the ministers being dead, and others held captive, as security to the people with the king: a people's government formed, under the protection of a people's guard—those news going forth to the kingdom, would make it the people's own, and bring the 'tyrant' masters everywhere to sue for peace and protection from their injured working men and women. Everywhere they would have to disgorge the ill-gotten wealth of 'tyranny', and yield it to those whose labour had earned it.

Those who planned this great scheme of operations, saw no difficulty in its accomplishment, if they had bold men enough to strike the first blows. These they felt sure of obtaining; only they were not certain of getting access to Lord Melbourne and the government offices. But at last, as the time approached, that difficulty was removed. An intimation was conveyed to them, that Lord Melbourne would, on the 21st of April, receive the deputation and the petition. This was satisfactory. He was set down as 'done for', and the work almost as good as begun; there only remained the selection of the men who were to do it, and follow it up.

The reputation which I had acquired (forced upon me, I should say) through the affair in the Scots Greys, as 'one who was supposed not likely to stick at trifles', turned their attention upon me. One of them had a good deal of conversation with me, before he made any propositions about joining a secret committee. I had signed the petition in favour of the Dorsetshire labourers, and did not withhold my opinion of their sentence, that it was excessive for their crime, and that there was a meanness about the manner of their prosecution unworthy of the dignity of justice.

I was urged to join the union. I replied, that I belonged to no trade; to which it was rejoined, that I might join the general union—it was not necessary to belong to a trade society. They required two or three hundred men like myself—so the intimation gradually proceeded—strong, energetic, not afraid of trifles, ready on any emergency, with a weapon or without one, to act or direct others to act. They had some good men already; and if I joined them, they thought I might bring some more. They had the great elements of necessity ready and in abundance—money, arms, and ammunition. And then followed a great deal about bishops, the House of Lords, the throne, the landed gentry, and the 'tyrants', who lived on the profits of labour; that none of them could be endured longer; that as I had suffered in the army from 'tyrants', I should be ready, they thought, to avenge myself, and serve my country, now that an opportunity was about to present itself.

I inquired when that opportunity was to come; in what shape it was to come, and what they expected two or three hundred men to do. They said I would know if I joined the union, and became one of them in the secret committee. I said that I understood the tailors' union, which took the lead of all the others in London, was managed entirely by tailors; and that the general committee of the trades was composed of delegated members from each trade. They replied, that such was the case; and that so far as the trades' societies, simply as such, were concerned in the present movement, no other committees were required. But that other things, not of trade importance, but of national importance, must now be done; for now was the time to do them. The country, they said, was never so well organized, as regarded working men (which was quite true), as at that time. More noise had been made about the political unions at the time of the Reform Bill, and, no doubt, rich 'tyrants' belonged to them, who did not belong to the trades' unions; but this fact was all the better. This was supposed by the 'tyrants' to be exclusively a trade movement; the 'tyrants' would be off their guard, as regarded any grand national effort to obtain freedom at one blow; and that one blow would be struck under cover of the trades' movement.

I replied, that if they would tell me what the two or three hundred men they spoke of, were supposed to be able to do, I would judge more correctly of the probability of my taking a share in the enterprise. To this, one who had not before spoken to me, said, 'Scotchman-like, always cautious.' 'I have not always been cautious,' I replied; 'but I think caution is desirable in any such purpose as that which you have foreshadowed to me.' 'We do not think the worse of you,' said one of the first speakers, 'for your caution; but we must also be cautious; and before we can go farther, you must join our body.' I said, I had no objection to become a member; and accordingly I was made a member.

This was on a Saturday night. We were to meet in a house near Drury Lane on the Sunday night, when I was to be introduced to the secret fraternal committee. The interval I spent in anxious cogitation as to the step I was about to take. I called to mind words which had fallen from the talkative unionist who first conversed with me. He had spoken of the ease with which possession might be taken of all the government offices, from Downing Street to the Horse Guards: how easy it was to get access, and catch the 'tyrants' in their offices, and hold them there; how easily the guards could be disarmed; how easily, if this were done on a day when all the working men of London were on the streets ready to assist, the palace could be taken, King William and Queen Adelaide made captive, and, with the 'tyrants', held as hostages until the army capitulated and gave up their arms to the people. I had treated such supposed possibilities as the mere ravings of a political lunatic; but I now called such sayings as these to mind, and pondered deeply and intensely upon them, and supposed that the person, whom I had believed to be a mere utterer of idle words, had really been trying to sound me for an opinion upon such a project.

I hesitated to go to Drury Lane on the Sunday night, and yet the desire to know more of that secret committee, of which they sought to make me a member, was irresistible. I went: and reached, soon after dark, the wall of that mean grave-yard in Drury Lane, the very earth of which smells of death. I stood there for a time, uncertain whether to go into the house appointed, which was not far distant. The thoughts of treason—of the Cato-street conspiracy—of conspirators hanged, beheaded, drawn, and quartered—came into my mind; and as the cold wind of March searched through my clothes, rose up in my face, and went over my head into the grave-yard, and came back again with the smell of death, it gave me the thought that I would be better to die at once, and go to such a mean, but not dishonoured, grave as that foul yard afforded, rather than go into the house to join conspirators. Then I said to myself, I had no intention of joining them: I did not even know if they were conspirators. Again, I said, if I go among them, even to know what they are, and the officers of justice come upon us all, and find proofs on them of treason; would not the officers, and all London, and all the world believe, that the worst man there was myself, my political and military character being marked, and despised by everybody save those very traitors or their political followers. No, said I; it must not be; I must not go.

As I thus reasoned with myself, a person took me by the arm, and said, 'What, is that you? Why don't you come on? I was looking for you an hour ago. We have been all waiting for you.'

'It won't do,' I said.

'What won't do?'

'To proceed farther in the business spoken of last night.'

'Oh! come along; you don't know what the business is. Here are many friends of yours waiting to see you.'

'Who are they?'

'Many; some you know, and some you don't know; excellent fellows all of them; the best men in England; you may depend on them.'

I considered for a few minutes, and felt that the only chance against me, if I went into the house on that night, would be the chance of the police còming, and taking us all prisoners, and that of their finding anything treasonable in the house. I thought the first chance, upon which the last depended, was very remote, owing to the open way in which the trades' unionists met everywhere in London; and, as I was determined not to be sworn to the performance of any act, until I knew explicitly what it was to be, and that if it was treason, or any political adventure whatever, that I would have nothing to do with it, I moved on, and entered the house.

In one apartment smoking and general conversation were going on, and liquor of some kind was on the table, with papers printed and written. I was hurried to a private room, but not before some persons had come forward to shake me by the hand as a brother unionist, and to introduce others whom I did not know. Some of these last were foreigners, who spoke English with difficulty. But they seemed to be quite familiar with my name, and with the affairs, military and political, in which I had been engaged, and shook me by the hand warmly; one of them advanced to embrace me as a brother democrat, but my appetite for embraces would not bear it, and I retreated from him. But, in addition to the disgust I felt at the offer of that reception (which, I believe, is a custom in some countries, and probably in the country where this foreign democrat came from), I had now little doubt that I was amongst conspirators, while the long beard and moustache of this man seemed to me so Judas-like, that I strengthened myself in the resolution to have as little to do with them as possible.

In the private room I again heard anxious words pass, as to the certainty that was now felt of the deputation, and the 'glorious band' that was to accompany it, being admitted to the presence of the cabinet ministers. I was hailed as a brother. At that time, I was thin of flesh, and my tall and broad body of skin, muscle, and bone, arrayed in clothes which did not bespeak me to have much stake in the property of the country, together with that energy of action, and those democratic opinions which I was supposed to possess, made me, no doubt, seem a very likely person to join in a very desperate adventure. They probably, like every other person in London who knew me at that time, gave me no credit for being a *thinking* man; nor were any of them, so far as I had opportunity to judge, of the thinking order of men, or likely to give a man credit for his superior powers of reflection. Nor were they liberal enough, democrats though they were, to tolerate any one's spoken thoughts that were not in accordance with their thoughts.

It was proposed to me, as I was a believer in God, to be sworn, as the preliminary act to any other business. I said, I saw some persons in the private room, and two or three more in the room outside, who were professed unbelievers, who glorified in unbelief, and ridiculed me and all others who held to the faith of our fathers; were they to be sworn? or, if not sworn, how were they to be bound? or, if they were sworn, what dependence was to be placed upon them, if they did not believe in the sanctity of an oath? To which it was replied, that they were all good men and true; they believed in the moral obligation, if not in the sanctity of oaths; that, without any personal imputation upon myself, it was thought that the word of a good democrat, he being a conscientious unbeliever, was quite as good as the oath of any Christian or other conscientious believer; it was a sense of virtue, in the one, that made him keep his word; it was a fear of punishment, in the other, which made him keep his oath. I replied, that I must know more of some of the unbelievers than I had been accustomed to see of them, before I could put any trust in their sense of virtue; at all events, if the business to be performed by me was such as I must be sworn to the performance of, I would not engage in it with others who were not sworn. Moreover, I said, I cannot swear to the performance of it, until I know what it is to be.

I was exceedingly glad that the subject of oaths had come before us before going farther, as I saw in it a loop-hole of escape. I had resolved to find an opening for a retreat, and this was opened for me unexpectedly. Desirous, however, to know something more of the purposes of the conspiracy, as I was thus far in it, I pressed to know what the business to be done by me was, before I engaged upon my oath to do it. Upon which, as much was told as confirmed me in the opinion I had formed, of the design being to take the cabinet ministers and government offices by surprise, when the deputation and the 'glorious band' went into the presence of the ministers, with the great memorial; of the 'glorious band' I was to be one, and one of its leaders, if I would accept the dignity and the danger.

I expressed unwillingness to be engaged in any enterprise of that kind, with persons whom I did not know. I was told that I need not distrust them, some of the best men of England were present in this house, and others were coming to take the lead. There would be some of the boldest and best of the democrats from Birmingham, and there were already some present from Sheffield and Nottingham; all of them were in the secret, and they only wanted a few more such as myself. There were also, they said, some glorious fellows who had been in Paris during the 'three days', and who knew what fighting was, and how to conduct street warfare; and there were Poles, also, the best men in the world for a gallant enterprise.

I said I was resolved not to be sworn to take share in such business, until I knew who were to be engaged in it, and until I had maturely considered it. And having said this, I moved to go away; but they were not inclined to let me go until I had engaged farther with them. It was urged that I should swear to hold within myself whatever secrets I had learned there. To which I replied, 'that is, I suppose, that I may not inform against you.' They rejoined, 'Yes, that is it.' Then, said I, 'My word of honour I hold to be as good as the word of any one of you, and I give my word upon my honour, that I will not divulge your designs or your names.' 'That will scarcely do,' said one; 'you should join with us now, heart and hand, body and soul, before you leave us, and then we shall have no doubt of you.' Said another, 'It is all right with Somerville, don't any of you fear; he has given too many good proofs of his devotion to democracy, for us to mistrust him; let him take his own way; we shall soon have him with us.'

Infatuated creatures! they did more in that half hour, by the revelation of their crimes and folly, to shake my faith in the wisdom of an ignorant democracy, than any amount of philosophic teaching or argument could have done. I left them, and went to my lodgings, and tumbled into bed; lay awake all night, and got out again in the morning unslept, restless, unhappy, and loaded to the very earth with the weight of the horrible secret that had been confided to me. Had I been able to give it back to them, to throw off its burden, and bid them keep it; able to forget it, and to believe that the secret committee of the great trades' unions was as innocent in its purpose as I had believed it to be, I should have felt myself to be a happy man.

Several days passed, and I was again and again applied to, but I pleaded illness. Indeed, I was ill, though not so sick but I might have gone out. I tried to read and think; I could think, but could not read. I felt that I was taking the right course in staying within doors. But, again I asked myself, was I doing my duty in only saving my own neck from the gallows, and reputation from ignominy? Was it not my duty to save those who would be victims of the conspiracy, if it succeeded—the ministers of government, the sovereign, the royal family, everybody who was not of the order of the trades' unionists? and the unionists themselves (most of them innocent of the conspiracy), who would be hanged if the attempt were made, and did not succeed? Was it not my duty to avert, if I could, the commission of the greatest crimes ever contemplated in political conspiracy?—to save the greatest commercial nation, and the most solid political institutions on the face of the earth, from the most perilous of impending convulsions? I prayed to Almighty God, to direct me what to do. What I did, and its effects, are related in the next chapter.

[27] The 'Tolpuddle Martyrs'.
[28] Somerville's old acquaintance the Judge Advocate General.
[29] Later the site of the Caledonian Market.

CHAPTER XXIII

The Plot Frustrated

THE morning of Monday, the 21st of April, came, and with it an assemblage of thirty thousand unionists, on Copenhagen Fields— a series of meadows on the northern side of London. The trades present were thirty-three in number; some of them consisting of a few hundreds of persons only, others of more than one thousand; the tailors alone being about five thousand. The onlookers, who crowded to the field to see the trades arranged in columns, under their respective colours, amounted to twenty thousand, before eight o'clock in the morning. During the day, the numbers attracted to look on as the procession moved through the streets, amounted, probably, to more than one hundred thousand.

From what I had been unwillingly compelled to know of the designs of the conspirators (only a few of whom were in the procession), I wrote private letters to all the daily newspapers, requesting them to caution the innocent members of the unions against appearing in the streets on that day, hinting at a reason why; but, as that caution might be futile (the infatuated unionists seldom listening to counsel that did not come from their own chiefs), the mere sight-seers, and all women, persons in charge of children, and heads of families who could control their servants, were implored to restrain, and be restrained, from exposing themselves in the streets. The newspapers were fervent in their warnings; and the effect was, that, probably, more than half of the sightseers who would have been out, were restrained, and staid within doors. Many of the unionists also took the caution, and remained away; for, in addition to the warnings of the newspapers not to join the procession, they heard the secret injunctions of some leaders, and saw the suspicious preparations of many of their fellow-workmen, to be prepared for what they called resistance; and they remained at home.

The killing of Colley, the policeman, while the police were employed to disperse a political meeting in Coldbath Fields, in the previous year, by a stab of an instrument which was alleged to have been a dagger, and the impunity of the assassin, together with the verdict of '*justifiable homicide*', by the coroner's jury, was frequently referred to now. That verdict, and the applause by which the public received it, proved that the public (so it was reasoned) were favourable to resistance, should the government use force against them, the unionists. And further, it was suggested and reasoned, that working men could not be blamed for carrying with them their work-tools, or any part of them. A dagger had been effective at Coldbath Fields; but they need not incur the expense or the danger, nor excite the suspicion of the government 'tyrants' by each man providing himself with a dagger. The carpenters could carry a chisel; the tailors, a pair of shears, with a keeper to hold the shears close above the joint; the coal-heavers, if they had no particular instrument by which they earned their bread, had good knives to cut their bread, or, if they had them not, they might have them. No one could blame them for carrying each a knife. Any man, of any other trade, might have a knife. The tailors, accordingly, about five thousand in number, appeared upon the ground under their banners, and formed their columns, most of them having a pair of shears in their pockets, so fastened with a keeper of leather or string, as to leave their points bare, and make both blades one. And many, in addition to the shears, carried a bare bodkin, that they might the *quietus* make of all or sundry of those who took arms against them. The carpenters carried chisels; the shoemakers, their knives and awls; and most of the other trades, something. Those members of the trades who were seriously alarmed at hearing the injunctions to carry such instruments, remained away. Fewer than one-half of the tailors in London were present.

But of those who carried their shop-tools, or other instruments, very few, if any, knew of the design, and certainly not of the details of the conspiracy, and preparations for assassinating the cabinet ministers. The members of unions with sharp tools, carried them, under the advice of leaders, who alleged, that an attack of the police or military, or of both, might be made upon them, as in Coldbath Fields. Those who were to execute the business at Whitehall, kept their secret to themselves, and were only to reveal it with the commission of the first act of the conspiracy. To do their work, they were differently armed—had more formidable weapons than shears, awls, knives, or chisels.

Besides writing to the newspapers, stating that I knew there was imminent danger, and urging on the editors to caution all mere sightseers from going near the line of procession; I wrote a letter, signed with my name and address, to Lord Melbourne, in which I related the personal danger he would be in, as well as the political danger to the state, if he admitted any deputation of unionists to an interview on that day, and especially a deputation accompanied by what might appear to be promiscuous followers. As I kept no copy of my letter (having good reasons relating to my personal safety for not doing so) I cannot now give the precise information conveyed; but as the letter is still (so I have reason to believe) in the archives of the Home Office, those who have the privilege of obtaining a sight of, or the publication of, government papers, may see it. Such papers are considered sacred, and are not made public without the writer's consent. In this case, the writer does not keep the matter secret himself. In the hope of teaching working men a lesson, which they may never learn from other teachers, of giving them a solemn warning of the danger their mad-headed leaders have placed them in, while they blindly followed; the writer of this 'state paper' runs the risk of publishing what he now does, and has no objection to the publication of that letter, should any of those whose criminal intents were frustrated by it, choose in parliament to move for it, or those whose lives were saved by it, think fit to produce it.

At what particular time Lord Melbourne changed his intention, and resolved not to admit the unionists, as he had intimated to them he would do, I have no means of knowing. At what particular time the government and the commander-in-chief changed their preparations, I cannot tell; but I know that they did change their preparations, and that very materially.[30] During the Sunday night, detachments of cavalry marched into London from Hounslow and Croydon; several regiments of infantry were brought from Chatham, Woolwich, Windsor, and more distant places; and, most formidable of all, while London was still, and in darkness, and the dreaming madmen of politics saw visions of the deeds to be done with tailors' shears, shoemakers' knives, carpenters' chisels, their own pistols, and their own daggers, no less than twenty-nine pieces of artillery, with shells and shot, were brought from Woolwich, and quietly placed within the barracks in Birdcage-walk, in the palace of St. James's, on the parade-ground of St. James's-park, and within the closed gates of the Horse Guards. On the roofs of the government offices were placed light 'mountain guns', to throw shells into the streets commanding the thoroughfare at Charing-cross, on one side, and Parliament-street and Westminster-bridge on the other. The park gates were closed against the public. No sentries were mounted in the ordinary way outside the Horse Guards. The military guard at the Bank of England was largely strengthened; and at all military stations in the metropolis the troops were under arms. The metropolitan police were armed, and retained in quarters, or in positions out of public view. The police magistrates were early at their respective offices. General officers on duty sent out their aide-de-camps in plain clothes, to reconnoitre in the streets and at Copenhagen Fields. The military forces drawn to the metropolis for the emergency, in addition to the usual complement of Life Guards and Foot Guards, were detachments of the 12th and 17th Lancers, two troops of the 2nd Dragoon Guards and the 1st Royal Dragoons, eight battalions of infantry, and twenty-nine pieces of field ordnance.

On the morning of Monday, the lord mayor, in obedience to a communication from Lord Melbourne, calling on him to make preparations to preserve the peace of the city, as there were reasons to apprehend a breach of it, summoned a court of aldermen, which met at an unusually early hour. Summonses were also sent to the members of common council, all of whom, then in London, attended with alacrity. After a brief deliberation, messengers were sent to the householders, requesting their attendance at Guildhall, to take upon themselves, by oath, the duty of special constables. The aldermen retired to their several wards, to order preparations there, except those who remained to swear in the constables. At Guildhall, in a brief period of time, the avenues of the court were crowded with householders, and five thousand were sworn in. The aldermen then re-assembled, with the lord mayor, at the Mansion House, receiving reports every half-hour, or oftener, from the numerous messengers employed to observe the unionists at different points of procession. Some persons were with the deputation, whose absence would have better satisfied the conspirators than their presence: one of these was the Rev. Dr. Wade, rector of Warwick, a clergyman of the church, who had more pleasure in listening to that applause which his speeches of extreme and eccentric politics ministered to his gratified ears in London, than in ministering to his parishioners in Warwick, in return for the liberal income which the endowments of the church brought to his non-resident pockets. Another was Mr. Robert Owen. Another was Mr. John Smith, more distinguished for making his liberal politics conducive to a liberal sale of gin, beer, and tobacco, than most other radical publicans in London.

Another was the Rev. J. E. S.[31], who, of all men known to me, had the most disproportionate superabundance of metaphysical intellect to his animal or matter-of-fact nature. Another was Mr. B. D. C.[32], the printer of the organ of the trades' unions (an unstamped paper). As a printer of unstamped papers, Mr. B. D. C. was brought into collision with the government, as other smugglers have been, before a reduction of stamp duty or custom-house duty rendered illegal printing or other smuggling unprofitable. Through the fame of that collision with the government, he was selected by the unionists of Birmingham, acting for other towns, to be their London printer and publisher. But no man within the British shores was more innocent of the designs of the conspirators of the 21st of April than he, though he printed for them, and walked in the procession. And, as I have thus referred to him, I shall add, that, after knowing him personally for fifteen years, though sometimes questioning the taste or the justice of some of his papers, or political opinions, and thinking that he had got into difficulties with the stamp office and the government, losing his type and presses by confiscation, when he might have quietly and thrivingly printed (but it was he, and his like, who caused the newspaper stamps to be reduced from fourpence); having known him fifteen years, and had trade dealings with him, I have known no tradesman more scrupulously exact, honest, or honourable; no man more benevolent or kindly helpful to those whom he could assist, than he is.

There were others, whom I need not particularize, in the foremost places of management, who were not welcome there. The Rev. J. E. S. had gone into the idealism of metaphysics until he was a far way past the borders of orthodoxy; that was a qualification for him to be admitted where he was; just as the printer was qualified, because he had refused to pay taxes; or as the reverend rector of Warwick was qualified, because he railed at the corruptions of the church, of which, however, he was a non-resident sinecurist; or as the apostle of socialism was qualified, because, in propounding new theories, he found fault with every institution on the face of the earth—political, social, and religious; or as the political publican was qualified, because, to sell beer and gin, he drew large custom to his house by preaching to the customers who drank and paid, and grumbled at the government and the country, that he was not satisfied with any party or creed—tories, whigs, radicals, republicans, churchmen, nor dissenters; that he was not satisfied with the borough of Marylebone, nor with London, nor with England, nor with the world, nor with heaven, nor with hell; that neither God, devil, nor man could satisfy him. The travels of the Rev. J. E. S. had led him across the Tweed of his country; his wanderings in metaphysics had led him beyond the Tweed of his religion; and, being far from satisfied with some existing institutions, he was thereby qualified to be an associate of the leaders. But he was a philosopher, and had proved, not to the conviction of the leaders, but to the conviction of most thinkers, that mankind are by nature monarchists; that there never was, and cannot be, a republic; that though the designation of the sovereign, and duration of the reign, and descent of the sovereignty, may be changed, in the nominal republics, still they are monarchies—perhaps it might not be amiss to say they are elective despotisms. Such opinions, in favour of the principle of monarchy, and of the limited and harmless monarchy of Britain, drew around him their disfavour. But there were causes of wider difference. The thin spirituality of his nature, ideal and metaphysical, gave him no feeling in common with the gross sensuality of some of them. They had put off religious belief, torn the garment, cast it away, followed after it, trampled on it, gloried in their nakedness, and they hoped, before long, to cast off political restraint. So far, metaphysical and speculative political philosophy might have contemplated them as interesting objects of abstract study. But they had gone much farther than to strip themselves of religion, and glory in the nakedness of their unbelief. Morals of the most ordinary quality, the mere social courtesies of life, were thrown aside. The reverend philosopher was constrained to tell some of them one day, that though it might be denied, that the state had any legitimate right to define and enforce a system of religion, or a code of morals, there were moral usages upon which all men were agreed, upon the observance of which society could only be held together; and, that they, by wilfully, openly, and vauntingly rending those moral observances from their conduct, proclaimed themselves the unfittest of men to become national reformers, or to continue to be trades' union leaders.

He and the others to whom I have alluded, and others not alluded to, were present at the arrangements on Copenhagen Fields. Dr. Wade was arrayed in canonicals, as an Oxford doctor in divinity. He called silence while he opened the business by prayer; but a shout of derision, led by Mr. ——, prevented him. Mr. ——, in his turn—the proposition having been made to go to the houses of parliament—was shouted down by derisive cries, when he reminded them that a law existed declaring the presence of an armed or hostile multitude at the doors of parliament, to be treason.

No prayers were said. No legal advice about treason listened to. At nine o'clock, when the massive columns were formed, colours and horsemen at their heads, and they had become impatient to be led off, a rocket was fired as the signal of advance. They wheeled off in sections of sixes towards Battle-bridge; proceeding through Gray's-inn-lane, Guildford-street, Russell-square, Keppel-street, Tottenham-court-road, Oxford-street, Regent-street, the Quadrant, Waterloo-place, Pall-mall, Charing-cross, to Whitehall. Mr. Robert Owen, who started with the procession from the field, and who had sought to have the honour of being the head of the deputation, and spokesman at the Home Office—an honour not conceded, left the procession in Tottenham-court-road, and taking a near cut by St. Giles's to the Home Office, presented himself as one of the deputation, sent forward to arrange for the reception of the rest. On the arrival of the rest, Mr. Phillips, the under-secretary in the Home Department of government, gave them audience, and Mr. Owen proceeded to speak. They denied his authority, and Mr. Phillips declined to hear him. He retired. Mr. Phillips then informed them that the petition, though respectfully worded, could not be received, accompanied by such an assemblage of people; nor could Lord Melbourne consent to give them an audience. The petition, he said, would be accepted, and presented to the throne, if left at the Home Office, in an ordinary manner. The deputation retired.

The petition, which had been carried in a triumphal car on a platform by twelve men, was placed in a hackney coach, and carried away; while the procession moved onward, by Westminster-bridge, and St. George's-road, to Kennington-common. As it approached the common, a squadron of cavalry stationed there moved out of sight. Those were the only soldiers which, at any time during the day, were visible to the public.

I reckoned the unionists at the Lambeth side of Westminster-bridge, and found that they marched past at the rate of about two hundred a minute. The whole passed any given point in about two hours and a half, which showed the number in procession to be thirty thousand. Some of the unionist leaders published the number in procession at two hundred thousand; none of them would admit the number to be under one hundred thousand. Some of the newspapers estimated them at eight or ten thousand. *The Times* stated the number at thirty thousand, and gave a reason for that estimate. The mode of reckoning, adopted by the reporters of that journal, was the same as mine, and the result was the same.

At six o'clock in the evening, the aldermen of London dined with the lord mayor in peace; the five thousand special constables went to their homes; the military retired to their country quarters, or, remaining in town, took off their accoutrements, 'eased springs', and put their arms in the rack. The unionists dispersed to their homes, or to their lodges in the public-houses, all tired, most of them satisfied with the procession, though not with the home minister; some of them bitterly expressing their vexation.

How far the warning of danger, conveyed to the secretary of state, had contributed to his safety, and that of the country, it is not for me to say. Each reader of these facts must judge; some believing more of their effect, some believing less. The ministers were neither assassinated nor assaulted. The king, the queen, the royal family, the lords in waiting, and the maids of honour, were not captives to be held until the army would disband itself. The nation was not enveloped in revolution and ruin; the Bank of England stood upon its coffers of gold undisturbed, and, though the augmented military guard remained during the night, the directors, with their governor, like the aldermen with the lord mayor, went to dinner in peace; nor, in the absence of a successful revolution of the highest magnitude, as designed, were there the smaller crimes of foiled attempts at treason, with the trial and execution of state criminals.

Next morning, about the time of breakfast, I was told that a gentleman was at the door who wanted to see me. I went to him. He said he came from Bow-street; that Sir Frederick Roe, the police magistrate, had sent for me. I went with him. I was taken into a private room, where Sir Frederick Roe came and seated himself, and bade me be seated. He said he had received a communication from Lord Melbourne, directing him to obtain from me the particulars of that danger to the government, of which I had writted in my letter. I said that the danger was now past; that, as the government had acted on my suggestion, and the home secretary had not received the unionists as he had intimated to them he would do, there was no necessity for me to do or say more; I had done all which my duty as a citizen required me to do. Sir Frederick Roe said that, no doubt, Lord Melbourne was obliged to me for the service I had done; still it was dangerous that such persons and designs as I had warned him to beware of, should be allowed to remain undiscovered. He inquired if I was sworn to secrecy. I replied that I was not; but it was not my intention to say more upon the subject. He said he would like to see me again; and, in reply to an objection I made to coming again to Bow-street, as I might possibly be watched, he appointed, as the place of interview, his own house in Langham-place, Regent-street.

I proceeded there on the evening of the next day, as appointed; but in the meanwhile had firmly resolved not to make any disclosures upon the political lunatics, of the conspiracy, beyond what I had already done; namely, that I had considered it my duty to put the cabinet ministers on their guard against a conspiracy, in which I had been solicited, but in which I had refused to take a part; and, that having fulfilled that duty, I would not be prevailed upon to do more. Sir Frederick put many searching questions to me at this interview, and urged that the danger might be as great now as before, for aught I knew, if I did not know what the conspirators were now doing. I replied, that I did not know what they were now doing; but they had been disappointed in having an opportunity to do that which they intended. On parting, he remarked, that I might possibly change my mind, and return and say more; that I would find him at his house, in Langham-place, at six o'clock any evening. I again, and finally replied, that nothing in fear or favour would induce me to say more than I had said. I was not sent for again; nor did I return. From that day in April, 1834, until this present day of writing (21st January, 1847, at Dublin), my knowledge of those matters here related, has remained within myself.

[30] Somerville's detailed knowledge of these precautions implies that he was very much deeper in the confidence of the authorities than he admits: in fact that he was a spy.
[31] The Rev. J. E. Smith (1801-57)—'Shepherd Smith'—a Scot and disciple of Robert Owen, who later worked for *The Family Herald*.
[32] B. D. Cousins.

THE AUTOBIOGRAPHY
OF A
WORKING MAN

by

Alexander Somerville

Edited with an introduction by JOHN CARSWELL

THE court martial and flogging of 'Somerville, the Scots Grey' was a *cause célèbre* in the early nineteenth century.

The autobiography of this independent Scot is notable for its vigorous realism and for its account of the society in which he lived. The first chapters give a vivid picture of childhood in rural Scotland as the son of poor farm labourers, and of his life as a young workman in Edinburgh at a time when Trades Unions were first being formed. He then describes how he joined the Scots Greys and gives a most entertaining and surprisingly unembittered account of the regimental life of a dragoon.

A keen and ambitious soldier, in 1832 he was posted to Birmingham, then in a state of political excitement over the Reform Bill. Chartists under Thomas Attwood were rumoured to be planning a march on London to present their petition. The Scots Greys were to stop them on the road and Somerville was a 'fatigue man' employed in turning the grindstone for his comrades to 'rough sharpen' their swords. With several friends he composed an anonymous letter to the press stating that while they would do their duty if riots took place, the Scots Greys could not be depended upon to suppress peaceful demonstrations. Authorship was easily traced and, 'framed' on a military charge, he was sentenced to receive two hundred strokes. His detailed description of the flogging (only one hundred lashes were administered as he was 'a young soldier') is a masterpiece of restrained and objective writing, and his full report of the court martial, and the Court of Enquiry that popular outcry enforced, is of great interest. Supporters purchased his discharge, and he became a journalist, playing at least one more dramatic part in politics.

John Carswell, in his introduction, explains the historical context of the narrative.